Using Physical Activity and Sport to Teach Personal and Social Responsibility

Doris L. Watson • Brian D. Clocksin

Human Kinetics

Library of Congress Cataloging-in-Publication Data

Watson, Doris, 1965-
  Using physical activity and sport to teach personal and social responsibility / Doris L. Watson and Brian D. Clocksin.
      p. cm.
  Includes bibliographical references and index.
  1. Physical education and training--Sociological aspects--Study and teaching. 2. Responsibility--Study and teaching. I. Clocksin, Brian, 1971- II. Title.
  GV342.27.W38 2013
  306.4'83--dc23
                            2012027081
ISBN-10: 1-4504-0472-3 (print)
ISBN-13: 978-1-4504-0472-3 (print)

The web addresses cited in this text were current as of October 8, 2012, unless otherwise noted.

Acquisitions Editor: Scott Wikgren; **Developmental Editor:** Ray Vallese; **Assistant Editor:** Derek Campbell; **Copyeditor:** Joyce Sexton; **Indexer:** Sharon Duffy; **Permissions Manager:** Dalene Reeder; **Graphic Designer:** Nancy Rasmus; **Graphic Artist:** Dawn Sills; **Cover Designer:** Keith Blomberg; **Photographs (cover):** © Human Kinetics; **Photographs (interior):** © Human Kinetics, unless otherwise noted; **Photo Asset Manager:** Laura Fitch; **Visual Production Assistant:** Joyce Brumfield; **Photo Production Manager:** Jason Allen; **Art Manager:** Kelly Hendren; **Associate Art Manager:** Alan L. Wilborn; **Illustrations:** © Human Kinetics, unless otherwise noted; **Printer:** United Graphics

Printed in the United States of America   10   9   8   7   6   5   4   3   2   1

The paper in this book is certified under a sustainable forestry program.

Human Kinetics
Website: www.HumanKinetics.com

United States: Human Kinetics
P.O. Box 5076
Champaign, IL 61825-5076
800-747-4457
e-mail: humank@hkusa.com

Canada: Human Kinetics
475 Devonshire Road Unit 100
Windsor, ON N8Y 2L5
800-465-7301 (in Canada only)
e-mail: info@hkcanada.com

Europe: Human Kinetics
107 Bradford Road
Stanningley
Leeds LS28 6AT, United Kingdom
+44 (0) 113 255 5665
e-mail: hk@hkeurope.com

Australia: Human Kinetics
57A Price Avenue
Lower Mitcham, South Australia 5062
08 8372 0999
e-mail: info@hkaustralia.com

New Zealand: Human Kinetics
P.O. Box 80
Torrens Park, South Australia 5062
0800 222 062
e-mail: info@hknewzealand.com

E5329

Contents

Foreword

Paul M. Wright, PhD
Northern Illinois University

David Walsh, PhD
San Francisco State University

As individuals who were trained by Don Hellison in his Teaching Personal and Social Responsibility (TPSR) model and who have made it the primary focus of our professional careers, we have a vested interest in how this work is interpreted, described, and shared. With that said, we are honored to have been invited by Doris and Brian to write a foreword to this book, *Using Physical Activity and Sport to Teach Personal and Social Responsibility*. We have known Doris and Brian as colleagues and friends for many years and are not surprised at the quality of writing, organization, and insight they have poured into these pages. The content, their interpretation of this work, and the way they have connected it to related topics make this a relevant and timely contribution for anyone interested in implementing TPSR with kids or training others to do so.

We assume most people interested in this text have already read some of Don Hellison's books, chapters, and articles about the TPSR model. If you haven't, we recommend that you do. These are the best resources for understanding the goals and underlying values of the model. Some of you may be familiar with the research articles on TPSR, the number of which is rapidly growing. These are great resources for understanding the theoretical and empirical support for the model. However, based on our perception and feedback from countless practitioners over the years, this body of literature is lacking resources in the middle—i.e., detailed, step-by-step examples of how to organize and implement instruction based on TPSR. This is why we need Doris and Brian. They have done an excellent job reviewing the current research and capturing the true "kids first" spirit of the model, but what makes this book such an important contribution is the second and largest section that is focused on using TPSR in physical activity and sport settings.

What you will find in this book, and in no other that we are aware of, is a series of chapters devoted to specific sports and other physical activities integrated with the TPSR model. The activities covered in these chapters are as varied as adventure education, tennis, and yoga. In each case, a fully detailed and consistently organized description is provided, showing not only how a teacher could guide students through skill development in that area but also how teachers can gradually hand over the reins of responsibility to them. These chapters are rich with specific examples of how to share responsibility with kids in any given lesson, but perhaps even more important is that instead of being presented as isolated examples, they are presented so that you can see the flow of instruction using the model over time. For example, which responsibility goals and empowerment strategies should you focus on (and how) in the first few lessons of a golf unit versus the last few lessons of a team handball unit? With the structure of these chapters, you'll get these answers and many more.

In addition to taking the reader through the developmental stages of teaching a given unit, Doris and Brian highlight connections to Mosston's spectrum of teaching styles in these chapters. This connection to core physical education pedagogy is another great strength of this book, especially as it applies to physical education teachers and teacher educators. For this audience, it is also important to note that promoting personally and socially responsible behavior is identified as one of six national content standards for K-12 physical education (NASPE 2004). We would argue, however, that this area of content is not as well understood and implemented as the other standards are. With this in mind, there are few resources as concrete and practical as this book to help people in the field of physical education to see exactly how they can teach this mandated content.

We believe the book is a great resource for physical educators working in schools, and this book also applies directly to coaches and youth workers in other settings, such as after-school programs or summer camps. In fact, much of the development of TPSR over the years has occurred in extracurricular programs. To highlight these varied applications, Doris and Brian invited a number of prominent TPSR practitioner-researchers to share vignettes in which they describe their programs and ways they have interpreted and adapted the model to fit their settings and meet the needs of the kids they are teaching.

In writing this book, Doris and Brian draw upon years of experience, not just studying TPSR but using it with kids. On top of this, they both have experience as teacher educators and have trained people to use this model. Their practical experience, as well as their broad knowledge of education, youth development, and related fields, made them the right authors for this book.

In the end, *Using Physical Activity and Sport to Teach Personal and Social Responsibility* is a valuable resource for anyone interested in TPSR. This book is an excellent complement to Hellison's writing and also establishes important links between TPSR and related topics such as caring, social emotional development, and mattering. For all these reasons, this book "matters," and we applaud Doris and Brian for their contribution.

Preface

In June of 2010, Brian and I participated in the second annual Teaching Personal and Social Responsibility (TPSR) Conference in Springfield, Massachusetts. In its second year, the conference was the brainchild of Don Hellison—the originator of the TPSR model—along with assorted suspects (check the About Us link on the TPSR website at www.tpsr-alliance.org). Designed to present the key components of the TPSR model to teachers and youth workers, from novice to expert, the conference focused on how the model has been used and can be used in school as well as out-of-school settings, barriers to the model's implementation, collaboration efforts, and assessment strategies. Another topic that received a lot of attention was the ways in which TPSR can be implemented. The program allowed participants to watch as three sets of instructors skilled in TPSR taught a 90-minute session to kids enrolled in a summer sport camp. The gym was divided into three areas, and participants could observe sessions on martial arts, basketball, or soccer, all using the TPSR model. Afterward, participants had a breakout session with the instructors to process what they saw and what had been done.

Where do I begin to integrate the model in my curriculum? Should I process the components in the same order that all of you did? What if I'm not skilled at teaching martial arts, basketball, or soccer—then what do I do? As the flurry of questions continued, it became evident to Brian and me that while many participants may have understood the TPSR model conceptually, they may have had less understanding of how to implement it. Certainly, experiencing the model over time with kids in a teaching or sport setting would help those new to TPSR get a handle on its use. However, we are not certain this is the best or most helpful way to go!

As physical education teacher educators and as instructors of out-of-school programs for at-risk youth, we have over 25 years of experience using the model within our undergraduate physical education teacher education (PETE) curriculum as well as implementing the TPSR model in sport settings. Thus, this book is written as a complement to Don Hellison's *Teaching Personal and Social Responsibility Through Physical Activity, Third Edition.* We are writing for preservice physical education teachers as well as their PETE professors. We are writing for physical

education instructors who have taught in the trenches for years and those who have just come to the TPSR model. We are writing for professionals in out-of-school and community-based programs who seek to create greater connections with the youth they serve. This book is written for anyone who believes in sport and physical activity as a hook that brings youth to a deeper awareness of their own personal potential and their place in their communities as responsible participants.

As a complement to Hellison's text, *Using Physical Activity and Sport to Teach Personal and Social Responsibility* will provide teachers and practitioners with bridges between the content and techniques spelled out in Don's book and their own practices in the actual teaching setting. The book is divided into three parts.

Part I consists of chapters 1 to 3 and lays the foundation for the implementation of the model. Chapter 1 presents the history and evolution of the TPSR model. The chapter also highlights how TPSR meets current National Association for Sport and Physical Education (NASPE) standards for teaching physical education as well as meeting the needs of beginning teacher candidates. Chapter 2 presents what we know about what works in youth development. The chapter synthesizes current literature concerning key concepts about motivational climate in a teaching or physical activity context and concludes with a look at current literature demonstrating effects of the TPSR model in the sport and physical activity setting.

Chapter 3 spotlights elements critical to the creation of a learning environment. The chapter examines the literature on socioemotional learning, caring, and physical activity toward creation of positive learning climates. Facilitating student-centered learning via altering one's teaching styles concludes the chapter and presents a tie-in to part II of the book, which focuses on implementation of the TPSR model in a variety of sports and physical activities—a shift from the theory of TPSR to the practice of TPSR.

Part II includes chapters 4 through 12 and centers on methods for teaching sport and physical activity via the TPSR model. A balance of individual, team, and lifetime activities serves as the foundation for this section and represents the types of sport and physical activities taught in K through 12 and youth sport settings. Chapters use the TPSR lesson plan format (awareness talk, lesson focus, group meeting, and reflection) in connection with each developmental level (stages 1, 2, and 3). In addition, these chapters include examples of activities using the styles of teaching discussed by Mosston and Ashworth (2002). Hands-on examples are provided as well as sample lesson components.

Lastly, part III of the book comprises chapters 13 and 14. Chapter 13 presents real-life examples of programs from teachers and youth workers who are currently using the TPSR model. The contributors describe their programs and explain how their programs maintain the TPSR core themes of student–teacher relationships, integration, transfer, and empowerment (SITE). Chapter 14 discusses how TPSR can underscore the creation of youth leaders in school and community settings.

We believe that the organization of the book will enable readers to naturally evolve their use of TPSR methods. Throughout, readers will consider conceptual frameworks associated with the TPSR model, examples of sport and physical activity lesson implementations, and ways to create additional teaching moments pertaining to responsibility in school and out-of-school settings.

The chapters in parts I and III end with a section that checks for understanding. These checks for understanding follow a processing style commonly used in adventure education that progressively moves the learner (you) through higher-order thinking questions. The process begins with "What?" questions that summarize the key aspects of the chapter. The "So What?" section expands on this line of questioning to ask learners to make connections between what they have learned and why it might be important or how it can affect their lives. We see these as good discussion-style questions to use in PETE classes and synthesis questions that practitioners can use to check on their understanding of what they have read. The final section, "Now What?", provides additional reading recommendations for practitioners and PETE faculty whose interest has been piqued and want to know where to go next.

The Foundation
of the TPSR Model

Introduction to the Personal and Social Responsibility Model

© Image 100

It is 1986 and I am sitting in the front row of my physical education methods course. Coach Williams is flipping the slide on the overhead projector (this is pre-PowerPoint days—imagine!) while presenting the concept of teaching personal and social responsibility (TPSR) as advanced by Dr. Don Hellison. I sit rapt with attention and think, "This is so cool! This totally makes sense!" Later during the summer as an instructor working for the National Youth Sport Camp, I begin to integrate Dr. Hellison's model into my soccer lessons. At first the kids look at me as though I am a freak: *Lady, you want us to do what? Talk about how we* feel? *Are you* crazy? *This is just soccer!* But slowly over the course of the summer, not only do the kids in my soccer classes begin to respond positively, but some of the other instructors are asking me what it is I am doing out there. I am hooked!

Flash forward to the fall of 2001, and I am in a gymnasium full of middle school girls, music is pumping, and the girls are shooting hoops with a few of the players from the (then) WNBA Utah Starzz (now the San Antonio Silver Stars). The Starzz have joined us for our afternoon of "U Move With the Starzz," an after-school program created for middle school girls to help them become more active. Brian is a new doctoral student working with me and five undergraduate students at the site. The music stops, signaling for the girls to huddle up so we can begin the afternoon lesson. When everyone is quiet, the student leader begins with a question, "What does it mean to respect someone?" The middle school girls sit quietly for a moment in thought; then a hand shoots up—"It means you don't be mean to someone." "Good, good," the student leader encourages. "But what does it mean not to be 'mean'?" Again, the young women think. "It means things like waiting for your turn or getting someone's ball when it rolls by you. You know, helping them out." This is my version of an awareness talk, a modification of the TPSR model (and Don encourages such modifications). The discussion ultimately creates teachable moments for both the girls and the student leaders for the day's lesson about offensive strategy but also about respect. Brian is hooked!

It is now fall 2012, and Brian and I are still out there working with kids and preparing teachers and youth workers to use the TPSR model. TPSR has grown quite a bit since 1986 in its conceptualization and use, not only as a result of lots of people reading the work by Don and his graduate students (notably Paul Wright and David Walsh) but also because teachers and youth workers have been using the model and adapting it to their context to meet the needs of the kids they serve. In this chapter we discuss the basics of the TPSR model. For a longer discussion, you are invited to read Don Hellison's *Teaching Personal and Social Responsibility Through Physical Activity, Third Edition* (2011). We also encourage you to do a little retro-reading and pick up a copy of *Humanistic Physical Education* (1973) by Don. This work lays the foundation for what is today known as TPSR.

Background

Approximately 30 years ago, Don Hellison reconceptualized the teaching of physical education. As a function of his work with youth in inner-city Chicago, Hellison adopted a more humanistic approach to teaching and working with young people (Hellison 1973). Recognizing that it was the activity or sport that drew youth in, Hellison began to focus on development of moral qualities that stemmed from teachable moments during the course of the class. He targeted attributes of personal well-being (e.g., control, effort, and self-direction) together with characteristics of positive social interactions (e.g., respecting the rights and feelings of others, caring for and helping others). Thus, TPSR emerged (Hellison 1973, 1985, 1995, 2003). The model possesses a strong foundation in humanism to create a student-centered approach that purports to facilitate development of student personal and social responsibility. The uniqueness of the model is situated in focusing youth on setting daily goals for their participation in class. Another important aspect of this model is that it encourages students to become more reflective in their decision making and provides them a voice with which to express their opinions, interests, and feelings. The underlying hope is that students will demonstrate appropriate behavior and activity choices through this type of instruction and will show greater concern for the well-being, safety, and quality of experience of their peers (Hellison 1995, 2003).

During the last 30 years, researchers have implemented the TPSR model across a variety of settings and with populations ranging from at-risk youth to intact sport teams. In the next chapter we look at what we know works, but first we discuss how the responsibility levels have evolved and how they relate to student development and characteristics. Through this understanding, physical educators can select learning experiences that meet the developmental needs of the learner and promote the development of responsibility. It is our belief that teaching personal and social responsibility is not simply a unit of instruction or behavior management tool but a guiding philosophy by which teachers create an environment conducive to learning for all students. We hope that through reading this book and integrating TPSR into your teaching practice, you will be hooked too.

Responsibility Levels

The responsibility levels have evolved over the years, but they retain a commitment to an interrelationship between personal and social well-being. These "values" provide an opportunity for participants to reflect on their responsibility as a progression through levels, thus moving the focus from responsibility for the self to responsibility for others over time. Understanding these levels provides insight into student characteristics and helps teachers adopt curricular choices. Figure 1.1 provides an overview of the responsibility levels. The bowl represents the amount of responsibility students can take on in relation to the level or levels they exhibit. Teachers can "fill" the bowl to the point of transfer by providing progressive and supportive experiences that increasingly allow students to demonstrate responsibility, share their voice, and reflect on these experiences.

Level I: Respect

Students at responsibility Level I are able to control their behavior to the extent that they do not interfere with the learning opportunities of others. They respect the rights and feelings of others to safely (emotionally and physically) engage in activities but may not participate by choice. Hellison (1995) describes this in the context of three subcomponents of Level I behavior: self-control (verbal and physical behavior), agreeing to peaceful conflict resolution, and inclusion as a right for all (p. 15). Students who are not able to meet these basic components of Level I have been described as Level 0 or irresponsible students. These are the students who disrupt the learning opportunities of others through bullying, verbal or physical abuse, or manipulation. Moving students from Level 0 to Level I can be a significant struggle but facilitates progression of other students through the responsibility levels.

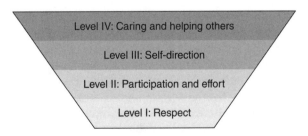

Figure 1.1 Responsibility bowl.

Level I students come prepared to learn, but they are often selective about the types of activities they engage in. They participate fully in activities they are good at or perceive as meaningful while disengaging in activities they perceive as meaningless or have limited skill in. The type (competitive or noncompetitive) and presentation of activities (teaching style and motivational climate) can influence student responses. Chapter 2 discusses the impact of teaching and motivational climate on student behavior.

Level II: Participation and Effort

Students at responsibility Level II maintain the respect for others' opportunities to learn while fully participating in activities. These students are willing to try new activities and to practice activities they are not skilled at. Level II students generally follow directions from teachers and are able to work in team settings. These students benefit from positive feedback and teaching styles that are primarily teacher centered and from practice sessions that are under teacher supervision. Hellison (1995) identifies three components of Level II behavior: exploration of effort, willingness to try new things, and beginning to define personal success.

Students in Level II are particularly influenced by the motivational climate in which tasks are presented. Teachers can expect these students to work cooperatively with other students during skill practice and application. Gradual shifting toward more student-centered teaching styles (e.g., task, reciprocal), under direct supervision, can occur as these students understand their role in the learning process.

Level III: Self-Direction

Students at responsibility Level III have demonstrated respect for their peers and the willingness to participate and give effort in a variety of tasks. These students are able to work independently toward self-identified goals and in cooperation with peers. Students at this level benefit from opportunities that promote self-regulation and teaching styles that encourage student responsibility. Using peer assessments and teaching episodes, having students self-assess, and developing goal-setting skills benefit learners at Level III. As students reach this level, the teacher's role can change from that of a "sage on the stage" to that of a "guide on the side" allowing for student-led learning opportunities.

Many students have not had the opportunity to set goals and develop plans to obtain their goals. Providing students with opportunities to set short-term performance goals, self-evaluate, and reflect on their experience helps in the development of goals. Students can then begin to set long-term goals and determine strategies for meeting these goals. Individual goal-setting skills can be transferred to group goal setting as students take on a greater role in the learning process. This provides motivation for students to move beyond Level III and to see how individual and group interactions play a role in learning.

Level IV: Caring and Helping Others

The willingness to positively help peers in the learning process is a key characteristic of Level IV learners. These students are able to lead learning experiences and assess their peers. They are ready for leadership opportunities during the lesson. This can involve facilitating the awareness talk or group meeting, leading warm-up or closure activities, or working with less skilled peers during the lesson focus. A continued shift toward student-centered teaching styles is needed to encourage the development of Level IV behavior in students. Students benefit from reciprocal styles of teaching that allow for teaching opportunities, peer interaction, and reflection.

Level IV learners need to be provided with opportunities to demonstrate helping and caring behaviors. The teacher needs to be willing to release some of the control to students at this level to foster these behaviors. Increasing the responsibility of the learner in the learning process facilitates the development of peer leaders. This in turn will transform the physical education classroom to a collaborative learning environment where peers support each other in the learning process, respect differences in learning, and understand the feelings and attitudes of others.

Level V: Transferring to Life Outside the Gym

Physical educators can promote transfer through awareness talks and group meetings and by exhibiting responsible behavior in all interactions with students. Integrating TPSR ideas into after-school and extracurricular activities can create a climate of responsibility that promotes transfer beyond the gym as well. Through the use of the pedagogical strategies discussed throughout this book, physical educators and youth leaders can develop learning experiences that provide students with opportunities to develop responsibility and reflect on how these experiences relate to life outside the gymnasium. The first step in this process is understanding the developmental readiness of learners to take on responsibility.

Level V students are able to make connections between the learning experiences in physical education and those beyond our doors. The teacher needs to incorporate experiences and reflections that promote transfer and to look for ways to provide leadership opportunities for these students. These students can benefit from teaching styles that promote goal setting and allow them to learn to self-assess and reflect on these experiences.

Developmental Stages

Expanding on the work of Hellison, Walsh (2008b) identified developmental stages of students as they progress through the responsibility levels (table 1.1). These stages form a foundation for curricular choices that support responsibility development and student–teacher interactions. Understanding the interaction between responsibility levels and developmental stages is essential for successful implementation of a responsibility-based physical education program. Think of the developmental stages as transition points for shifting responsibility from the teacher to the learner. As students demonstrate the ability to consistently perform at designated responsibility levels, the teacher introduces opportunities that promote greater levels of responsibility. Culminating with the creation of peer leaders, the developmental stages foster the development of responsibility by matching developmentally appropriate experiences with demonstrated behavioral readiness.

You will note that Level V is omitted from this table. It is our belief that connections to Level V (transfer) are infused throughout TPSR and are independent of curricular choices. Teachers and coaches need to make connections for the learner with what is occurring in the curriculum regardless of developmental readiness of the learner to take responsibility in the learning environment. As you will see throughout this book, the strategies for promoting transfer change as students move through the developmental stages.

Stage 1: Developing Responsibility

As we begin to introduce the TPSR model to a class, many students will be at Levels I and II. It is natural to have a period of transition as we begin the discussion of responsibility for personal and social well-being. Students who demonstrate primarily Level I behavior are classified as developmental stage 1 learners. Much of the time in this stage is spent making the students aware of what behaviors constitute each

Table 1.1 Developmental Stages as They Relate to Levels

Developmental stage	Responsibility level	Student characteristics	Teaching strategies
1	I	• Respects the right of others to learn • Controls behavior • Comes to class prepared	• Use teacher-centered teaching styles • Provide positive feedback for engaging students • Use behavior contracts • Provide opportunity for teacher–student relationship time
	II	• Tries new activities • Has positive interactions with peers • Follows directions • Needs some prompting to stay on task	• Move toward a student-centered teaching style (task) • Use team activities and cooperative games • Develop reflection skills
2	III	• Is able to self-regulate behavior • Can work independently and with peers • Stays on task, is able to set goals	• Use student-centered teaching styles (task, reciprocal, self-check) • Develop goal-setting and self-assessment skills
3	IV	• Is ready for leadership opportunities • Demonstrates interest in working with peers • Promotes personal and social responsibility	• Use student-centered teaching styles (reciprocal, self-check, guided discovery) • Provide opportunity for student leadership • Use peer assessment and instruction

level. During awareness talks and reflection time, the teacher can promote the students' use of behavioral self-assessment. Nearly the entire lesson (about 80 percent) is spent in teacher-directed activities that promote Level I and II behaviors. During this stage teachers are developing students' self-reflection skills and promoting a climate that allows students to have a voice.

Stage 2: Promoting Self-Directed Learning

The teacher transitions to a focus on developmental stage 2 once most of the students can demonstrate self-control and respect for others (Level I) and regular participation and effort (Level II). The task in this stage is to develop self-directed behavior (Level III)

and to identify students who are ready for leadership (Level IV) opportunities. Thus a greater amount of time (70 percent) is spent in activities that promote self-direction and leadership. Transitioning from teacher-centered to student-centered teaching styles helps to facilitate the development of Level III and IV behaviors by increasing the role of the student in the learning process. Teachers can introduce goal setting, self- and peer assessment, and peer-teaching episodes during this stage.

Stage 3: Creating Peer Leaders

The final developmental stage targets the development of youth leaders. The majority of students consistently demonstrate self-directed behavior (Level III), and further transfer of responsibility from the teacher to the learner is warranted. Students continue to take a leadership role in awareness talks and are provided opportunities to exhibit Level III and Level IV behaviors throughout the lesson. Using teaching styles and curricular models that promote student leadership facilitates development during this stage.

Themes

The first question we get, and one that provides motivation for this book, is consistently "I understand the model, but how do I begin?" Central to the implementation of the model are four thematic objectives that guide teachers in the delivery of responsibility-based pedagogy. They are student–teacher relationships, integration, transfer, and empowerment (SITE). The themes guide the creation of a climate of responsibility that is fostered through shared respect, modeling, and teachable moments. By keeping "SITE" of these themes, teachers can promote personal and social responsibility through any curricular activity.

Student Relationships

From the beginning, Don has promoted a humanistic approach to teaching that requires teachers to know their students. Grounded in work ranging from Maslow to Noddings, establishing an environment of caring that is emotionally and physically safe begins with the relationship between students and the teacher. Dedicating time to fostering student–teacher and student–student relationships is essential for creating a climate of respect. For students to buy in to a responsibility-based climate, we have to model, reinforce, and reflect upon what it means to respect the rights of others. This needs to occur daily, and students need a voice in the process.

Chances are you have begun to develop relationships with your students. Physical education offers a medium that is conducive to relationship development between teachers and students. Don recognized this 30 years ago and speaks to the importance of providing opportunities to foster relationships. This is the keystone of using the responsibility model as a philosophical foundation for your physical education and sport programs. Participants need to feel respected and need to feel that they have a voice in the learning experience in order to buy in. They need to see respectful behavior modeled and reinforced. As Maslow would say, their "love" needs have to be met if they are to feel a sense of belonging and in turn a willingness to respect others. Without positive student–teacher and student–student relationships, the best we can hope for from the responsibility model is for it to serve as a behavior management tool.

Building positive student relationships is one theme in TPSR.

Integration

We believe that responsibility-based instruction is a philosophy that should guide every aspect of your program. We speak to this throughout the book and provide you with strategies and resources to make such instruction a reality. For this to happen, teachers using the model must integrate responsibility roles, concepts, and expectations into every lesson regardless of the activity or skill being taught. For some this may be a paradigm shift, while for others it may be business as usual. Through an understanding of the responsibility levels and the developmental stages that students progress through, physical educators can select physical activity experiences that support and develop responsibility. We can maximize this transition by consistently providing students with guidance, opportunity, voice, and reflection on personal and social responsibility attributes and expectations.

A responsibility-based lesson plan provides the foundation to foster student personal and social responsibility. Walsh (2008b) identified key aspects of responsibility-based lesson planning. Table 1.2 describes the aspects of a responsibility-based lesson plan that we use throughout the book.

Teachers can use a variety of techniques and strategies to promote responsibility in students. The goal of this book is to provide you with practical ways to integrate the TPSR model throughout any unit of instruction you choose to use in physical education. Table 1.3 identifies six simple strategies you can start using today regardless of the content you are teaching.

Transfer

If we are to create students who can consistently perform at Level V, we need to help them make connections between what is done in the gym and how it applies to life in other settings. This is accomplished in our awareness talks, through group meetings, and through guided reflection experiences. Often overlooked in TPSR programming, transfer moves the model from a physical education curricular tool to a youth development process. Initially we must help students identify connections between their actions and behaviors in the gym and those outside of their time in physical education. Eventually students learn to make these connections reflectively and to make choices on their own that are consistent with the responsibility model.

Empowerment

Empowerment is an individual's sense of power in his or her life. For the model to work, the teacher must share responsibility with students, reinforce positive choices, redirect negative choices, and encourage

TPSR can teach students how their actions and behaviors in the gym can transfer to their lives outside the gym.

Table 1.2   Responsibility-Based Lesson Components

Component	Description	Strategies
Relationship time	Time to work on student–teacher and student–student relationships.	• Use icebreaker activities. • Provide opportunities for self-selecting partners and tasks. • Use peer leaders.
Awareness talk	Teacher-initiated discussion on integration of responsibility into the lesson. Sets the stage and expectations for learners. As learners move through the developmental stages, students take over these discussions.	• Use guided discussion and questioning on ways students can demonstrate responsibility during physical education. • Identify connections to promote transfer to life outside of the gym.
Lesson focus	The heart of the lesson, used for development of responsibility and skills.	• Vary teaching styles to match developmental readiness of students. • Provide opportunities for students to demonstrate responsibility appropriate to the levels they exhibit.
Group meeting	Group debrief on the lesson that identifies how students exhibit personal and social responsibility and checks for understanding of content presented. Students should have an increased role and voice in this process as they become developmentally ready.	• Provide opportunity for student voice. • Limit teacher contributions. • Use structured questions to begin the discussion. • Have partners and small groups engage in discussions and present back to the class.
Reflection	Dedicated time for individualized reflection on the learning experience and on personal and social responsibility behavior.	• Use student journals. • Use exit slips. • Guide questions initially to develop reflection skills in students.

self-reflection. As students reach Level III, we want them to feel ownership in their learning. For students to feel a sense of empowerment, they need to have a voice in the learning process and be supported by their peers and the teacher. Through the development of relationships, the creation of a climate of respect and responsibility, and a commitment to reflection, we can help students gain their sense of power to effect change in their lives.

Connection to National Standards

In 2004, the National Association for Sport and Physical Education (NASPE) revised its National Standards for Physical Education. Additionally, in 2008, NASPE identified National Initial Physical Education Teacher Education Standards. Both of these documents identified a commitment to teaching personal and social responsibility to students through physical education experiences. Thus it is the role of physical educators to promote responsibility in their students and to monitor that this is occurring. Using TPSR in support of these documents will strengthen physical education programs.

The National Standards for Physical Education comprise six standards that should guide physical educators as they shape their curricula. Standard 5 specifically addresses "responsible personal and social behavior" in physical activity settings. The description of the standard states that the "intent of this standard is achievement of self-initiated behaviors" (NASPE 2004, p. 39) (Level III) with respect for others (Level I) as a key. As the learner transitions from elementary school to and through high school, expectations for positively influencing the behavior of others (Level IV) in physical education and sport

Table 1.3 Strategies for Promoting Responsibility in Students

Strategy	Description	Implications
Restroom pass	Create a "pass" that allows students to go to the restroom without asking the teacher. Students are free to go to the restroom whenever the pass is available.	Students are allowed to self-regulate with respect to their needs. If they struggle with self-regulation, this provides the teacher with teachable moments for discussing responsible and irresponsible behavior.
Water break rule	Allow students to get a drink of water whenever they feel the need as long as no one else is getting a drink.	Students can self-regulate their drinking needs, eliminating the necessity for a whole-class water break.
Instant student-directed activity	Post a warm-up or skill practice task for students to complete when they arrive in the gymnasium. This allows students who get ready quickly to be active and learning instead of having to wait for those who are slower.	Strategy provides additional skill practice episodes to promote student motivation and may encourage students to get ready faster. It also promotes Level III (self-direction) behavior.
Equipment choice	Allow students to self-select the equipment they will use for a task (e.g., inclusion style). Provide choices of equipment that will challenge the learner at the appropriate level.	Strategy creates a mastery climate in which students can find success in skills according to their developmental readiness. Students perform the same general task (e.g., catching a self-tossed item) but use an appropriate object in skill practice (e.g., balloon, beach ball, beanbag, tennis ball).
Peer teaching episodes	Create learning and teaching episodes that allow students to teach and provide feedback to their peers. Use of a reciprocal style can motivate learners, increase feedback, and promote learning across the cognitive and psychomotor domains.	Strategy promotes Level IV (caring, helping) behavior and can be used to create leadership roles (i.e., peer mentoring). Teacher needs to provide criteria sheets and develop the evaluation skills of the learners.
Peer assessment	Allow students to evaluate their peers. In tandem with teaching episodes, have the peer evaluate others' performances using a checklist or rubric.	Strategy promotes Level IV (caring, helping) behavior and provides additional feedback to the learner. Teachers need to develop the evaluation tool (checklist, rubric) and train students in its use.

Adapted, by permission, from M. Parker, J. Kallusky, and D. Hellison, 1999, "High impact, low risk: Ten strategies to teach responsibility," *Journal of Physical Education, Recreation and Dance* 70(2): 26-28.

settings increase. Table 1.4 provides an overview of outcomes for NASPE standard 5 as they relate to TPSR levels.

The National Initial Physical Education Teacher Education Standards (NASPE 2008) identify program elements as the skills and knowledge that physical education teacher candidates should acquire in teacher preparation programs. Element 4.6 identifies the ability to "implement strategies to help students demonstrate responsible personal and social behaviors" as a part of the effective communication and pedagogical skills that teacher candidates should pos-

sess. Additionally, a number of other elements make connections between TPSR and effective pedagogy.

- Elements 3.4, 3.5, and 3.6 speak to the physical educator's ability to plan and manage "fair and equitable" learning experiences.
- Elements 4.5 and 4.6 highlight the physical educator's ability to effectively implement routines that maintain a "safe and effective" learning environment.
- Speaking to the physical educator's impact on student learning, element 5.3 highlights the

need for the use of the "reflective cycle" to support "student learning" and instructional goals.

- Professionally, elements 6.1, 6.3, and 6.6 identify the need to "demonstrate behaviors" and "communicate" in ways that convey respect and a belief that all students can become physically educated individuals.

Together, the NASPE documents provide justification for implementing and an imperative to carry out a responsibility-based physical education program not simply as a stand-alone unit but as a philosophical foundation across the K through 12 physical education experience. It is the role of the physical educator to provide opportunities and support for responsible student choices and actions.

Table 1.4   Standard 5 Sample Outcomes Aligned to Responsibility Levels

Grades	Level I	Level II	Level III	Level IV
K through 2	• Works in a diverse group setting without interfering with others • Accepts all playmates without regard to personal differences	Enjoys participating alone while exploring movement tasks	Practices specific skills as assigned until the teacher signals the end of practice	Shows compassion for others by helping them
Grades 3 through 5	Assesses and takes responsibility for own behavior problems without blaming others	Works productively with a partner to improve performance	Works independently and productively for progressively longer periods of time	Takes seriously the role of teaching an activity or skill to the team
Grades 6 through 8	Shows self-control by accepting a controversial decision of an official	Is able to accomplish group or team goals in both cooperative and competitive activities	• Makes responsible decisions about using time, applying rules, and following through with decisions made • Remains on task in a group activity without close teacher monitoring	• Makes decisions about modifying a soccer game to allow all members to participate • Seeks out, participates with, and shows respect for a peer of lesser skill ability
Grades 9 through 12	Slides into a base in a way that avoids injury to a defensive player	Chooses to participate in an activity because of personal enjoyment rather than only when friends are participating	Makes enlightened personal choices for engaging in physical activity over the life span	• Invites less skilled students to participate in a warm-up activity prior to class • Shows leadership by diffusing conflict during competition

Summary

In relation to the rest of this book, this chapter should serve as a reference on the TPSR model. Through an understanding of the theoretical foundations of the model and the developmental characteristics of students across levels and stages, teachers can provide meaningful responsibility-based instruction that promotes personal and social well-being in our students. This will fill the bowl of responsibility and make connections to promote the transfer of these attributes to the lives of our students beyond the gymnasium or practice field.

What?

Our goal in writing this chapter was to provide you with an overview of the TPSR model and its evolution. We hope that just as the model hooked us, you see the potential of the model for creating an environment that is student centered and physically and emotionally safe—one in which all students have the right and opportunity to learn.

So What?

1. The levels provide a framework for discussing personal well-being and social interactions with our students. Explain the levels as they relate to personal well-being and social interactions.
2. Identify general teaching strategies for working with students within the TPSR model.
3. David Walsh identified three developmental stages related to the TPSR model that serve as a guide for teachers implementing the model. Explain the three stages as they relate to the TPSR levels and how understanding these stages will help teachers plan learning experiences.
4. Explain the responsibility lesson plan format. What is the role of the teacher and the student in each phase of the lesson? How do these role responsibilities change as students move through the levels?

Now What? Suggested Readings

Compagnone, N. (1995). Teaching responsibility to rural elementary youth: Going beyond the urban at-risk boundaries. *Journal of Physical Education, Recreation and Dance, 66,* 58-63.

Cutforth, N.J. (1997). What's worth doing: Reflections on an after-school program in a Denver elementary school. *Quest, 49,* 130-139.

Hammond-Diedrich, K.C., & Walsh, D. (2006). Empowering youth through a responsibility-based cross-age teacher program: An investigation into impact and possibilities. *Physical Educator, 63*(3), 134-142.

Martinek, T., McLaughlin, D., & Schilling, T. (1999). Project effort: Teaching responsibility beyond the gym. *Journal of Physical Education, Recreation and Dance, 70*(6), 59-65.

Walsh, D. (2008). Helping youth in underserved communities envision possible futures: An extension of the teaching personal and social responsibility model. *Research Quarterly for Exercise and Sport, 79*(2), 209-221.

What Works

An often-heard expression in education is "Good teachers are born, not made." We believe that this statement derives from the tension between theory and practice, between what we know and what we do. Certainly, both theory and practice are important to us as teachers and coaches; but rather than a reliance on one or the other, it is a balance of the two, or better yet, the connection of theory to practice that lends itself to our professional development. In this chapter we seek to make just that connection, between what has been identified as good practice in our gymnasiums and why it is relevant to positive youth development.

Don Hellison began the third edition of *Teaching Personal and Social Responsibility Through Physical Activity* by asking the question, "What's worth doing?" Hopefully, if you are reading this book, you have already answered that question and perhaps have a better one: "*Why* is it worth doing?" Why is it worth altering your curriculum, the way you teach, or the climate you create in your gymnasium when you could just as easily replicate the "roll out the ball—busy, happy, and good" programming that is still prevalent today? Why expend the energy? Because you know in your gut that it *does* matter! It matters to you as a professional with integrity and passion for sport, physical education, and physical activity. It matters to you because you have seen how sport can change kids' lives, their values, and their behavior. You understand the big picture; sport is the hook that attracts kids, and through purposeful planning and intentional, conscious manipulation of curriculum, you know that the impact of sport on kids is not accidental. Why is it worth doing? Because you know that sport, physical education, and physical activity really can make a difference in the lives of youth. But perhaps you don't know *how.*

We just used the word manipulation, which often carries a negative connotation. We use the word to imply purposeful and conscious planning to instill something beyond the X's and O's of teaching sport and physical education. Sport and physical education beyond the ball are more important today than ever before. According to studies over the past 15 years, violence against and instigated by youth has slowly decreased (Cook & Laub 1998; National Center for Health Statistics 2012; Vivola, Matjasko, & Massetti 2011). Despite this trend, youth today are still growing up in what Garbarino (1997) termed "socially toxic environments"—a social context that has become poisonous to the well-being of kids. Social toxins include poverty, disruptive family lives, absence of adult role models, alienation, communities that are violent and drug ridden, and a host of other factors (Bradshaw et al. 2009). Thus youth today are con-

stantly bombarded with messages and realities that undermine their sense of security. Cumulatively, these social toxins result in youth who are disruptive, aggressive, emotionally inconsistent, and generally difficult to work with. Therefore, teachers need strategies beyond simple classroom management that will enable them to facilitate development that is not just physical but also social and emotional.

In her book *Smart and Sassy: The Strengths of Inner-City Black Girls* (2002), Joyce West Stevens draws an analogy between the great jazz vocalist Sara Vaughan and inner-city black youth. Vaughan was nicknamed "Sassy" because of her irreverence and strong independent streak, and West contends that the word can be used to describe the multifaceted personalities of urban black girls in particular and urban youth in general. We believe the analogy can be generalized to all youth in the 21st century. Thus, it can be said that the way in which youth navigate their daily lives is akin to that of jazz vocalists or—better yet, if we are talking about the 21st century—hip hop artists who lean heavily on improvisation or the ability to recognize subtle and not-so-subtle nuisances in context and alter themselves to meet those challenges.

As we have reflected on the goals of the work we do with kids as well as the physical education teachers and youth workers we hope to influence, we are grounded in the contributions of a few notables to the literature on youth development and sport. The next section of this chapter explores ideas that have supported us professionally in our work toward positive youth development.

Although the TPSR model is often presented as an instructional model in a physical education curriculum, its usefulness for us became apparent in a physical activity setting outside of school. The programs were composed entirely of large numbers of kids from underserved communities that surrounded our university, with class sizes ranging from 30 to 60. The scenario is little different for physical education teachers and youth workers today. A common criticism of both physical education and physical activity programs for underserved youth has been that they tend, ironically, to underserve these youth. Often we are no more than pedagogical traffic cops as we keep large diverse groups of kids moving safely somehow, some way in our gymnasiums. In addition, traditional curricular and pedagogical approaches tend to be problematic because they focus on "fixing troubled youth" rather than working with their strengths, assets, and competencies. An example of this was highlighted in an article on urban youth in the *Journal of Physical Education, Recreation and Dance* that encouraged reducing choice in the classroom as well as limiting teacher use of humor with students to underscore who is really in charge (Clements 2009). Our belief is that the TPSR model offers a paradigm shift in how we approach physical education and, more importantly, how we interact with the youth we are charged with educating.

We are not naïve enough to believe or suggest that many teachers, particularly from urban settings, are not faced with daunting tasks daily and must seek a professional barometer that allows them to maintain a safe teaching environment for all. It is our belief that a safe environment is one with caring adults that philosophically believe that "these young people are not the problem; in fact, they do incredibly well, given the negative influences they have to navigate through and the minimal institutional support available to them . . . they need programs that work" (Hellison & Cutforth 1997, p. 224).

Motivational Climate

Although most people would agree that a physical education or physical activity context is grounded in competition, it is possible to conceptualize that context in a more cooperative way. We can think of the physical education or activity setting as like a coin. On one side, the setting is competitive and focuses on individual talents and successes. On the other side, the setting can be seen as one that is cooperative, with individual and group goals dictating what

success means. The two sides of the coin give rise to two different goal structures; the one that predominates becomes the motivational climate perceived by the participants, or the *perceived motivational climate* (Ames 1992; Ames & Archer 1988). As noted by Newton, Duda, and Yin (2000), the presence and extent of social comparisons, evaluative practices, rewards and punishments, and the value placed on effort by a teacher or coach differentiate between the two distinct elements of the motivational climate. It is believed that youth are influenced by their interpretation of the cues the teacher or coach provides and by which side of the coin those cues are perceived to have come from.

If a teacher or coach behaves so as to emphasize personal mastery, focuses on effort as the key to success in combination with cooperative learning, and rewards optimal individual effort, he is said to be creating a task-involving climate. Research in the physical education or activity setting has linked perceptions of a task-involving climate to greater intrinsic motivation (Standage, Duda, & Ntoumanis 2003), more mature levels of moral reasoning (Ommundsen et al. 2003), and more positive sportsmanship attitudes (Fry & Newton 2003).

On the other side of the coin, a teacher may create an ego-involving climate by encouraging interpersonal competition, basing rewards on optimal ability, punishing mistakes, and promoting rivalry between students. The response of students in a context they

A task-involving climate can facilitate a more cooperative learning environment.

perceive as ego involving has been associated with more negative attitudes toward teachers and coaches as well as a general lack of positive sportsmanship behaviors (Fry & Newton 2003).

Given the differences in response to a task-involving versus an ego-involving context, it seems apparent that physical educators ought to strive to create an environment in which youth perceive the climate as more task involving. Indeed, the literature supports that participants in task-involving motivational climates tend to be more persistent, prefer to engage in more challenging tasks, experience greater feelings of enjoyment, and report stronger beliefs that effort is an important part of doing well in sport (Solomon 1996; Treasure 1993; Wallhead & Ntoumanis 2004).

As physical educators, if we recognize that the ways in which we organize and conduct our lessons influence the youth we are teaching or coaching, we can also begin to recognize that we can do more as a consequence of manipulation of the environment than simply develop outstanding athletes or skilled movers. If you believe that context matters (and we do!), then it is possible to recognize that you can alter or adjust the elements of how you work to facilitate positive youth development. We think this is really at the core of understanding TPSR—the model can be modified to fit the creativity of the teacher and the population of the school and program for which it is being used. This is done not just to develop better physical performance but also to help youth better understand themselves through the lens of physical activity and sport.

What We Know About TPSR

The TPSR model is unique in that it focuses youth on setting daily goals for their participation in a physical activity setting. Another important aspect of this model is that it encourages students to become more reflective in their decision making and provides them with a voice in which to express their opinions, interests, and feelings. As Don (2003, p. 11) puts it, "TPSR does not mean getting inside the kids' heads but getting them inside their own heads." The underlying hope is that students will demonstrate appropriate behavior and activity choices through this type of instructional approach and show greater concern for the well-being, safety, and quality of experience of their peers (Hellison 1995, 2003).

Although the TPSR model has been around for more than three decades, not a great deal of research on TPSR has been published until recently. In the rest of this chapter we present a snapshot of the literature in an attempt to provide you—the teacher, coach, or youth worker—with evidence beyond our convictions that TPSR can and has made a difference in the lives of youth, specifically youth development. The studies presented here have explored the implementation and efficacy of the TPSR model both within and outside the school setting and at both the primary and secondary grade levels.

In what was probably the first published TPSR study, DeBusk and Hellison (1989) examined the impact of a TPSR-based after-school program on delinquency-prone fourth-grade boys. The findings

TPSR helps kids learn to set daily goals for their participation.

provided evidence of some change in the boys' affective behavior as well as of a positive influence on the teacher's attitudes toward the youth. In a similar study by Martinek, Schilling, and Johnson (2001), youth in an after-school program that used a TPSR-based curriculum were able to apply goals associated with effort to different tasks in the classroom. The authors noted, however, that the youth struggled to set personal goals in the classroom.

In a review of their own work and in partial response to criticisms regarding a lack of empirical support for the model, Hellison and Walsh (2002) conducted a retrospective qualitative analysis of the use of TPSR in a before-school program spanning 25 years. The authors provided an analysis of 26 studies employing the personal responsibility model, highlighting some of the ways in which the strategy had been used, various populations that had been studied, and data in support of its effectiveness. They noted four key findings from the review.

1. Improvements in in-program goals were found in the areas of self-control, effort, self-worth, and self-direction.

2. Aspects of transference of TPSR goals to outside the program included improvement in self-control, effort, and self-esteem in the classroom. Also noted was a reduction in classroom reprimands, discipline referrals, and dropout rates.

3. A heightened concern for others, development of self-reflection and self-confidence, and interpersonal skill development were enhanced through cross-age teaching opportunities in TPSR programs.

4. Overall, participants in TPSR programs reported having more fun, a greater sense of belonging and feelings of safety, and an increased appreciation of the value of interaction with a caring adult.

Specific to the physical education setting, Li and colleagues (2008) investigated the relationship of the TPSR model to intrinsic motivation in an urban high school. The authors found that the higher levels of personal and social responsibility in the youth correlated to higher levels of enjoyment of physical education. In the first (and we believe only) published article of its kind, Wright, White, and Gaebler-Spira (2004) used the TPSR model in an adapted physical education class. They found that the young people reported an increase in positive social interactions and feelings about the program as well as an increased sense of their ability.

Schilling (2001) investigated underserved youths' perceptions of commitment to an after-school program that used Hellison's model of responsibility. Interviews and focus groups identified program organization, personal characteristics, development of interpersonal relationships, and program environment as key factors tending to engender commitment to the program.

Buchanan (2001) examined the impact of implementation of Hellison's responsibility model on staff at a summer sport program. The research design incorporated qualitative methodologies and included both ethnographic interviews and observations. Data revealed that the staff identified three contextual barriers to implementation of the model: understanding and implementation of the model, perceptions of respect and disrespect, and issues of control.

Tables 2.1 and 2.2 provide information about these studies and other published research relating to TPSR, ordered from most recent to oldest. The key terms listed are those noted in the publications by

Table 2.1 TPSR School-Based Research

Authors	Year	Key terms	Grade or age
Wright & Li	2009	Youth development, urban youth, physical education	High school
Li, Wright, Rukavina, & Pickering	2008	Personal and social responsibility, intrinsic motivation, self-direction	Middle school
Wright & Burton	2008	Responsibility, life skills, tai chi, high school	High school
Wright, White, & Gaebler-Spira	2004	Empowerment, adapted physical education, martial arts, cerebral palsy	Elementary
Martinek, Schilling, & Johnson	2001	At-risk youth, underserved youth, personal and social responsibility	Elementary
DeBusk & Hellison	1989	Delinquency, responsibility	Elementary

Table 2.2   TPSR Out-of-School-Based Research

Authors	Year	Key terms	Grade or age
Walsh, Ozaeta, & Wright	2010	Responsibility model, youth development, at-risk and urban youth, transference	Elementary
Walsh	2008a	At-risk youth, career club, underserved youth, youth development	Middle school
Walsh	2007	Youth development, personal and social responsibility	Elementary
Hammond-Diedrich & Walsh	2006	Urban youth, leadership, cross-age teaching	11-15 years
Hellison & Wright	2003	After-school programming, at-risk youth, underserved youth, youth development	11-22 years
Watson, Newton, & Kim	2003	Values-based programming, adolescent physical activity	10-15 years
Hellison & Walsh	2002	Responsibility model, youth programs, youth development	Multiple
Schilling	2001	Underserved youth, resiliency, sport program	12-15 years
Buchanan	2001	After-school programming, at-risk youth, underserved youth, youth development	Adult

the authors. We strongly encourage you to undertake reading beyond this chapter on the efficacy and implementation of the TPSR model both within and outside school settings.

Summary

Teaching physical education is difficult work. We often teach in a context that few others in the school must endure, with large class sizes, heterogeneous abilities, lack of equipment, and general apathy for our discipline. This scenario could be compared to one in which a classroom teacher is charged to teach math to 25 students with one math book, one pencil, and one piece of paper. Yet teaching physical education is one of the most rewarding endeavors in the school setting. When we allow ourselves to step beyond "busy, happy, and good" physical education practices and recognize that physical education reaches beyond the psychomotor, cognitive, and affective domains, we challenge ourselves to connect with our students and help them connect with themselves and each other through movement. This is worth doing!

What?

Our goal for chapter 2 was to highlight some of the notables who have directed our teaching beliefs and practices. We are also very aware that the teaching beliefs and practices of all of us are influenced by the work of countless others, both through published findings and direct interactions and observations. We believe that the published work is an element critical to teacher and professional development because it creates the bridge that links theory to practice, connects our passion to our reason, and inevitably facilitates the development of physical educators who seek positive youth development.

So What?

1. Discuss the term *socially toxic environment* and provide three to five examples of what this might look like.
2. Compare and contrast task-involving and ego-involving motivational climates.
3. Don Hellison said that TPSR is not about getting inside the heads of kids but rather getting them inside their own heads. What does he mean by this statement?
4. Summarize the findings from the TPSR research highlighted in this chapter. How might these findings influence your teaching strategies?

Now What? Suggested Readings

Murgia, C., & McCullick, B. (eds.). (2009). Engaging urban youths in physical education and physical activity. NASPE symposium. *Journal of Physical Education, Recreation and Dance, 80,* 25-45.

Noddings, N. (2003). *Happiness and education.* New York: Cambridge University Press.

Palmer, P. (2007). *The courage to teach.* San Francisco: Jossey-Bass.

Creating a Positive Learning Environment

TPSR professionals have debated the efficacy of the model in a physical education setting. Because of the nature of the teacher–student relationship, some people argue that TPSR cannot be used effectively in such a setting. For example, the often very large class sizes in physical education do not lend themselves easily to a sound teacher–student relationship. Likewise, having large numbers of youth in a class or program tends to result in greater variability with regard to skill, development, or both, thus creating an environment in which it is challenging for teachers to connect with their students. Lastly, given the large, often heterogeneous grouping in a typical physical education class, teachers (particularly new teachers) feel it is necessary to create an environment where they can rule with an "iron fist." In fact, the sport pedagogy literature that supports this notion often portrays effective teaching as high in management, discipline, and control (Parker 1995).

All in all, the typical physical education context can be a tough place to implement TPSR so as to facilitate youth development. This chapter highlights elements that we feel connect with the core themes of the TPSR model and that underlie the creation of a positive learning environment. A brief discussion on teaching across the spectrum (Mosston & Ashworth 2002) concludes the chapter as a segue to part II of the text, in which we weave TPSR into various sports and physical activities. But first, we examine some of the literature on development of positive student–teacher relationships.

Caring

Many of us became teachers because we felt drawn to the content, whether that was science, history, or, in our case, sport and physical education. Many more of us came to teaching because we also care about kids. We care about their well-being on the intellectual, physical, social, and emotional levels both inside and outside of our programs. It is this combination—love of the content and the kids—that author Parker Palmer notes is the stuff good teachers are made of: "Good teachers join self and subject and student in the fabric of life. Good teachers possess a capacity for connectedness" (Palmer 2007, p. 11). Palmer goes on to note that good teachers are able to weave a web of connections between the students, the content, and themselves so that eventually students can weave their own connections. Sometimes as teacher educators we mention helping our students develop or enhance their "bag of tricks," but good teaching is not about method alone. Being a good teacher is also about recognizing the importance of the connection between ourselves and the learner.

Nel Noddings is our hero! (Yes, professors have heroes, too.) She dared to care before caring was cool. Noddings (1995) provided justification for focusing on the social emotional needs of the learner when she commented on the nation's ardent push for emphasizing only academic standards in middle school, stating, "We will not achieve even that meager success [academic success] unless our children believe they themselves are cared for and learn to care" (p. 675). Noddings has written extensively on the importance of caring in the school setting (Noddings 1984, 1988, 1992, 1995).

If we step back a little farther, we can see the place of caring in the evolution of survival even before Noddings weighed in on the topic. In his book *Born to be Good* (2009), Dacher Keltner supports the notion that caring—among other noteworthy emotions (sympathy, love, gratitude, compassion)—is grounded in our genetic makeup. Using evolutionary biology and psychology and a large dose of Darwinian theory, Keltner argues that the foundation of survival is caregiving, rather than the often-touted survival of the fittest. As our hominid predecessors developed or evolved, characteristics such as narrower hips to support upright walking resulted in earlier birth patterns. Consequently, infants were more dependent on mothers, fathers, and communities and for longer periods of time. Keltner and others suggest that this change resulted in the need for more extended and more sophisticated caring. Additional examination of primates, our closest genetic relatives, supports this notion of the organization of communities around the need to care. Thus, Keltner states, "Caregiving is a way of life in humans and has been wired into our nervous system in the form of emotions such as sympathy and filial love" (Keltner 2009, chapter 4 "Survival of the Kindest").

If we consider the need to have cooperative communities that actively support the critical need for caregiving as a means by which to ensure survival, it is not too far-fetched to consider caring as advanced by Noddings over the last few decades as a plausible necessity for creating positive student–teacher and student–student relationships.

Noddings (1988, 2010) has also underscored the need for caring in our educational practices as a function of the reality of the changing demographics in the United States as well as globally. By 2020, more than two-thirds of the school population will be students of color—African American, Latino, Asian, or Native American (Meece & Kurtz-Costes 2001). Relatively recent statistics showed that 69 percent of students in urban areas were students of color (Johnson 2002) and that 33 percent of students had limited English proficiency (Futrell, Gomez, & Bedden 2003).

However, approximately 82 to 84 percent of public school teachers were white, and 75 percent of public school teachers were women (U.S. Department of Education 2003); only 32 percent of teachers felt they could adequately address the needs of children from diverse backgrounds, and less than 15 percent of teachers were fluent in a language other than English (Sachs 2004). Given this mismatch between who is doing the teaching and who is doing the learning, it is critical to develop a pedagogy that underscores a caring context or a context that connects.

Caring for someone requires engrossment or attention (Noddings 1984, 1988, 1992, 2010). Engrossment and attention refer to the acts of fully attending to another, or being open and able to receive another without judgment. Thus, to suspend one's judgment via the act of caring suggests that a caring person sets aside his own values and seeks to understand or attend to another. Or, as Noddings notes, we engage in motivational displacement—our needs are put aside as our "motive energy flows toward the needs . . . of the cared-for" (Noddings 2010, p. 391). This is a relational concept, and in order for the act to be labeled truly caring, it is necessary that the cared-for have some recognition of the efforts of the carer. It is through this reciprocity that both the carer and

cared-for develop trust, sympathy, and respect, and in this way community is formed.

Social Emotional Learning

Social emotional education refers to a curriculum focused on developing social emotional competencies, including the abilities to understand, process, manage, and express one's social and emotional life (Cohen 2001; Goleman 1995). This growing body of research and teaching practice points out what many teachers and parents have known for a long time: that it is as important for kids to learn how to "read" themselves and others as it is for them to learn how to read words. Social emotional learning (SEL) is characterized by the following core concepts (Cohen 2001):

1. Reflective capacities or enhancement of awareness of ourselves and others

2. Enhanced awareness of ourselves and others used toward increasing our ability to solve problems

3. Enhanced awareness of ourselves and others used toward increasing our ability to learn and be creative in a variety of contexts

4. Creation of safe, caring, and responsive environments

5. Strong collaboration between school, home, and community that is sustained over the long term

Hundreds of SEL programs exist in educational settings across the country. One such program is the Child Development Project (CDP). The CDP is a comprehensive program aimed at assisting schools in becoming "caring communities" of learners (Battistich et al. 2000; Battistich, Schaps, & Wilson 2004; Battistich et al. 1997; Solomon et al. 1996). CDP has pulled from a number of theoretical perspectives, including socialization, motivation, and learning, to develop school-wide interventions and programs that focus on promoting positive development in elementary-aged children. CDP is implemented school-wide and includes the components of classroom community building, facilitating cooperative learning, literature-based reading and support, and developmental discipline (Dasho, Lewis, & Watson 2001). Central to CDP's approach is a focus on creating a climate of caring, promoting personal and social understanding, and highlighting helping behaviors. The creation of a caring school community has been linked to greater enjoyment of school, prosocial attitudes, concern for others, and prosocial moral

By 2020, kids of color will make up most of the population of U.S. public schools.

reasoning, as well as lower antisocial behaviors, student drug use, and delinquency (Battistich & Hom 1997; Battistich, Schaps, & Wilson 2004; Battistich et al. 1997; Solomon et al. 1996).

Cohen (2001) brings the point home when he suggests that we remember our best and worst elementary school experiences. The best experience is often a time in which we felt recognized, understood, supported, and cared about. The worst experience tends to have been a time when we felt misunderstood, anxious, alone, and shamed. Cohen observes that "in both cases relationships provided the context for learning" (Cohen 2001, p. 21). Thus, when programs focus on the development of social emotional competencies in kids, they allow for the creation of learning environments that are caring and that facilitate connecting kids to themselves and others. Within the general education realm, caring has been shown to positively influence the learning process (figure 3.1).

Caring and Physical Activity

While evidence of caring in an educational context has been shown in the literature, much less such evidence has been noted in the physical activity setting until rather recently. The work of a group (or a "gaggle," as Don Hellison likes to call them) of sport sociology and psychology professors known as "the Posse" provides us with an empirical examination of caring in relation to motivation in physical activity contexts. The work of Fry, Gano-Overway, Guivernau, Kim, Magyar, Newton, and Watson (named here in alphabetical order) was initially based on the TPSR model in connection with notions around motivational climate (task vs. ego) and recognition of the value of keeping SITE of the TPSR themes. As the work has evolved, the Posse has demonstrated not only that kids recognize a caring climate but also that when they do, the results include a positive impact on their respect for the teacher and classmates, improvement in their prosocial behavior and enjoyment, and an increased likelihood of continuing in the physical activity program (see figure 3.2).

We encourage readers to check out this literature, but for the purposes of this chapter it suffices to say that through the instructional approaches we use or manipulate, we change the context of our gymnasiums from one that is defined primarily as competition and self-serving to one in which cooperation, communication, and support for others are primary. As noted in chapter 2, the climate of the gymnasium is attached strongly to our methods as educators and sport leaders. The last section of this chapter lays the groundwork for part II of the book by illuminating key elements of Mosston and Ashworth's spectrum of teaching styles (2002) and concludes with a brief discussion of the value of teaching through physical activity as it connects to the TPSR model.

Student-Centered Learning

A major aspect of the TPSR model is its focus on student–teacher and student–student relationships. An easy way to think about this is to ask ourselves as teachers, How do I invite the views, thoughts, or input of my students into my teaching? Given how we invite our students to share in the methods we use to teach, we are creating a situation through which we relinquish control and thus enhance student–teacher and student–student relationships.

A way to think about how we invite students into our teaching is to use the spectrum of teaching styles by Mosston and Ashworth (2002). The spectrum places the teaching context on a continuum (figure 3.3). The continuum is anchored on one end by

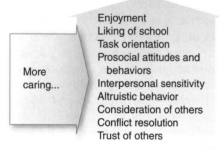

Figure 3.1   The impact of caring on the learning process (Battistich & Hom 1997; Battistich et al. 2000; Battistich et al. 1995; Battistich et al. 1989; Battistich et al. 1999; Solomon et al. 1996).

Figure 3.2   The impact of caring in physical activity programs (Magyar et al. 2007; Newton, Fry et al. 2007; Newton, Watson et al. 2007; Newton et al. 2006; Watson, Newton, & Kim 2003).

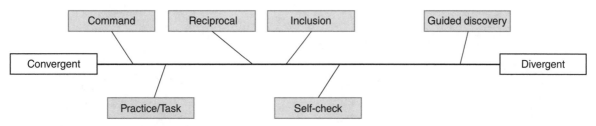

Figure 3.3   Continuum of teaching styles.

teaching styles that are convergent or that come to a common goal. The opposite end of the continuum is anchored by teaching styles that are divergent or that have many goals or possible answers.

Mosston conceptualized the teaching spectrum on the basis of the decisions the teachers made; as he states, "Teaching behavior is a chain of decision making" (Mosston & Ashworth 2002, p. 4). For Mosston, the spectrum identified teaching and learning options. Thus, the goal of the spectrum was for teachers to become proficient in generating a variety of teaching contexts based on the content focus, objectives, and learner needs. Movement along the teaching continuum is based on manipulation of the three phases of teaching: preimpact, impact, and postimpact.

- The preimpact phase entails establishing the lesson objectives and focus. It is often the teacher who is primarily in charge of this aspect of teaching.

- The impact phase is the actual execution of the teaching. This includes elements such as the pace of the lesson and the types of learning activities. Obviously, these aspects can also be primarily teacher centered; but within the spectrum, it is when we step away from the center in the impact phase that we begin to elicit a more student-centered approach.

- The postimpact phase includes evaluation of the student's performance both during and after completion of the task.

As the teacher begins to release control of the various phases to the student, the style of teaching changes and typically moves from the convergent end of the continuum toward the divergent end.

Mosston identified 11 styles of teaching, labeled styles A through K. The first five styles (A through E) represent teaching decisions that foster and support reproduction of past knowledge; these styles are called command, practice/task, reciprocal, inclusion, and self-check. The rest of the styles (F through K) represent options that foster production of new knowledge; these styles are called guided discovery,

convergent discovery, divergent discovery, learner-designed individual program, learner-initiated, and self-teaching.

Here we briefly discuss the styles incorporated into part II of this book. For a more detailed discussion of all the styles (A through K), the reader is directed to Mosston and Ashworth (2002).

Command

Response is influenced by telling students what to do, telling them how to practice, and directing practice.

Most effective approach when:

- Goal is to learn and perform specific skill
- Teacher is looking for a specific response
- Teacher has limited experience working with a group
- Time for organization is limited

Practice/Task

The teacher presents information through tasks, often organized into stations, that provide the teacher with the flexibility to maintain control over the teaching phases (teacher-centered) or begin to release some control to the students.

- Involves different students (often individually or in pairs) practicing different tasks at the same time
- Involves stations and task cards
- Works well when students need to practice skills they have already been taught

Most effective approach when:

- Teacher explains stations or tasks beforehand
- Teacher makes managerial aspects clear
- Teacher frequently checks with students
- Students start with only a few stations or tasks
- Students work well independently
- Students are able to function without close supervision

Giving kids choices helps increase motivation and engagement.

Reciprocal

Teacher designs and communicates tasks, and students assume roles of providing feedback and assessment to peers.

Most effective approach when:
- Skill to be taught is simple
- Cues for observation are clear
- Performance is easily measured

Inclusion

The teacher designs tasks; students are allowed to choose the level at which they begin the tasks that best meets their needs or ability levels. Learners make a decision based on self-assessment of their entry point (e.g., size of ball, distance to goal). When the learner meets that goal, she can challenge herself again at a new level.

- Accommodates individual learning differences
- Individualizes further because choices are presented
- Is really a developmentally appropriate approach

Most effective approach when:
- Criteria for self-evaluation and assessment of success are clear

- Performance is easily measured
- Students work well independently

Self-Check

Similar to the reciprocal style, the teacher designs and communicates the task; however, in this style students assume a self-teaching role as they perform the task and then self-assess and reflect upon their performance.

- Carryover from task and reciprocal styles
- Decisions shifted to the learner in the impact and postimpact phases
- Learners weaned away from external feedback; they provide their own feedback as they self-monitor their progress on task
- Learner decides the context based on feedback from self-evaluation

Most effective approach when:
- Teacher values the learner's ability to develop self-monitoring capacity
- Teacher trusts the student to be honest
- Learner can identify own limits, successes, and failures
- Learner can use self-check as feedback
- Learner can work independently

Guided Discovery

Teaching is through questioning, designed to let students think and solve problems. Two versions:

- Convergent inquiry: Students discover the same answer to a series of questions.
- Divergent inquiry: Students find multiple answers to a problem.

Most effective approach when:

- Students are encouraged to think independently to discover new and different approaches to performing skill
- Students are encouraged to solve questions related to teamwork and strategy as they relate to skill performance
- Students are encouraged to explore a movement when they are not yet ready to learn a mature version of the skill

Once we make the decision to alter the style of teaching, we are also making the decision to give the student a greater role in the lesson and thus are facilitating development of personal and social responsibility. As noted in table 1.1 (chapter 1), each teaching style connects the student to a different TPSR level focus and underscores the student's awareness and recognition of his personal and eventually social responsibility. Thus, as noted in this book and by Don, it is critical that TPSR be integrated within all aspects of your lessons and content. Incorporating divergent teaching styles allows students to make decisions within the learning context. This approach is unique in that it engages the learner in the discovery and production of options within the subject matter (Mosston & Ashworth 2002).

For example, when youth are afforded the opportunity to set their own learning pace during lesson practice, select the type(s) of equipment that best match their ability level, and work in small collaborative groups, this allows them to work on skills of self-direction, participation, cooperation, and goal setting (TPSR Levels II and III). Divergent teaching styles also create opportunities for students to learn how to assess their own performance as well as to assess and provide feedback to each other through peer or reciprocal learning (Levels III and IV).

Alteration of one's teaching style is crucial by its very nature to creating a caring environment. Therefore incorporation of the styles of teaching serves to create an environment ripe with teachable moments that enhance and connect to the TPSR model. Whether students are learning sport skills or life skills, infusion of the strategies presented here will help teachers develop youth who are responsible and caring members of their school and community.

The choice of teaching style depends on a number of factors, including the following:

- **Teacher beliefs:** It is difficult to loosen control; is the teacher comfortable doing so?
- **Goals of lessons:** Are the skills or tasks familiar to the students or are they completely new?
- **Teacher skill and preference:** Is the teacher confident about her teaching skills?
- **Student characteristics:** Do students work well independently without supervision?
- **Nature of content:** Are students familiar with the content? How complex is it?
- **Context of teaching:** How much equipment and space are available?

Summary

As physical educators, coaches, or program coordinators, we are tasked with teaching *about, within,* or *through* movement (Arnold 1999). While we debate about which facet to focus attention on, recent calls to enhance the social and moral development of youth through physical education have resulted in such a focus for two of the six national standards in physical education (NASPE 2004): A physically educated person should demonstrate personal and social responsibility (standard 5) and should value physical activity for health and social interactions (standard 6). Certainly as evidenced in the discussion in this chapter, a number of approaches and programs within general education address this need. While Noddings' work has contributed greatly to the argument, it is the work of such programs as the Child Development Program that gives legs to the philosophy that caring can and does lay the foundation for critical learning to take place. Within the realm of physical education and activity, the work of the Posse has shown that caring within a physical activity setting is equally important.

Pedagogical modifications inclusive of shifting one's teaching style(s) from convergent to more divergent provide impetus for the creation of care in the educational setting as students get opportunities to have choice, voice, and connection. It is then possible to maintain SITE of the core values of the TPSR model. Recognizing the importance of facilitating caring relationships via our pedagogy provides for the formation and maintenance of student–teacher and student–student relationships. Integration of this philosophy will be seen throughout the curriculum as a function of our pedagogical choices, and students with choice, voice, and connection are empowered and are more apt to demonstrate the behaviors of personal and social responsibility outside our gym-nasiums and programs. Ultimately, however, it is our responsibility as teachers to recognize and be willing to change our approach to teaching in the interest of creating a more positive learning environment.

What?

Our goal for chapter 3 was to give you the big picture of a positive learning environment as it relates to education and physical education. Clearly, caring for youth is not an idea specific to TPSR, and it is not enough for us to simply say that we care; we must also be mindful of the environments we create that aid us in ensuring that students learn and develop beyond becoming skillful movers. We hope that our brief discussion of Mosston and Ashworth's styles of teaching has resonated in a way that will encourage you to create such an environment. In addition, we hope that part II of this book will take you a little further not only in the thought process but also in the action process.

So What?

1. Draw three columns on a piece of paper. In the first column, list some negative images of today's students. In the second column, list some of the fears faced by young people in today's society. In the third column, list the positive attributes that you've observed in today's students.
2. How do these lists relate?
3. What are some of your fears in the gymnasium? Do your lists relate to these fears?
4. How might this exercise inform your teaching?

Now What? Suggested Readings

Holt, N.L. (ed.). (2008). *Positive youth development through sport.* New York: Routledge.

Mahoney, J.L., Larson, R.W., & Eccles, J.S. (eds.). (2005). *Organized activities as contexts of development.* Mahwah, NJ: Erlbaum.

Shields, D., & Bredemeier, B.J. (1995). *Character development and physical activity.* Champaign, IL: Human Kinetics.

Using TPSR in Physical Activity and Sport Settings

Introduction to Part II

Part II presents strategies for integrating TPSR levels and themes into physical activity and sport content areas. Chapters 4 through 12 represent the wide scope of curricular choices available to teachers or youth workers in physical education or recreation settings and are not intended to be exhaustive. Nor are these chapters designed to provide extensive content related to the given topic; rather the intent was to identify strategies for implementing TPSR across a wide variety of sport and physical activities. We believe that responsibility can be infused into any lesson and at any grade level.

Each chapter in part II walks readers through the developmental stages discussed in chapter 1 and shows how student characteristics and expectations at these stages influence the responsibility lesson. Table 1 outlines this progression in each lesson plan component (awareness talk, lesson focus, group meeting, and reflection) through the three developmental stages.

We use the TPSR lesson plan format introduced by Clocksin and colleagues (2011) to assist in organizing this model within the developmental stages, levels, and themes. The chapters in part II are organized according to the developmental stages using the lesson plan format. The characteristics of each lesson plan component was presented in table 1.2. Model in Action examples are used throughout each developmental stage to illustrate how responsibility shifts from the teacher to the student during each lesson component.

Processing Strategies and Tools

Each chapter in part II provides examples of processing strategies and tools you can use to help students generalize from their experiences in any unit. It is through processing that we can enhance the learning experiences of our students and create a foundation of reflection and transfer that is vital for the implementation of the TPSR model. The strategies and tools presented next and revisited in chapters 4 through 12 are ones you can use to promote a climate of reflection and communication.

Frontloading is a processing technique used to set the stage for the learner for a particular task or initiative. For example, before starting a task, teachers can point out to the group that success in the task requires the group to communicate clearly and work as a team. This draws the attention of the learner toward the communication and teamwork attributes of the task. Teachers can also directly or indirectly guide students through a "debrief" of their experience through questioning. As students become familiar with their role in the learning process, guiding questions ("What?" questions, such as "What are ways we show respect when a teacher is talking?") and questions that apply concepts within the context of the lesson ("So what?" questions, such as "Why is it important for you to listen to all the instructions before starting?") are a way to engage students in the reflection process. As students enhance their ability to reflect, we introduce questions that make a connection between the experience and life beyond the classroom context. These are transfer-related questions ("Now what?" questions, such as "Are there other situations where it is important to understand the instructions before starting?"). We can use these processing strategies throughout a TPSR-based lesson.

Many students are not used to having a voice in the learning process or being asked to openly share their thoughts and feelings. We can use props or simple strategies for prompting student responses and developing a climate of reflection and sharing. The following are eight ideas that we use throughout part II. When chapters mention these ideas, refer back to these descriptions to refresh your memory about how they are used.

Buzz Words

Buzz words are a great way to introduce students to sharing their voice in class. The group meeting leader identifies a question or topic, and students quickly give a "buzz word" response (i.e., a one- or two-word summary). This works well in a circle format, allowing each student to quickly share his response while minimizing the time spent on reflecting. For example, the group meeting leader might say, "Give me one word that summarizes what you focused on during that task." As students move through the developmental stages, buzz words can be followed by probing questions to elicit more fully why a student chose a particular buzz word or to link back to the lesson theme.

Table 1 Developmental Sequence and Lesson Components

Developmental stages	Relationship time	Awareness talk	Lesson focus	Group meeting	Reflection
Stage 1	Activities focus on individual traits (self-control, respect, and effort) within the context of group interactions.	• Students have a voice • Teacher leads • Identify expectations of the teacher for the students	• Teacher leads • Present opportunities to exhibit respect and the willingness to participate with effort • Begin using teaching styles that allow students to make choices and demonstrate self-direction (e.g., practice/task style)	• Teacher is primary leader • Provide opportunity for students to voice how they or others demonstrated behaviors consistent with the responsibility levels • Students are introduced to their responsibilities in the class environment	• Students reflect on their role in meeting the responsibility levels • Use guided response sheets (e.g., rubrics, picture charts) • Use informal checks • Students self-evaluate performance in the lesson
Stage 2	Activities transition from individuals performing within the context of the group to individuals positively interacting with partners and small groups in self-guided learning experiences.	• Student voice increases • Students begin to lead with help from teacher • Identify expectations of students for other students	• Teacher leads most of the activities • Provide opportunities to exhibit self-direction • Transition to student-centered teaching styles (e.g., task, reciprocal, self-check)	• Students begin to lead • Present opportunities to set group goals and expectations • Peer review boards may be formed to reinforce student expectations	• Students reflect on their role in meeting the responsibility levels • Begin using open-ended responses • Use journal writing • May include reflection outside of class
Stage 3	Activities transition from individuals positively interacting with partners and small groups to collaborative learning experiences led by student leaders with the support of the teacher.	• Fully developed and led by students • Identify expectations of students toward individual and group goals	• Students begin to take greater leadership roles • Provide opportunities to demonstrate caring and leadership • Transition further to student-centered teaching styles that allow greater student responsibility for learning	• Completely student led • Present opportunity to voice observations and expectations • Reinforce responsibility expectations • Peers may mitigate disputes	• Students reflect on their role in meeting the responsibility levels • Open-ended questions make a connection to life beyond the gym (transfer) • Use journal writing • May include reflection outside of class

Show of Hands

With show of hands, students are simply asked to respond to questions by agreeing (hands up) or disagreeing (hands down). "Raise your hands if you were able to make at least 7 out of 10 shots." This technique works well for developmental stage 1 students as they learn appropriate ways to share their reflections on activities during the group meeting. You can follow up show-of-hands questions with questions that ask students to explain (e.g., "Why did so many of you struggle to make 7 out of 10 shots?").

Thumbometer

The thumbometer is another easy technique that gives students a way to safely share their views and teachers a way to get a sense of how students are responding to the activities. Students use their thumbs to answer simple questions posed by the teacher. For example, following a skill practice you might say, "Give me a thumbs up if you were able to successfully complete the task every time, a sideways thumb if most of the time, and a thumbs down if that task was difficult for you." The questions can be modified to fit the context of the lesson and can be easily linked to the lesson theme.

Metaphor Cards

Metaphor cards (http://store.training-wheels.com/metcar.html) are designed as props for students to use when reflecting on an activity. One side of the card has an image (e.g., a picture of a boy building a sand castle) and the other a single word (e.g., "collaboration"). The student can use either the image or the word to frame her response to a question posed by the group meeting leader.

Deck of Questions

Teachers can develop a deck of question cards for student leaders to use to guide their peers in reflecting on the day's lesson. These can be a set of generic "What?", "So what?", and "Now what?" questions, or they can be tailored to link back to the theme of the lesson, thus providing a connection between the reflection and transfer beyond the classroom experience.

Deck of Cards

The suit of the card guides the student response. For example:

- Heart: something you felt during the activity
- Clubs: something the group struggled with
- Spades: something the group did well
- Diamond: something you valued in another student during the activity

Chiji Processing Dice

Like other processing props, Chiji dice (www.chiji.com/products.htm) encourage student communication during debriefing. The set of four dice includes a control die (determines who will speak) and three progressive dice that ask "What?", "So what?", and "Now what?" questions. Teachers can customize the questions on the dice to better address the experiences presented in the lesson. Consider using one of the dice to link discussions back to the theme and another to set the stage for the students' reflection on how the theme can be transferred beyond the classroom experience.

Position Stands

In position stands, the teacher names an action or behavior observed during the lesson and asks students who modeled that action or behavior to stand up. For example, following a putting drill in golf, you could use position stands to check on student practice:

- "Stand up if you were successful at hitting the ball into the correct zone most of the time."
- "Stand up if you took your time to properly address the ball before putting."
- "Stand up if you took a practice putt before each real putt."

Each position stand offers a topic for further discussion with the students, for example:

- "What strategies did you use to putt the ball into the correct zone?"
- "How does addressing the ball help our putting?"
- "Why should we take a practice putt?"

Starting With Adventure

We believe that adventure education theory and practice (chapter 4) provides a natural connection to the TPSR model. The activities used in an adventure curriculum provide a medium for starting discussions on responsibility and a reflective learning cycle. We use these activities when starting with groups that are new to the TPSR model or as a way to refocus a group that is struggling with implementation of the model. As you move through the other activity chapters, you will notice the underpinnings of adventure pedagogy that serves to facilitate student relationships, integration of content, transfer of learning experiences, and the empowerment of students in the learning process. All chapters in part II implement the TPSR model and highlight ways to adapt the presentation of the content to facilitate prosocial behavioral changes in youth.

Keeping SITE

As discussed in chapter 1, the key to TPSR is keeping SITE of four thematic objectives (student–teacher relationships, integration, transfer, and empowerment) throughout your lessons and program. Each chapter in part II concludes with a series of questions based on these themes to serve as a SITE check for understanding.

Teaching Personal and Social Responsibility Through

Adventure Education

Considering the similarities in the basic tenets of adventure education and physical activity programming that promotes personal and social responsibility, the merits of including adventure activities in physical education programming are numerous. Adventure education uses activities, challenges, and initiatives to create an environment where participants routinely set goals (individual, group, or both), challenge themselves, and take risks to achieve those goals as they commit themselves to an experience-based learning episode. Adventure education also provides an opportunity for teachers to use student-centered teaching styles (guided discovery, self-check, inclusion) and assesses affective development consistent with the TPSR model.

Adventure education has evolved out of the early teachings of Kurt Hahn and the philosophy of Outward Bound. Learning occurs as students are exposed to risk (perceived and actual; physical, emotional, or both) and provided with the support and experiences to successfully complete the task. Learning through individual and shared experiences is the foundation of experiential learning and an essential part of adventure education. It is through these experiences that individual and group assets are developed and fostered. These activities also have the potential to create a learning environment that promotes positive social interaction, develops reflective learners, and lays the foundation for discussion of personal and social responsibility. To maximize this potential, adventure educators use the experiential learning cycle (figure 4.1) developed by Kolb (1984). As physical educators we commonly use an experiential teaching model by giving students concrete experiences from which to learn. Often embedded in these experiences are opportunities for students to observe their peers and reflect on their performance. We often fail to take the time to help students generalize these experiences to other content within physical education or transfer learning to contexts beyond the gymnasium.

As a teacher of physical education, you understand the potential for reaching children through physical activities and sport. However, we often miss opportunities to maximize the attributes of the activities we choose. Adventure educators accomplish this through processing techniques that encourage students to collectively and individually reflect on the experiences. Adventure educators use a continuum of processing techniques that range from letting the activity speak for itself to indirectly frontloading the experience (Gass 1995).

Developmental Stage 1

As we discussed in the beginning of this book, students in the first developmental stage are often working on consistently exhibiting Level I (respect) and Level II (participating with effort) behaviors. By its very nature, an adventure education curriculum should place students in a novel and somewhat unsettling state as they deal with risk (perceived and real) and challenge. The dynamics of the group can be greatly affected by the sequence of activities we present during our adventure program. During this stage the teacher takes the predominant role, leading the awareness talk, choosing developmentally appropriate tasks and challenges, structuring the group meeting, and providing reflection opportunities. Students are guided by challenge-by-choice and full-value contract principles as they form, storm, norm, and perform in their new roles in the group (Tuckman 1965). For those unfamiliar with adventure education, challenge-by-choice is a foundational philosophy whereby participants choose their level of challenge. This can be related to the role they take (e.g., leader, spotter) and whether they engage in an activity (e.g., fear of climbing, physical injury). The role of a full-value contract is to create a climate of support for one's own abilities and the abilities of others. In demonstrating their understanding of the full-value contract, participants avoid negative self-talk (e.g., "I can't") and abstain from using language and actions that discount the contributions of others.

Relationship Time

Much of adventure programming works through the affective domain. This allows opportunities for social interactions throughout most games and initiatives. Deinhibitor games (icebreakers) set the stage for learning experiences in adventure. They provide an

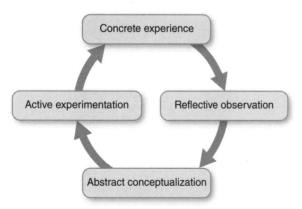

Figure 4.1   Kolb's experiential learning cycle.

opportunity for students to interact, develop relationships, and have fun. Throughout this section we provide examples of relationship time activities that foster interactions between students. Relationship games begin every lesson we teach. They can vary in length but all serve the purpose of creating an environment that fosters acceptance and interaction. When working with developmental stage 1 learners, consider selecting activities that place the focus on individual traits (self-control, respect, and effort) within the context of group interactions.

The Race Is On activity (Model in Action 4.1) gives students the opportunity to demonstrate respect (Level I) and participate with effort (Level II). There is often a point in the game when two students arrive at the same spot at the same time. This provides the opportunity for conflict, but also conflict resolution and compromise. Transition from this activity to the awareness talk by drawing the students' attention to the similarities they exhibited during the game. "I noticed that many of you moved when Lilka said she liked to play soccer and Michael said he liked ice cream. It appears that we have a lot in common. I also liked that when Katie and Jay arrived at the spot at the same time, they were able to quickly decide who got to stay." With comments like these, we can help students be aware of the concept of respect (understanding similarities we have, peaceful conflict resolution, compromising). Similarly, we can link the students' effort in moving during the game to Level II.

Awareness Talk

With students in the first developmental stage, the teacher takes the primary role during the awareness talks. He identifies the theme, guides the questioning, and makes the connection to the lesson focus. Commonly used themes during developmental stage 1 include respect, self-control, participation, effort, and effective communication. Here we use The Race Is On activity (Model in Action 4.1) to illustrate adventure-based awareness talk techniques that can move students from a relationship activity to the lesson focus. Although it is often effective to use relationship time activities as a means to start the awareness talk, there are times when we may just want to establish a warm-up protocol, play a game, or practice a concept that reinforces the previous lesson but may not link to the awareness topic of the day. Just as we use instant activities, relationship activities can be an opportunity for students and the teacher to interact for the pure purpose of establishing relationships and a sense of belonging (more on this in chapter 14).

MODEL IN ACTION 4.1

The Race Is On

DESCRIPTION

We have used this activity with nearly every group we have worked with that was larger than 15 people. For students from second graders to graduate students, this game offers an opportunity to learn about peers, warm up, and have a bit of fun. Participants stand on poly spots (or similar floor markings) in a large circle. One person (usually the teacher first) stands in the middle of the circle. She says "The race is on if you . . ." and adds something that is true about herself, such as "like ice cream," "have a sister," "are wearing red." All participants for whom the statement is true must leave their poly spot and find a new one. They may not return to their original spot or the spots adjacent to their original spot. The person in the middle also attempts to find a spot, leaving someone new in the middle.

EQUIPMENT

Poly spot for each participant.

VARIATIONS

- With larger groups (40+), have participants sit back-to-back on the spots. If they agree with the statement they jump up, run to a new spot, and sit back-to-back with a new partner. We often use this to transition to a partner activity.

- With groups that are relatively new to each other, have participants state their names when they are in the middle. "Hi, my name is Brian, and the race is on if you. . . ."

Initially you may need to make direct connections between learning experiences. One technique is to "speak for the experience" (Gass 1995). In The Race Is On example, you would generalize the lessons learned from the activity to the theme and subsequent activities. These are examples of statements you might use:

- "I was surprised to see how many moved when David mentioned liking to swim and Jasmine mentioned having a sister. It appears we have a lot in common in this class."
- "I noticed that everyone did a nice job moving safely around the area."
- "It was great to see Michael and Alyssa work out who got to stay on the spot without the need for me to get involved."

In speaking for the experience, you can generalize what occurred in the activity. However, this assumes that all students interpret the experience in the same way. While this is rarely the case, by speaking for the experience the teacher can highlight key aspects that she observed and link directly to lesson outcomes.

"Debriefing the experience" (Gass 1995) is a second technique that can draw the attention of the learner to the cognitive and affective attributes of an activity. This technique uses a series of questions to get participants to reflect on their experiences. In The Race Is On example, you would begin discussion after the activity to determine what happened ("What?" questions), what it means ("So what?" questions), and how it can be generalized to other learning experiences ("Now what?" questions). These are examples of questions you might use:

"What?" Questions

- "What did you need to do to safely participate in this activity?"
- "What did you learn about your classmates?"

"So What?" Questions

- "Why is it important to learn about other students in your class?"
- "How can knowing about others affect how we treat them?"

"Now What?" Questions

- "How can you learn more about each other outside of class?"
- "What are ways we can use our similarities or differences to have success in the activities we do in the future?"

The depth of debrief will depend on the experience of the group in sharing their thoughts, the types of questions asked, and the time available for reflection. Initially using "What?" questions may help students voice their thoughts, since these questions typically

Adventure activities teach cooperation and teamwork as well as attributes like respect, pride, judgment, and character.

require simple, short responses that address what happened. Debriefing the experience goes beyond speaking for the experience as it allows individual students to reflect on their interpretation of the experience.

Selecting relationship activities that can be used to stimulate discussion during the awareness talk is a way to link concrete experiences to the lesson that follows. The shared experience of the group during the activities and subsequent reflection can make students aware of the theme of the lesson and provide teachable moments from which to guide this discussion. As we move through the developmental stages, student awareness talk leaders can also benefit from having an experience to use as a guide for the awareness talk. In this case the awareness talk leader is in essence frontloading the lesson experiences to come.

Lesson Focus

The theme identified during the awareness talk often sets the stage for what will occur during the lesson focus. Teachers can select tasks or use pedagogical strategies that provide opportunities for students to make a cognitive or affective connection between the tasks and the theme. Adventure educators often categorize activities based on the attributes they possess. Generally we use four primary attribute categories in adventure education (teamwork, problem solving, trust, and communication) with an understanding that a single activity might address more than one attribute (e.g., teamwork and communication). We can draw the attention of the learner to the attributes by using a variety of processing techniques.

The teaching style we use can also influence how the students perceive the task. With students in developmental stage 1, it is often beneficial to maintain a somewhat teacher-centered approach. That being said, to truly draw meaning from adventure activities we often need to allow students to work through challenges with little teacher guidance. To meet their developmental needs, select challenges that provide opportunities for them to demonstrate respect (Level I) and participate with effort (Level II) while using a style that transitions them to working independently with their peers (Level III). In the examples that follow, you can use the command or guided discovery style of teaching to present adventure tasks across the attribute themes (e.g., trust, teamwork, communication, problem solving). The style you choose will be influenced by your teaching philosophy, the learning styles of your students, and the context in which the lesson is presented.

Sequencing learning experiences to match the developmental level of learners is essential for creating a positive learning environment. Within adventure education, the sequence provides opportunity for group cohesion and the development of trust in self and peers. Table 4.1 identifies a sequence of adventure activities and possible connections to the TPSR model. A number of activities can be used to promote learning across the sequence. The sample

Table 4.1 Sequence of Learning Experiences in Adventure Education

Day	Learning sequence	Link to TPSR levels
1	Deinhibitor games, icebreakers	Respect, participating with effort
2	Name games	Respect
3	Attribute activities Trust	Respect, caring, leadership
4	Communication	Respect, participating with effort, caring, leadership
5	Problem solving	Respect, participating with effort, caring, leadership
6	Teamwork	Respect, participating with effort, caring, leadership
7	Social responsibility activities (low initiative)	Respect, participating with effort, caring, leadership
8	Personal responsibility activities (individual activities such as high elements)	Respect, participating with effort, self-direction

activities listed in this section were selected to illustrate adventure activities that provide opportunities for students to demonstrate developmental stage 1 behaviors. By modifying how the activities are presented, educators can use these activities with any developmental level.

There is some debate as to when, and how best, to develop trust in participants during adventure activities. Some believe that trust is developed through shared experiences. Others believe that through planned trust activities we can foster a sense of trust between and within participants. Either way, trust (emotional and physical) is central to adventure-based programming and serves as a foundation for advancing students through the responsibility levels. The Self-Spot activity (Model in Action 4.2) demonstrates how adventure-based activities can be used to foster trust and how this connects to the levels of responsibility we discuss throughout this book.

As teachers we have a variety of pedagogical strategies at our disposal. Modifying the teaching style can be a useful tool to integrate personal and social responsibility into physical education and sport settings. In doing so, we begin to shift the responsibility for learning from the teacher to the student. We expect students in the first developmental stage of the TPSR model to need more guidance from us throughout the lesson. Using teacher-centered instructional styles allows students to concentrate on being respectful and participating with effort without the expectation that they will work independently (Level III) or demonstrate caring for others and leadership (Level IV).

Table 4.2 presents considerations for teaching Self-Spot activities using two teaching styles and shows how they connect to the TPSR model.

These instructional styles give students the opportunity to directly demonstrate personal and social responsibility; they also provide teachers with teachable moments to reinforce respect, effort, caring, and leadership consistent with the TPSR philosophy. The trust attribute of adventure activities is ephemeral and requires consistent attention, and it is often a talking point during processing of the experience.

Command (Direct) Style

Presenting the self-spotting activities through a command style of teaching allows you to direct the students through the progression of tasks. This encourages students to perform the task in the same way at the same time and allows you to check student performance. For these self-spotting tasks and other

---

MODEL IN ACTION 4.2

Self-Spot

DESCRIPTION

This pair of activities is used to start a spotting sequence and demonstrates to students their ability to self-support their body when falling.

Activity 1: Wall Walk

Working in pairs, one student (faller) stands on the floor mat at arm's-length distance from the wall. Her partner sits directly behind her, using his heels to push the mat against the wall. The faller places her hands on the wall, takes a step back (8 to 10 inches, or 20 to 25 centimeters), and walks her hands down the wall (a total of 8 to 10 inches). The process is repeated until the student feels she has reached her limit, at which time she reverses the process and walks her hands back up the wall. Partners then switch roles and the process is repeated.

Activity 2: Wall Fall

Starting as in the Wall Walk, the student falls into the wall, catching herself with her hands. She pushes off the wall to return to a standing position and takes a step back (8 to 10 inches). The process is repeated until the student feels she has reached her limit. Partners then switch roles and repeat the process.

EQUIPMENT

Flat wall surface, floor mats.

VARIATION

Have the student repeat the process using only her dominant or nondominant hand.

Table 4.2 Developmental Stage 1 Instructional Strategies

Instructional style	Teaching considerations	Links to TPSR
Command (direct)	• All students perform task together. • Teacher is in position to see all students. • Provides order for new tasks and high-risk activities. • Class progresses together. • Limits opportunity for student voice. • Does not accommodate student differences. • Assumes students will "solve" task in the same way. • Limits opportunity for students to demonstrate self-direction. • Limits student–student interaction.	• Students can demonstrate respect (Level I) for the teacher (e.g., following directions, staying in control) and for peers (e.g., not interfering with their practice, anchoring the mat for partner). • Students can demonstrate participation with effort (Level II) by staying engaged with the self-spot activities. • Students can begin to demonstrate self-direction (Level III) by progressively challenging themselves throughout the self-spot activities (e.g., distance they fall).
Guided discovery	• Student solves problem presented by the teacher (cognitive engagement). • Teacher is free to work with students who need extra attention. • Provides opportunity for students to solve task in unique ways. • Provides opportunity for students to voice opinion to peers. • Leads to greater variance in performance. • May decrease practice time. • May increase risk for injury.	• Students can demonstrate respect (Level I) for the teacher (e.g., following directions, staying in control) and for peers (e.g., not interfering with their practice, anchoring the mat for partner). • Students can demonstrate participation with effort (Level II) by staying engaged with the self-spot activities. • Students can begin to demonstrate self-direction (Level III) by progressively challenging themselves throughout the self-spot activities (e.g., distance they fall).

tasks that have an element of risk, the command style may establish protocols by which students can safely complete the task. You may choose to present these activities as described next. You can increase control over this activity by having all students move through the steps at the same time (e.g., "step back," "walk hands," "step back").

Wall Walk   Provide a demonstration of the task and identify cues (i.e., hands at shoulder height, arms extended, body straight, catch and absorb). Position students in pairs around the gym.

1. Arm's length away from wall, hands touching wall, perform wall push-up.
2. Step back and walk your hands down the wall.
3. Repeat stepping back and walking your hands down the wall until you reach your limit.

4. Reverse—walk up the wall with your hands, step in.

Wall Fall   Provide a demonstration of the task and identify cues (i.e., hands at shoulder height, arms extended, body straight, catch and absorb). Position students in pairs around the gym.

1. Arm's length away from wall, hands touching wall, perform wall push-up.
2. Step back, fall to wall, perform wall push-up, return to standing.
3. Repeat until you reach your limit (demonstrate fall escape—stepping forward with one leg to decelerate the body).
4. Start over and use only one arm.
5. Repeat with the other arm.

Guided Discovery Style

Presenting the self-spotting activities through a guided discovery approach allows the teacher to engage students in both the cognitive and psychomotor domains. The teacher guides the students through the progression of tasks. Through questioning or the presentation of a problem, you can have students converge on the solution for safely performing the self-spotting skill progression. For these self-spotting tasks and other tasks that have an element of risk, a guided discovery approach may increase the risk of injury. With these tasks you should get students to converge on the best solution, verbalize what this would look like, and then demonstrate. Through this process you can guide students to determine the learning cues for successful skill performance (i.e., hands at shoulder height, arms extended, body straight, catch and absorb). Note in the following how a subtle change in presentation style can alter the way in which students learn.

Wall Walk   Position students along the wall (their partner supporting the mat as described earlier).

1. Can you make a triangle with only your feet touching the ground and only your hands touching the wall? How low can you get your body?
2. Does it work better to have your arms straight or arms bent?
3. Can you do it with only one hand touching the wall?
4. Only one leg touching the ground (two hands on the wall)?

Wall Fall   Position students along the wall (their partner supporting the mat as described earlier).

1. Take a step back; without moving your feet, can you place your hands on the wall?
2. Take another step back; does your technique still work?
3. What are ways we can slow the body down as we fall into the wall?
4. Is it easier with the body bending or staying straight?
5. Can you take another step back? What can we do while falling into the wall to stop ourselves if needed? What if you took a step forward? (Use this as a teachable moment to discuss the idea of keeping ourselves safe while practicing self-spotting techniques. It is better to fail at the aim of the task [keep feet set] but

keep ourselves safe if we have overestimated our abilities.)

6. Continue until you think you have reached your limit.
7. Can you start over and only use one arm? What do you have to do to maintain balance?

Group Meeting

A group meeting during the first developmental stage is facilitated by the teacher but provides an opportunity for students to have a voice in the learning process. From an adventure education perspective, the group meeting serves as the culminating debrief session for the lesson. This offers an opportunity for the teacher to make connections between the activities presented during the lesson and the theme and for students to voice how they and their peers met the responsibility expectations of TPSR. This aspect of the lesson need not take a great deal of time, but it is essential for connecting the responsibility attributes of the activities to student learning.

During developmental stage 1, the teacher takes the primary role in facilitating the group meeting, but student voice should be encouraged and prompted. Use techniques that allow students to quickly and safely provide input (e.g., buzz words, show of hands, thumbometer). It is during this stage that you must establish the protocols for group meetings (i.e., Who gets to talk? What is appropriate to discuss?).

For example, during Self-Spot (Model in Action 4.2), you can ask students to rate their performance using the thumbometer (thumbs up if they did better than they thought they could, thumbs sideways if they did about what they expected, and thumbs down if they did not do as well as they had hoped). On the basis of the students' responses, you can ask for examples of student action to illustrate their ratings. You can also ask students to speak to positive performances they noticed in their peers; they might say, for example, "I was so impressed with how far Isabella was able to walk down the wall" or "I appreciated how Matthew encouraged me to go farther than I thought I could." You can then link these discussions back to the theme ("Our theme today focused on respect, and I heard a lot of good examples of how we recognized the efforts of others and challenged ourselves in today's activities"), or set the stage for the reflection portion of the lesson, or both.

Reflection

The reflection time is an opportunity for students to self-reflect on their actions and what they observed in others throughout the lesson. During developmental stage 1, the focus is typically on self-reflection around Level I and II behaviors. This can be accomplished through a variety of formats (e.g., student drawings, journal assignments, rubrics) in class or outside of class time. Consider partnering with the classroom teacher to create a writing assignment linked to physical education experiences that gives students an opportunity to reflect on their learning experiences and the TPSR levels. For Self-Spot, this could include the following:

- Ask students to draw the ideal body position when doing the self-spot activity.
- Have them describe the characteristics of a good self-spotter.
- Ask them to rate their performance with regard to effort (3, pushed myself; 2, tried hard; 1, took it easy).

Developmental Stage 2

Once students are consistently demonstrating Level I and II behaviors, the teacher should transition to the second developmental stage. Within the adventure education curriculum, this means providing opportunities for students to work collaboratively with their peers with little guidance from the teacher (Level III, self-direction). During the second stage, you begin to call on students to take a role in the learning process and begin to relinquish some control of the class to students during awareness talks and group meetings. Through this process, some students may begin to demonstrate a desire to take leadership roles (Level IV). However, most will continue to need some guidance in keeping self-directed.

Relationship Time

As we transition to developmental stage 2, students have consistently demonstrated an ability to perform with respect (Level I) and to participate with effort (Level II). You have begun to offer students opportunities to demonstrate self-directed learning behaviors (Level III) through planned activities and a gradual transition to student-centered teaching approaches. These opportunities for self-direction take center stage during developmental stage 2, and relationship time activities should transition from individuals performing within the context of the group to individuals positively interacting with partners and in small groups in self-guided learning experiences.

The Partner Duck Duck Goose activity (Model in Action 4.3) gives students the opportunity to continue to demonstrate respect (Level I) and to participate with effort (Level II) while working collaboratively with their partner without direct supervision from the teacher (Level III). When students are asked to physically touch (tag) another student, there

Students begin to take leadership roles.

MODEL IN ACTION 4.3

Partner Duck Duck Goose

DESCRIPTION

This is a nice variation on a traditionally inactive game that gets students' heart rates up and gets them laughing. Have each student find a partner. Standing with one foot on the center line (or poly spot) facing his partner, one student begins by tapping his partner's shoulder and saying "duck." The second student then taps back, also saying "duck." This continues until one student says "goose," at which point the tapper (the one who said "goose") flees his partner by running to the end line on his side. If the person fleeing reaches the end line without being tagged by his partner, he gets a point. If the chaser is able to tag the player who is fleeing, the chaser receives the point. First player to 5 points wins, and then the students find new partners.

EQUIPMENT

Markings for a center line and two end lines. When the activity is outside, you can use a poly spot for the center line and two cones on each side for end lines.

VARIATIONS

The variations are endless with games like these. For example, students can

- say even and odd numbers, chasing when an odd number is called;
- say multiples of 5, chasing when a number that is not a multiple of 5 is called;
- say capitals and states, chasing when a state is called;
- vary the locomotor pattern; or
- complete a fitness task (for example, try to be the first one to finish 40 ski jumps).

is potential for disrespectful behavior (e.g., hitting too hard, pushing). Transition from this activity to the awareness talk by drawing the students' attention to the level of effort and self-control you observed during the activity.

- "Whose heart is racing? I am impressed with the level of effort I noticed during this activity."
- "It was nice to see how quickly you got set back up for the next round."
- "I appreciate that everyone used good tagging techniques; I did not see any pushing or hard tags."

With comments like these we can bring to students an awareness of the concept of participating with effort (committing to trying during both new and familiar activities).

Awareness Talk

During the second developmental stage, the teacher begins to share the responsibility for the awareness talks. The teacher identifies the theme, asks one or more students to guide the questioning, and draws

the connection to the lesson focus. Commonly used themes during developmental stage 2 are self-control, self-direction, goal setting, and problem solving. Here we use Partner Duck Duck Goose (Model in Action 4.3) to illustrate adventure-based awareness talk techniques that can move students from a relationship activity to the lesson focus.

Using students to help guide the awareness talk is key in the development of youth leaders (Level IV). Following the activity, you can use student leaders to "debrief" so as to draw the attention of the learners to the cognitive and affective attributes of an activity. These are examples of questions you might provide to the student leader:

"What?" Questions

- "What did you need to be successful in this activity?"
- "Was it easier to chase or flee?"

"So What?" Questions

- "How did your body positioning influence your ability to chase or flee?"
- "How could you be more successful in activities?"

"Now What?" Questions

- "How are chasing and fleeing used in sports and activities you participate in?"
- "What strategies did you use in this activity that can help you find success in other activities that involve chasing or fleeing?"

By providing a selection of questions, you maintain the direction of the conversation while giving students an opportunity to comfortably explore what it is like to take a leadership role in class.

Lesson Focus

The lesson focus during developmental stage 2 begins the shift from a teacher-centered to a student-centered teaching style. The logical sequencing of adventure education activities promotes student responsibility to the group that fosters self-direction and leadership and caring behaviors consistent with TPSR Levels III and IV. As the students begin to take on the group roles that have been established through the curricular choices made by the teacher, they begin to need less guidance from the teacher to finish and reflect upon tasks. Because student behavior is ephemeral, reinforcement of Level I and II behaviors may be required, but a majority of class time can be spent with activities that promote self-direction (Level III) and offer leadership roles for students (Level IV). The Impulse activity (Model in Action 4.4) is an example of an activity that helps students transition through responsibility levels.

Table 4.3 presents considerations for teaching the Impulse activity using two teaching styles and shows how these connect to the TPSR model. With use of a teacher-centered (i.e., command) teaching style, the activity primarily reinforces responsibility Levels I and II. Through the processing of the activity, you can make connections to responsibility Levels III and IV behaviors that you observed during the activity. However, if you use a more student-centered approach (e.g., guided discovery), you can foster self-direction and leadership behavior in students.

You can make connections to Levels III and IV in the debrief of the activity, but you will be able to call upon concrete examples of behaviors you observed during the group trials. "I was impressed at how Matthew got the attention of the group and suggested that everyone turn their heads as they pass the impulse." In so doing you can link the behavior (e.g., leadership) to subsequent tasks and to experiences beyond the classroom, thus providing an opportunity for transferring the lessons learned. Impulse usually creates a variety of teachable moments that can be discussed (processed) throughout the activity. Students have a tendency to start an impulse without first receiving it or to forget to transfer the impulse when they do receive it. Both of these situations lend themselves to a discussion on staying engaged with the activity (participating with effort). Some students will squeeze hard as they transfer the impulse. Draw their attention to being a self-regulated (Level III) learner and demonstrating caring (Level IV) for their classmates. Additionally, squeezing hard causes a delay in the transfer of the impulse.

MODEL IN ACTION 4.4

Impulse

DESCRIPTION

This activity works on the group's ability to successfully communicate through movements rather than verbally. Participants sit in a circle holding hands. The leader starts an impulse by squeezing the hand of one of the people next to him. That person transfers the impulse to the next using a similar hand squeeze. This continues until the impulse travels around the circle and makes it back to the leader.

EQUIPMENT

No equipment is needed for this activity. It is usually performed in a seated circle.

VARIATIONS

To add a level of challenge to this activity, try one or more of the following:

- Send an impulse in both directions.
- Send multiple impulses simultaneously or with a pause in between.
- Time how long it takes for the impulse to return to the start.

Table 4.3   Developmental Stage 2 Instructional Strategies

Instructional style	Teaching considerations	Links to TPSR
Command (direct)	• All students perform task together. • Teacher is in position to see all students. • Provides order for new tasks and high-risk activities. • Class progresses together. • Limits opportunity for student voice. • Does not accommodate student differences. • Assumes students will "solve" task in the same way. • Limits opportunity for students to demonstrate self-direction. • Limits student–student interaction.	• Students can demonstrate respect (Level I) for the teacher (e.g., following directions, staying in control) and for peers (e.g., not sending a fake impulse, keeping the impulse moving). • Students can demonstrate participation with effort (Level II) by staying engaged with the Impulse activity. • Students can demonstrate self-control by sending the impulse only when they receive one.
Guided discovery	• Student solves problem presented by the teacher (cognitive engagement). • Teacher is free to work with students who need extra attention. • Provides opportunity for students to solve task in unique ways. • Provides opportunity for students to voice opinion to peers. • Leads to greater variance in performance. • May decrease practice time.	• Students can demonstrate respect (Level I) for the teacher and peers (e.g., following directions, staying in control). • Students can demonstrate participation with effort (Level II) by staying engaged in the Impulse activity. • Students work as an independent group (Level III), identifying a leader (Level IV) to initiate the impulse, and reflect on strategies after each trial.

Being mindful of the activities used during this stage gives the teacher opportunities to alter the teaching style and encourage greater student responsibility. This allows for students to begin leading the group meeting segment of the lesson and speaking to how the lesson activities address any themes identified during the awareness talk.

Command (Direct) Style

Presenting Impulse through a command style of teaching allows you to direct the students through the task. This will encourage them to perform the task in the same way and allow you to provide congruent feedback throughout. For Impulse, the command style may help minimize off-task behavior and would look something like this:

The teacher describes how an impulse is transferred (hand squeeze) and sets limitations (i.e., no talking, stay connected). Students are positioned in a seated circle so that they are able to hold the hands of the students next to them.

Teacher: "We have been hired by the electric company to test a new electricity transportation system. The system is designed to quickly transfer electricity along the power lines. Our job is to demonstrate this process for the board of directors. I will start the impulse by gently squeezing the hand of Marcus or Rachel [the students sitting next to the teacher]. Once one of them receives the impulse, he or she needs to transfer the impulse to the next person, so Marcus would gently squeeze David's hand or Rachel would gently squeeze Katie's hand. Each person then transfers it to the next person until it returns back to me. You should squeeze only when you receive the impulse, and you need to use a gentle squeeze to transfer the impulse. The board meeting will be in progress during our demonstration, so we are not allowed to talk while we do the demonstration. The president expects us to complete the demonstration in 9.42 seconds or less. Let's practice."

Impulse provides you with the flexibility to maintain control of the activity (i.e., starting the pulse, processing the trials to identify strategies) or release some of the control to the students (i.e., student leader begins the pulse, student-led processing and reflection). You will probably need to help students generalize the experience to the theme for the lesson and help them transfer what they have learned to subsequent tasks in the lesson.

Guided Discovery Style

By presenting the Impulse activity through a guided discovery approach, the teacher engages students in both the cognitive and psychomotor domains. Through questioning or the presentation of a problem, you can have students converge on the solution for successfully completing the task. With this task you should get students to converge on the best solution, verbalize what this would look like, and then demonstrate. These subtle changes, described next, promote opportunities for student leadership.

Teacher: "We have been asked to demonstrate the transfer of electricity to Mrs. Kalny's kindergarten class. For this demonstration we will sit in a circle and hold hands. Mrs. Kalny also asked us not to talk during the demonstration so she can explain what is happening to her students.

- "How can we show the electricity being transferred around the circle?"
- "Michael wants to squeeze hands to transfer the electricity. Should we see if this will work?"
- "The pulse seems to have been lost somewhere in the circle. What can we do to help show the progress of the impulse?"
- "Anna thinks we should turn and look as we transfer the pulse to the next person; let's give that a try."

Group Meeting

The group meeting during the second developmental stage should continue to provide students with an opportunity to have a voice in the learning process. From the perspective of adventure education, the teacher transitions from speaking for the experience to guiding students to find meaning in the experiences. Debriefing questions during this stage can go beyond the "What?" questions highlighted in the first developmental stage to include "So what?" and a few "Now what?" questions. In posing questions

like these, the teacher can help students integrate and transfer lessons learned in the activities to experiences beyond the classroom.

This aspect of the lesson may warrant a greater time commitment during developmental stage 2 than needed during developmental stage 1 because students take a more active role in the group meetings. During developmental stage 2, the teacher shifts much of the responsibility to the students for the facilitation of the group meeting; however, you should be prepared to redirect responses and initiate guided questioning. Use techniques that allow students to respond quickly and safely (e.g., metaphor cards, deck of questions). Initially during this stage you may need to reinforce the protocols for group meetings, but you should shift this responsibility to the students as leaders emerge. For example, during Impulse (Model in Action 4.4), you may give one student a deck of questions or metaphor cards to use to guide her peers in reflecting on the day's lesson.

Processing props often encourage student communication during the debriefing experience in that they provide a tangible object from which to frame responses: "I chose the snail card because we started out pretty slow but the way everyone was listening when I talked made me feel safe, like the snail shell, to give my ideas." You can link these discussions back to the theme ("Our theme today focused on communication, and I heard a lot of good examples of how we communicate effectively with others") and set the stage for the reflection on how the theme can be transferred beyond the classroom experience.

Reflection

The reflection time at this stage is an opportunity for students to self-reflect on their actions and what they observed in others throughout the lesson. During developmental stage 2, the self-reflection typically focuses around Level III and IV behaviors. You can achieve this focus through a variety of formats (e.g., student drawings, journal assignments, rubrics) in class or outside of class time. Consider using a two-part reflection in which students identify questions to reflect upon during class (e.g., Why was communication important during the Impulse activity? What actions did I or my peers use to demonstrate effective communication?) and write their responses to the questions during their next class (classroom teacher partnership) or after school (homework). This gives students time to informally reflect on the experience before speaking for the experience. For the Impulse activity, consider asking students to

- draw a three-panel comic strip that shows effective communication,
- describe the characteristics of a good communicator, or
- rate their performance with regard to communication (3, listened to others and clearly explained my ideas; 2, listened to others or shared my ideas; 1, talked over people to share my ideas or did not share the ideas I had).

Developmental Stage 3

Transitioning students to developmental stage 3 within the confines of physical education settings can be difficult. At this stage students should routinely demonstrate behaviors consistent with Levels I through III and actively seek out opportunities to lead. Students are increasingly afforded opportunities to lead their peers in skill development, awareness talks, and group meeting settings. These opportunities for caring and leadership take center stage during developmental stage 3.

Relationship Time

Relationship time offers an ideal opportunity for the initial transition to student leadership. As such, relationship time activities should shift from positive interactions between partners and in small groups to collaborative learning experiences led by student leaders with the support of the teacher. This setting allows students to experiment with leading in partner and small-group activities, often with peers they feel most comfortable with, thus providing a safe environment for developing leadership skills.

The Fifteenth Plate activity (Model in Action 4.5) gives students a chance to work independently during the relationship time activity. Expectations and instructions can be posted for students as they enter the gym. Each pair of students selects a group leader to acquire the necessary equipment and set up the game. The teacher is free to move among the students and discuss strategies during game play. Additionally the teacher can use students to demonstrate or answer questions for their peers.

Awareness Talk

During the third developmental stage, the teacher releases the responsibility for the awareness talks to student leaders. The student leaders identify the theme, guide the questioning, and draw the connection to the lesson focus. Commonly used themes during developmental stage 3 include self-direction, leadership, and transfer. Here we use the Impulse

---

MODEL IN ACTION 4.5

Fifteenth Plate

DESCRIPTION

This game works equally well as a paper-and-pencil game and as an action game. Each pair of partners gets 15 plates (poly spots, or a piece of paper with 15 large circles in a row). Working with their partner, students take turns selecting one to three plates in a row (cannot skip plates). The object of the game is to make your partner take the 15th plate. Students play for best three out of five, alternating who goes first.

EQUIPMENT

Fifteen "plates" (poly spots, paper plates, paperclips, or pennies) per pair. I like to print out sheets with multiple 15-circle game sets for students to play in their own space in the gym.

VARIATIONS

As already noted, you can have students act this game out or play using the pattern printed on paper. These are other variations:

- Assign a physical activity (or a math problem, a spelling word, for example) to each plate (e.g., one push-up, two sit-ups, . . . , 15 lunges).
- Arrange the poly spots in a four-by-four square. Each player can take one to four spots in any row or column (spots must be taken in a single row or column, no diagonal moves), with the goal to have the partner take the last spot.

activity (Model in Action 4.4) to illustrate adventure-based awareness talk techniques that can move students from a relationship activity to the lesson focus.

In speaking for the experience during the Impulse example, the student leaders would generalize the lessons learned from the activity to the theme and subsequent activities. The following are examples of statements they might use.

- "I liked seeing Makeeba taking a leadership role during the activity. Several of you did not listen to the ideas she presented, however. This led to several debacles that could have been prevented."
- "It was great to see everyone stop and listen when Neil gave his idea."
- "I liked that Lilka offered suggestions for modifying Neil's plan after he was done and that the group put the plans into action."

By speaking for the experience, the student leaders can generalize what occurred in the activity. Following the activity, the student leaders can "debrief" so as to draw the attention of their peers to the cognitive and affective attributes of an activity. These are examples of questions they might use following the Impulse activity:

"What?" Questions

- "What did you need to be successful in this activity?"
- "In what ways did you work together?"

"So What?" Questions

- "Why was communication important with this activity?"
- "How can working as a team make you more successful in activities?"

"Now What?" Questions

- "How can being a good listener help you with school?"
- "In what other activities is teamwork important?"

A third technique is to draw the attention of the learner to the attributes of the activity before the activity begins. When we do this we are "frontloading" (Gass 1995) how students will react and reflect upon the experience. In the Impulse example, the student leaders could select one attribute of the activity (e.g., teamwork, communication, problem solving) and set the stage for the activity. Examples of statements a student leader could use to frontload the Impulse

activity are "For this next activity we will need to work together as a team," or "Groups that have the most success in this activity do a great job communicating." Upon completion of the activity, the student leader can quickly speak to what he observed or use debriefing questions related to the attribute he frontloaded to enhance the reflection of his peers.

Lesson Focus

The transition to developmental stage 3 activities is characterized by opportunities for students to take leadership roles in the classroom, for peer facilitation of awareness talks and group meetings, and for increased reflection on strategies for transferring lessons beyond the classroom experience. During adventure education programming, the facilitator (i.e., teacher) presents the challenge to the group and then steps back to allow time for the group to work through the problem. The teacher may step in to redirect the group but does so through questioning that guides the group toward self-discovery of solutions. Adventure programming is uniquely suited for introducing students to this level of responsibility and may provide teachable moments as instructors begin to integrate responsibility throughout their curriculum. The activities presented in this section demonstrate ways to promote student leadership and provide strategies for encouraging transfer to other aspects of the curriculum.

The Ten-Person Pyramid activity (Model in Action 4.6) gives students an opportunity to demonstrate responsibility Levels I through IV. It is important to note that an element of risk exists with activities like this that require direct contact between students and movement off the ground. You as the teacher must understand spotting strategies and determine whether your students are ready for this level of responsibility.

While some groups will be able to safely construct a vertical 4-3-2-1 pyramid, most will struggle initially. While the activity calls for students to construct a 4-3-2-1 pyramid, it does not require a vertical orientation. Most participants will make that assumption; however, a horizontal pyramid also meets the requirements. One purpose of this activity is for students to learn to listen attentively to the instruction and to ask questions to clarify instructions before jumping into a task. The key to this activity is to think of alternative solutions to problems.

Table 4.4 presents considerations for teaching Ten-Person Pyramid through two teaching styles and shows how they connect to the TPSR model. It shows how changing the teaching style can elicit leadership and problem-solving skills in students.

MODEL IN ACTION 4.6

Ten-Person Pyramid

DESCRIPTION

This game deals with the ability of the group to work together and problem solve. Divide the class into groups of 10 students. Additional students can serve as spotters or advisors during the construction of the pyramid. Each team of 10 is required to construct a 4-3-2-1 pyramid using the 10 students in the group. Remind the group about spotting, full-value contract, and challenge by choice.

EQUIPMENT

A large exercise mat or open grassy space.

VARIATION

Ask students to complete the task without talking.

With either approach we can discuss how the group came up with strategies and how they decided which strategy worked best. Discuss the role of learners in the learning process. The Ten-Person Pyramid activity usually creates a "leadership" opportunity in that the student who talks the loudest often becomes the leader for the group. It is common for other students to have ideas for the solution but fail to voice their opinions or fail to be heard. This gives rise to opportunities to discuss the role of a leader, the right of participants to be heard, and their responsibility to hear others.

At this developmental stage, students have demonstrated the ability to work independently while putting forth effort and to show respect for their peers. By properly selecting and sequencing activities, you can provide opportunities for the development of leadership skills. These skills can be carried over to the group meeting segment of the lesson, increasing the contribution of students to the learning process.

Convergent Discovery Style

Presenting Ten-Person Pyramid through a convergent discovery style of teaching allows student groups to discover the solution to the task through problem solving and trial and error. This encourages students to work together during the task and provide feedback to their peers throughout. You can provide prompts or ask questions that assist students in their reflection on what works best to solve the problem presented. For the Ten-Person Pyramid activity, the convergent style may provide opportunities for students to demonstrate leadership skills and encourage group interaction. The following is an example of how this activity could be set up and discussed.

Teacher: "The school board has asked that we integrate scientific concepts into physical education.

Today we are going to use geometric shapes to demonstrate bases of support and stability. Your challenge is to construct a 10-person pyramid. The pyramid will have a 4-3-2-1 configuration. You may use only the 10 people in your group to construct your pyramid; you cannot use equipment, walls, and so on to support the pyramid."

- "How did you decide on who would make up the base of the pyramid?"
- "Did Tori volunteer to be the top of the pyramid?"
- "Let's take a break and talk through the strategy you have selected."
- "Is this the only way to solve the problem?"

Divergent Discovery Style

Presenting Ten-Person Pyramid through a divergent discovery approach allows the teacher to engage students in both the cognitive and psychomotor domains. In the following example you will notice a change in the focus of the activity. Through questioning or the presentation of a problem, you can have students diverge on solutions for successfully completing the task.

Teacher: "Each group is being asked to construct a 10-person pyramid. You may use only the 10 people in your group—no using the walls or equipment to help support the pyramid."

- "How will you organize your group?"
- "What should your finished product look like?"
- "Are there other possible solutions to this problem?"

Table 4.4 Developmental Stage 3 Instructional Strategies

Instructional style	Teaching considerations	Links to TPSR
Convergent discovery	• Student solves problem presented by the teacher (cognitive engagement). • Teacher is free to provide spotting suggestions. • Provides opportunity for students to work toward a "best practice" solution. • Provides opportunity for students to voice opinions to peers. • One student can dominate the group. • May lead to some students "checking out" during the task.	• Students can demonstrate caring (Level IV) by respecting the rights of other students in alignment with challenge by choice. • Students can demonstrate leadership and caring (Level IV) by organizing the group to try out ideas for completing the pyramid task.
Divergent discovery	• Student solves problem presented by the teacher (cognitive engagement). • Teacher is free to offer prompts or questions to groups struggling to "solve" the task. • Provides opportunity for groups to solve task in unique ways. • Provides opportunity for students to voice opinions to peers. • Leads to greater variance in performance. • May necessitate additional spotting during this task.	• Students can demonstrate caring (Level IV) by respecting the rights of other students in alignment with challenge by choice. • Students can demonstrate leadership and caring (Level IV) by organizing the group to try out ideas for completing the pyramid task.

Group Meeting

The group meeting during the final developmental stage should give students a chance to lead the reflection on the learning experiences. Adventure education activities uniquely allow teachers to transition from speaking for the experience to guiding students to find shared meaning in the experience. Debriefing questions during this stage can go beyond "So what?" questions to greater emphasis on "Now what?" questions that guide students toward the integration and transfer of lessons learned in the activities to experiences beyond the classroom.

The teacher continues to transition to a guide on the side by allowing students to take a greater role in this aspect of the lesson. When this occurs, opportunities for leadership persist beyond the lesson focus and create a climate of shared reflection. While shifting much of the responsibility to the students during developmental stage 3, you should continue to redirect responses and initiate guided questioning. Continue to use techniques that promote peer-to-peer responses (e.g., deck of cards, Chiji processing dice). During this stage students should reinforce the protocols for group meetings. For example, during Ten-Person Pyramid (Model in Action 4.6), you may give each student a card from a standard deck of cards or use Chiji processing dice as props to encourage student responses.

Reflection

The reflection time at this stage continues to be an opportunity for students to self-reflect on their actions and on what they observed in others throughout the lesson. During developmental stage 3, attention centers on how students can transfer the responsibility attributes they are developing in physical education to life beyond the gym. This can be accomplished through a variety of formats in class or outside of class time. As with the reflection during developmental stage 2, consider using a two-part reflection in which students identify questions to think about during class (e.g., Why was teamwork important during the Ten-Person Pyramid activity? What actions did I or my peers use to demonstrate effective leadership?) and write for homework about how they can use these concepts beyond the physical education setting. This provides time for students to reflect on the experience and begin to think about how they can integrate these concepts in other aspects of their lives.

Keeping SITE

As discussed in chapter 1, the key to TPSR is keeping SITE of four thematic objectives (student relationships, integration, transfer, and empowerment) throughout your lessons and program. Using the content from this chapter, reflect on the following questions:

Student Relationships

1. What aspects of the variation in teaching styles assisted in enhancing student–teacher relationships? How?

2. What aspects of the variation in teaching styles assisted in enhancing student–student relationships? How?

Integration

1. What elements within this chapter facilitate development of personal responsibility in students? How?

2. What elements within this chapter facilitate development of social responsibility in students? How?

Transfer

1. What elements within the chapter might assist in transfer of TPSR outside of the class but within the school or program? How?

2. What elements within the chapter might assist in transfer of TPSR outside of the school or program? How?

Empowerment

1. What elements of your lessons support an empowering pedagogy for students?

2. What pedagogical choices can you make to promote autonomy and a sense of control in your students?

Teaching Personal and Social Responsibility Through

Volleyball

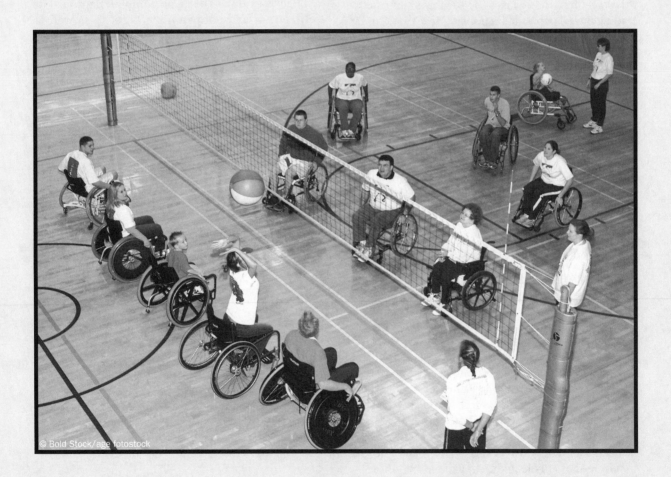

© Bold Stock/age fotostock

Volleyball: Steps to Success by Bonnie Kenny and Cindy Gregory (2006) is the primary source for this chapter. We have found the books in the Steps to Success series, including this one on volleyball, particularly helpful to our teaching. The activities and drills are easily modified to accommodate different teaching styles as well as to meet the differing needs of the TPSR developmental stages.

Developmental Stage 1

As we discussed in the beginning of this book, students in the first developmental stage are often working on exhibiting Level I (respect) and II (participating with effort) behaviors consistently. During this stage the teacher takes the predominant role in leading the awareness talk, choosing developmentally appropriate tasks and challenges, structuring the group meeting, and providing reflection opportunities. As the lessons progress, the teacher is mindful to provide students with opportunities to begin to transition to developmental stage 2 (TPSR Level III, self-direction).

Relationship Time

Although icebreaker games can set the stage for learning experiences in adventure education, we use them throughout the learning process in a variety of sport and physical activities to facilitate a more coordinated effort to build connections between the teacher and students. Icebreaker games provide an opportunity for students and teachers to interact, develop relationships, and have fun. Icebreakers can vary in length but all serve the purpose of creating an environment that fosters acceptance and interaction. A number of resources for icebreaker activities for all ages appear on the list at the end of the resources section in the back of the book. When working with developmental stage 1 learners, consider selecting activities that focus on individual traits (communication, cooperation, self-control, respect, and effort) within the context of group interactions.

The Mystery Move activity (Model in Action 5.1) gives students the opportunity to demonstrate self-control and cooperation (Level I) as well as to participate with effort (Level II). There is often a point in the game when a student is unable to identify who is leading the activity and begins to point madly at everyone. This bit of conflict can allow for the group to reset and to establish limits on the number of times a person can guess the leader before he switches places. It also gives the teacher and students the opportunity to compliment the student leading the activity, as well as the whole group on their cooperation, which provides a nice transition to the awareness talk.

MODEL IN ACTION 5.1

Mystery Move

DESCRIPTION

We have used this activity with groups ranging in age from 8 to 50 years and ranging in size from 5 to 35. Participants stand in a large circle. One person volunteers and moves outside the circle to stand with her back to the group. One person in the circle is designated the move leader. That person begins a movement, for example jumping in place or patting the head or waving the arms like a bird. The people in the circle imitate the movement of the leader. The volunteer is told to come back and stands in the center of the circle. The goal is for this person to figure out who is leading the moves. The leader changes movements to keep things fresh and fun. The people in the circle must change their movements in time with the leader, but not in a way that tips off who the leader is. Once the person in the center guesses who is leading the move, she gets back into the circle, the leader moves to outside the circle, and a new leader is selected to begin another round.

EQUIPMENT

None, or a poly spot for each participant.

VARIATIONS

- With large groups you can break into smaller circles.
- Incorporate music.

Awareness Talk

During the first developmental stage, the teacher takes the primary role during the awareness talks. He identifies the theme, guides the questioning, and makes the connection to teachable moments in the lesson focus. Commonly used themes during developmental stage 1 include respect, self-control, participation, effort, and effective communication. We like to use icebreakers during the relationship time, because they provide a leaping-off point from the activity to the remainder of the lesson. We also use the "What?", "So what?", "Now what?" method of structuring the awareness talk. This technique helps us draw meaning from the activity during the relationship time; it also models for students how they may direct the awareness talk as we eventually move to the side and allow them to lead this portion of the lesson (developmental stages 2 and 3). For example, in developmental stage 1, we might ask these questions:

- "What were some of the things we needed to do in Mystery Move to be successful as a group?"
- "What did you need to do to support the group?"

On the basis of responses from the students, we then lead them to extend their thinking by asking questions such as the following:

- "So what might be some things from the activity you might want to work on personally?"
- "What might be a couple things you know about yourself that you want to try to stop doing?"
- "Today we are starting our volleyball unit. What can you do in this unit to demonstrate some of those characteristics or behaviors?"
- "As you consider where you are, what are some goals you can take forward during today's lesson? Challenge yourself a bit!"

Lesson Focus

The theme identified during the awareness talk can set the stage for teachable moments throughout the lesson focus. You can select tasks or use pedagogical strategies that provide opportunities for students to make a cognitive or affective connection between the tasks and the theme. The teaching style you use can help to create a space for those teachable moments to occur. Although in developmental stage 1 it is often beneficial to maintain a somewhat teacher-centered approach (command style), we must also give students opportunities to work toward skill development in developmental stage 2. The style you choose will be influenced by your teaching philosophy, the learning styles of your students, and the context in which the lesson is presented. Here we provide an example of a lesson focus on a volleyball skill using two different styles of teaching.

Table 5.1 presents considerations for teaching the Dot Drills (Model in Action 5.2) activity using two teaching styles and shows how these connect to the TPSR model. The command style is more teacher centered, and the reciprocal style progresses a bit toward the divergent end of the teaching spectrum.

Command (Direct) Style

Presenting the Dot Drills activity through a command style allows you to direct the students through the progression of tasks. This encourages students to perform the task in the same way at the same time and allows you to check student performance. For each separate drill, provide a demonstration of the drill and identify cues:

1. Keep knees bent.
2. Move feet quickly from dot to dot.
3. Keep body in a ready position with hands and arms out.

The teacher starts and stops the students for each drill, demonstrating the new variation and establishing cues. Throughout the activity the teacher moves about the space providing feedback.

Reciprocal Style

To present the same drill in reciprocal style, organize students into pairs. Each pair has a Dot Drill diagram on the floor. Students also have task sheets that briefly describe each drill and provide cues. In addition, we suggest providing a list of possible motivation-type feedback phrases students can use, such as "Way to keep your feet moving" or "Great job! Keep with it!"

Each pair of partners begins when ready. One student completes one rotation of the drill while the partner observes and provides feedback. The feedback should relate to the cues identified on the task sheet. After one rotation of the drill, students switch roles; the observer becomes the doer, and the doer becomes the observer. This process is repeated for each drill variation. The teacher's role is to move about the space and assist the observers in accurately observing the doer. The teacher must step in to provide feedback if a safety issue arises. Otherwise, the teacher encourages or suggests feedback to the observer only if the

MODEL IN ACTION 5.2

Dot Drills

DESCRIPTION

This activity is used to improve foot speed as well as to strengthen muscles in the lower leg. You can use floor tape or nonpermanent floor paint; just be certain it will not move when stepped on. Setup follows the accompanying diagram. Each drill is performed six times.

Up and Back

Begin with left foot on dot A and right foot on dot B. With both feet, quickly jump to dot C, landing on both feet, and then split again so you land with left foot on dot D and right foot on dot E. Without turning around, come back the same way: Place both feet on dot C, then jump with left foot landing on dot A and right foot landing on dot B.

Right Foot

With weight only on right foot and beginning on dot A, move through each dot in order A to B to C to D to E, landing only on your right foot. When you get to the end, do not turn around; instead, repeat coming backward. This time you will go from dot E to D to C to B to A.

Left Foot

Same as right foot drill, only this time with just your left foot.

Both Feet

Using the same pattern as you did for both the right foot and left foot drills, this time follow the same pattern but jump on both feet.

Turn Around

Same as up and back, but this time at the end you make a quick 180-degree turn and face the direction you are returning in.

EQUIPMENT

Floor tape or nonpermanent floor paint.

VARIATION

Have students begin with fewer repetitions and build up to the total suggested (six).

Adapted, by permission, from B. Kenney and C. Gregory, 2006, *Volleyball: Steps to success* (Champaign, IL: Human Kinetics), 7.

observer is not providing feedback. Key to this style is getting the students to interact with minimal or no input from the teacher.

Group Meeting

Group meetings during the first developmental stage are facilitated by the teacher but provide an opportunity for students to have a voice in the learning process. This is the time for students to give input on how the lesson went, how their peers did, and even how the teacher did, all in relation to working on goals of developmental stage 1. Questions about how the activities challenged the students and how they felt participating in the lesson when the teacher used a given teaching style are good beginning points. Students can also be asked how they felt the class as a whole or just they and their partner or small group did. Lastly, you can ask how you as the teacher did and what you might work on for next session. As Don Hellison notes, this facet of the lesson tends to be foreign to students initially, as young people are not often asked to provide feedback to each other, much less to and about the teacher. Over time, students will

Table 5.1 Developmental Stage 1 Instructional Strategies for Volleyball

Instructional style	Teaching considerations	Links to TPSR
Command (direct)	• Students perform task together on teacher's cue. • Students progress through activity together. • Teacher is in position to see all students. • Teacher controls pacing of all facets of the activity.	• Students can demonstrate self-control and respect (Level I) for the teacher (e.g., following directions, staying in control) and for peers (e.g., not interfering with their participation). • Students can demonstrate participation with effort (Level II) by staying engaged throughout the Dot Drill activities. • Students can begin to demonstrate self-direction (Level III) by progressively challenging themselves throughout the Dot Drill activities (e.g., timing themselves, counting errors).
Reciprocal	• Students work in pairs and have specific roles (observer, doer). • Students have lists of task cues and feedback phrases. • Students work at own pace. • Teacher ensures that students are maintaining their roles and intervenes only if there is a safety issue.	• Students can demonstrate respect (Level I) for the teacher (e.g., following directions, staying in control) and for peers. • Students can demonstrate participation with effort (Level II) by staying engaged in the Dot Drill activities. • Students can begin to demonstrate self-direction (Level III) by progressively challenging themselves throughout the Dot Drill activities (e.g., increasing speed, decreasing number of errors). • Students begin to develop patience and tolerance for peers (Level IV).

feel more comfortable verbalizing their thoughts as this becomes a consistent part of the class.

Don suggests that teachers initially lay down some ground rules; they can do this in collaboration with the students. These are examples of group meeting ground rules:

- No blaming others—accept responsibility for yourself.
- Include everyone in the discussion.
- Be respectful of yourself and others (full-value contract).
- Use each other's names.
- Do not talk over each other.
- Wait for classmates to finish their comments.

These are only a few examples; again, we encourage teachers to solicit input from their classes about what the ground rules should include.

Another especially relevant issue concerning group meetings is time. If you do not have sufficient time to check in with all students, ask for responses on how things went from a few students. A common practice in many TPSR-based programs is to have the students keep a journal. They can do this as homework and turn in their comments the next day. This way you keep track of how things are going and get timely input from the class.

Reflection

Reflection time should flow fairly seamlessly from the group meeting time. Group meeting time focuses on student evaluation of the lesson, and reflection time focuses on evaluation of the students' roles as learners and support. Thus, questions can move from how the activities or style of teaching challenged or engaged the students to a focus on how they participated as independent learners, demonstrated respect, showed self-direction, and cooperated during the lesson. During developmental stage 1, the teacher directs the discussion. The thumbometer is a technique often used for reflection time. In response to questions from the teacher, students point their thumbs up, sideways, or down to indicate how well they did on a particular aspect of the lesson. These are examples of questions the teacher might ask:

- "During Dot Drill today, did you demonstrate cooperation with your partner by giving feedback?"
- "Did you show stick-to-itiveness during Dot Drill as it got harder?"
- "Did you show self-direction by challenging yourself during the drill?"

Students respond as a group by pointing their thumbs. The teacher notes where most of the participants are (e.g., more thumbs up than down) so as to facilitate activities toward the higher levels (Levels III through V). As Don notes in his work, it is important to acknowledge that kids have bad days, too, which means we should support them and encourage honest self-evaluation. We also want to underscore not blaming others for our behavior.

Lastly, the reflection time is when we can begin to encourage students to think about how they can demonstrate the levels outside of the class or program. Asking students where in their out-of-class or out-of-program lives they could demonstrate a given level of responsibility allows them to begin to conceptualize this transition. For some students, reaching a particular level outside of class but still within the school (which is a nice scaffold) might be all that is possible. In any case, we should begin to encourage students to think about responsibility concepts outside the class.

Developmental Stage 2

Once students are consistently demonstrating Level I and II behaviors, you should transition to the second developmental stage. This means providing opportunities for students to work collaboratively with their peers with little teacher guidance (Level III, self-direction). During this stage you begin to call upon students to take a role in the learning process. As you will see in this section, you begin to relinquish some of the control of the class to students during awareness talks and group meetings. As this occurs, some students may begin to demonstrate a desire to take leadership roles (Level IV), but most will continue to need guidance in keeping self-directed without individual supervision.

Relationship Time

Mystery Move (Model in Action 5.1) gives students the opportunity to continue to demonstrate respect (Level I) and participate with effort (Level II) while working collaboratively with their classmates without direct supervision from the teacher (Level III), especially if smaller circles are incorporated. Following the same format (What?, So what?, Now what?) but inviting more student leadership during the process, we navigate TPSR Level III and begin transition to Level IV concepts.

Developmentally appropriate practices within relationship time might include having students process the activities in smaller groups. This can help minimize the intimidation some may feel talking or taking more leadership in a large group. You can keep students in the same groups they were in during the activity or divide them into even smaller groups of three or four. Then, cue students to process the activity in their groups by providing them with an initial question for each stem (What?, So what?, Now what?), but encourage them to come up with their own. For example, once students are in their groups, you might suggest questions like "What were some of the main behaviors demonstrated during the activity?" and "What might also have been demonstrated but was not?" As students are talking, move about the space, providing encouragement or input only if they are stalled. Then cue them to move along to "So what?" and "Now what?" questions.

Awareness Talk

During the second developmental stage, the teacher begins to share the responsibility for the awareness talks. The teacher identifies the theme, asks one or more students to guide the questioning, and draws the connection to the lesson focus. Commonly used themes during developmental stage 2 include self-control, self-direction, goal setting, and problem solving.

Using students to help guide the discussion in the awareness talk is key in the development of youth leaders (Level IV). Following the activity, you can use student leaders to "debrief" so as to draw the attention of the learners to the cognitive and affective attributes of an activity. These are examples of questions you might provide the student leader following Mystery Move:

"What?" Questions

- "What did you need to be successful in this activity?"
- "Was it easier to be in the circle or in the middle?"

"So What?" Questions

- "How did your body positioning influence your ability to identify the move leader?"
- "What were a couple of things you did *not* do to give away who the leader was when the move changed?"

"Now What?" Questions

- "What are some things you can think about when trying to cooperate with someone?"
- "How can you tell that someone might want you to help them out with something even if they do not ask for help?"

By providing the students with a selection of questions, you maintain the direction of the conversation while giving students a way to comfortably explore taking leadership roles in class.

Lesson Focus

The opportunities for self-direction take center stage during developmental stage 2. Again, activities should transition from individuals performing within the context of the group to individuals positively interacting with partners and small groups in self-guided learning experiences.

Table 5.2 presents considerations for teaching the Pass to Self, Pass to Partner (Model in Action 5.3) activity using two teaching styles and shows how these connect to the TPSR model.

Being mindful of the activities used during this stage provides the teacher with opportunities for altering the teaching style and encouraging greater student responsibility. This allows for students to begin leading the group meeting segment of the lesson and speaking as to how the lesson activities address the theme(s) identified during the awareness talk.

Inclusion Style

When using the inclusion style, you initially demonstrate the skill correctly while identifying the cues the learner needs to focus on while performing the pass to self and pass to partner tasks. You also identify the options available for students in deciding how and where to enter the drill or task. For example, one student may choose to work independently on a single self-pass while another may perform three self-passes before passing back to their partner. Present varying distances as indicated by markers, differing types of balls to pass, and examples of challenges such as counting and timing. Task sheets provide a diagram of the activity as well as performance cues.

Students are placed in pairs and dispersed throughout the area. Allow time for the learners to assess their level though trial and error before beginning the drill. Each time, the learners reassess and set new challenges based on the levels available and the achievement of performance criteria. The teacher's role is to circulate throughout the learning space and provide feedback only on the decisions of the students. You can ask, for example, "How are you doing at the level you have selected?" The students' responses will help you inquire about the decisions made and about how successful the students feel they are. With this style it is important not to start out by overtly challenging the decision made by the student but to assist the student in accomplishing the level of challenge they selected.

Reciprocal Style

When using the reciprocal style, organize this activity using groups of three. Provide each group with a Pass to Self, Pass to Partner task sheet that briefly describes the drill and the cues. We also suggest providing a list of possible motivation-type feedback phrases that students can use. In addition, the task sheet should list clear role expectations for students to help them keep focus. For example, spell out what the observer ought to be observing (performance cues) and what the doers are doing (practicing). Specify a time or a number of passes for each facet of the activity. Once they have completed a drill variation, the students rotate their roles—one of the doers becomes the observer, and the observer becomes one of the doers. This process is repeated for each drill variation.

The teacher's role is to move about the space and help the observers accurately observe the doers. The teacher must step in to provide feedback if there is a safety issue. Otherwise, the teacher encourages or suggests feedback to the observer only if the observer is not providing feedback.

Group Meeting

The group meeting during the second developmental stage should continue to provide students with an opportunity to have a voice in the learning

MODEL IN ACTION 5.3

Pass to Self, Pass to Partner

DESCRIPTION

This activity works on learning correct balance, posture, and angle of platform for a forearm pass. Standing approximately 15 to 20 feet (4.5 to 6 meters) apart, in pairs, one partner passes to self and then to the other person. The partner receives the pass, passes to self, and then passes back. Start with 1-minute intervals and keep count.

EQUIPMENT

Volleyball, volleyball trainer, or beach ball depending on level.

VARIATIONS

- Catch the ball after it is passed and before you self-set (less difficult).
- Contact the ball twice before passing back to your partner (more difficult).
- Count how many times you make successful passes; try to beat each score.
- Team up with another pair for a four-way passing drill (see photo).

The Pass to Self, Pass to Partner drill helps students learn the correct way to do a forearm pass.

Adapted, by permission, from B. Kenney and C. Gregory, 2006, *Volleyball: Steps to success* (Champaign, IL: Human Kinetics), 39.

process but should facilitate their leading more of the discussion. Because you have modeled leading the discussion in developmental stage 1, you can help students assume more responsibility by asking questions such as these:

- "What sorts of questions did I ask you about the lesson?"

- "What questions do you have of your peers from the lesson?"

Another strategy is to have students write their questions or comments on slips of paper and then exchange with partners and engage in small-group discussions. You can then bring them back to the large group and ask for culminating thoughts from

Table 5.2 Developmental Stage 2 Instructional Strategies for Volleyball

Instructional style	Teaching considerations	Links to TPSR
Inclusion	• Students make individual choices to accommodate their ability (distance to partner, type of ball—volleyball, trainer, beach ball). • Students reassess abilities and make allowances as lesson progresses (e.g., stepping farther from partner, using a different ball). • Students' assessment allows them to rechallenge themselves or set goals (e.g., number of times to pass without a miss). • Teacher decides skill to be practiced and provides possible levels for the task.	• Students can demonstrate respect (Level I) for partner and self. • Students practice honesty in selecting appropriate level of entry (Level I). • Students demonstrate effort and participation (Level II) as they reassess and rechallenge themselves. • Students set goals and demonstrate self-evaluation as they reassess throughout the lesson (Level III). • Students learn to deal with agreement or discrepancy between their aspirations and actual performance (Levels II and III).
Reciprocal	• Students work in small groups and are assigned a specific role (observer, doers). • Students have lists of task cues as well as feedback phrases. • Groups work at own pace. • Teacher ensures that students are maintaining their roles and intervenes only if there is a safety issue.	• Students can demonstrate self-control (Level I) in relation to peers (e.g., not interfering with their participation). • Students can demonstrate participation with effort (Level II) by staying engaged in the activity. • Students can begin to demonstrate self-direction (Level III) by progressively challenging themselves throughout the activities (e.g., distance, number of hits before passing). • Students develop patience and tolerance as they work with peers (Level IV).

the day's lesson. Don't be disappointed if this developmental stage takes a bit more effort to engender. Be consistent and caring and be a good model for your students, and they will begin to assume more responsibility.

Reflection

Key to this stage is that students begin to lead more of the discussion. You can cue students to questions that address the particular levels they are working at for this stage (Level III) and begin to scaffold to goals for the next levels (IV and V). Examples include the following:

- "How did you feel you and your partner worked independently of teacher direction?"
- "What might you improve on?"

- "As we move toward more independence, what goals can you set to show more leadership in class?"

Students can begin to generate these types of questions once you have modeled them. We encourage you to note the many examples in *Teaching Personal and Social Responsibility Through Physical Activity, Third Edition*, of different ways to engage students in reflection time. Methods such as exit slips, journaling, and tapping in (students tap on a poster showing the levels to indicate where they are) can be quite effective and keep this part of the lesson fresh.

Developmental Stage 3

Transitioning students to developmental stage 3 within the confines of physical education settings can be difficult. At this stage students should routinely

As students progress through the levels we hope there is transfer of both TPSR and enjoyment of physical activity outside the gym.

demonstrate behaviors consistent with Levels I, II, and III and actively seek out opportunities to lead. Students are increasingly provided with opportunities to lead their peers in skill development, awareness talks, and group meeting settings. These opportunities for caring and leadership take center stage during developmental stage 3. Accordingly, relationship time activities should transition from individuals positively interacting with partners and small groups to collaborative learning experiences led by student leaders with the support of the teacher.

Relationship Time

As students begin to work within developmental stage 3, you can provide for them to lead the activities during this segment of the lesson. You can have volunteers or predetermined leaders identified so that they can be ready with an activity. In addition, the activity within this stage ought to include increasing amounts of problem solving as well as communication and working together.

Depending on how students form the knot, they may not be successful in their attempts. This provides multiple teachable moments for students as they must consistently communicate, work together, and

solve problems. When you have designated students leading the activity, this is a chance for them to provide guidance and cue their peers on behaviors that support this stage.

Awareness Talk

During the third developmental stage, the teacher releases the responsibility for the awareness talks to student leaders. The student leaders identify the theme, guide the questioning, and draw the connections to the lesson focus. Commonly used themes during developmental stage 3 include self-direction, leadership, and transfer. Here we use Human Knot (Model in Action 5.4) to illustrate. In the initial portion of the activity, it might be necessary to cue students to the sorts of things they work on while engaging in the activity. Use previous lessons as a scaffold. For example, "In the previous lessons we have focused on what types of qualities? As you engage in Human Knot, think about what sorts of skills we are focusing on and what you might bring to the awareness talk following the activity."

Again, since you have been consistent in modeling this aspect of the lesson throughout the developmental stages and have allowed for more and more

MODEL IN ACTION 5.4

Human Knot

DESCRIPTION

In groups of about six to eight, students stand shoulder to shoulder in a circle. Each person reaches across the circle and grabs hands with two different people. The group has now formed a human knot. The goal is to untie the knot without letting go of your grasp. The teacher's role is to watch and provide only safety feedback if warranted. If the group unties the knot quickly, have them reknot and incorporate the variations listed.

EQUIPMENT

None.

VARIATIONS

- Every other student cannot speak.
- Some students are blindfolded.

student leadership, it is highly likely that students will follow the "What?", "So what?", "Now what?" format they are familiar with. You then truly become a guide on the side. The teacher's nonverbal behavior can really be important here. Remain involved by demonstrating active listening, nodding your head, and making eye contact with whoever is speaking. This models to the students behaviors that they too can maintain in the process.

Lesson Focus

Developmental stage 3 activities should provide students with the opportunity for leadership experiences and provide strategies for encouraging transfer to other aspects of the curriculum. Model in Action 5.5 offers students opportunities to exhibit behaviors consistent with responsibility Levels I through IV.

Teaching strategies for developmental stage 3 include providing students with opportunities to emphasize previous levels but, more importantly, focus on Levels IV (caring and leadership) and V (outside the gymnasium). Table 5.3 presents considerations for teaching the H-O-R-S-E activity using two teaching styles and shows how these connect to the TPSR model.

Self-Check Style

With use of the self-check style, you would create a task sheet that includes the learning cues and description of the task or drill. You can demonstrate the activity and focus students on their task sheet. Once students are in pairs and have read their task sheets,

they can begin the activity at their own pace. Following each serve, students recheck the criteria noted on the task sheet relative to their execution of the serve. Each student is responsible for his own feedback based on the criteria for the skill. The teacher's role is to ask questions relative to the student's process of self-checking or self-assessing.

Convergent Discovery Style

Using the convergent discovery teaching style during H-O-R-S-E allows students to discover the solution to the task through problem solving and trial and error. This encourages students to work together during the task and to provide feedback to their peers throughout, thus facilitating student leaders. You can provide prompts or ask questions that assist students in their reflection on what works best to solve the problem presented.

Provide students with a description or demonstration (or both) of the activity. You do not present explicit learning cues but instead use questioning to help students understand how their execution arrives at success. Move about the gymnasium and question the students who are working together. Questions might include the following:

- What part of the hand is best for contacting the ball?
- Does it help to vary the distance to the net?
- What is the beginning place of the ball?
- What direction do your feet and hands point in at the end of the serve?

H-O-R-S-E

DESCRIPTION

Use tape or cones to divide the floor on one side of the volleyball net into six to eight sections. Students are in pairs for this activity. Server 1 calls out a zone across the net for server 2 to serve to. If server 2 hits the zone, then server 1 must hit the same zone or get a letter (H-O-R-S-E). If server 2 misses the zone, then she gets the letter. Next, server 2 calls out a zone for server 1 to hit. If server 1 hits the zone, server 2 must do the same or receive a letter. Players keep going until one server gets all the letters.

EQUIPMENT

Standard volleyball court, cones or marking tape for section designation.

VARIATIONS

- Vary the distance of the serve.
- Do the activity with no net to make it easier.
- Hit a specific target rather than a zone to make the activity more difficult.

Adapted, by permission, from B. Kenney and C. Gregory, 2006, *Volleyball: Steps to success* (Champaign, IL: Human Kinetics), 27.

Table 5.3 Developmental Stage 3 Instructional Strategies for Volleyball

Instructional style	Teaching considerations	Links to TPSR
Self-check	• Teacher values students' ability to self-evaluate their performance. • Teacher values students' ability to work independently of teacher and peers. • Students have demonstrated competency in the skill.	• Students can demonstrate caring (Level IV) by respecting the rights of other students. • Students can demonstrate transfer outside the gym (Level V) by gaining self-awareness about their proficiency. • Students can demonstrate leadership (Level IV) by maintaining honesty about their performance.
Convergent discovery	• Student solves problem presented by the teacher (cognitive engagement). • Style provides opportunity for students to work toward a "best practice" solution. • Style provides opportunity for students to voice opinions to peers. • One student can dominate the group. • May lead to some students "checking out" during the task.	• Students can demonstrate caring (Level IV) by respecting the rights of other students. • Students can demonstrate leadership by caring (Level IV).

Students use the questions from the teacher along with feedback from their peers to self-correct their performance. Thus, students work together collaboratively and emerge as group leaders.

Group Meeting

As with the awareness talk, this portion of the lesson is mostly student led. You can assist in cueing the students regarding the levels they are working on, as well as remind them of what sorts of questions have been asked in previous classes. Again, questions that focus on how the lesson was conducted, how the activity met the students' needs or provided challenge, and how the style of teaching engaged the students are examples of program-related discussion questions. You can encourage small-group discussion and then bring everyone back to the larger group. Most importantly, allow the students to direct this process while you remain as a support.

Reflection

Allowing students to lead the discussion using the various methods discussed in the chapter or in small groups provides them with the choice and leadership opportunities inherent to this developmental stage. Students might begin to read each other's journals and provide feedback, assist each other in goal setting, or create strategies to transfer the levels to experiences outside of the program. Again, the teacher remains connected to the process as an active listener and support.

Keeping SITE

As discussed in chapter 1, the key to TPSR is keeping SITE of four thematic objectives (student relationships, integration, transfer, and empowerment) throughout your lessons and program. Using the content from this chapter, reflect on the following questions:

Student Relationships

1. What aspects of the variation in teaching styles assisted in enhancing student–teacher relationships? How?
2. What aspects of the variation in teaching styles assisted in enhancing student–student relationships? How?

Integration

1. What are elements within this chapter that facilitate development of personal responsibility in students? How?
2. What are elements within this chapter that facilitate development of social responsibility in students? How?

Transfer

1. What are elements within the chapter that might assist in transfer of TPSR outside of the class but within the school or program? How?
2. What are elements within the chapter that might assist in transfer of TPSR outside of the school or program? How?

Empowerment

1. What elements of your lessons support an empowering pedagogy for students?
2. What pedagogical choices can you make to promote autonomy and a sense of control in your students?

Teaching Personal and Social Responsibility Through

Yoga

Teaching Yoga for Life by Nanette E. Tummers (2009) is the primary resource for content in this chapter. In addition to having produced a tremendous and enormously user-friendly resource, Tummers has included a section in which she infuses themes into yoga class—a sort of reverse of what we attempt here. Happy breathing!

Developmental Stage 1

As we discussed in the beginning of this book, students in the first developmental stage are often working on exhibiting Level I (respecting self and others) and Level II (participating with effort or stick-to-itiveness) behaviors consistently. During this stage the teacher takes the predominant role in leading the awareness talk, choosing developmentally appropriate tasks and challenges, structuring the group meeting, and providing reflection opportunities. As the lessons progress, the teacher is mindful to provide students with opportunities to begin to transition to developmental stage 2 (Level III, self-direction).

Relationship Time

We advocate the use of icebreaker activities throughout the learning process in a variety of sport or physical activities to facilitate a more coordinated effort to build connections between the teacher and students. Icebreaker games provide an opportunity for students and teachers to interact, develop relationships, and have fun. Icebreakers can vary in length, but all serve the purpose of creating an environment that fosters acceptance and interaction. When working with developmental stage 1 learners, consider selecting activities that focus on individual traits (communication, cooperation, self-control, respect, and effort) within the context of group interactions.

The People Find activity (Model in Action 6.1) gives students the opportunity to demonstrate respect for others (Level I) and self-control (Level II) and to begin to work toward self-direction (Level III). The game is simple and does not necessarily invite situations in which conflict may arise; it does support discussions that connect well with kids' recognition of self, others, and group.

Awareness Talk

During the first developmental stage, the teacher takes the primary role during the awareness talks. She identifies the theme, guides the questioning, and makes the connections to teachable moments in the lesson focus. Commonly used themes during developmental stage 1 include respect, self-control, participation, effort, and effective communication. We like to use icebreakers during the relationship time, because they provide a leaping-off point from the activity to the remainder of the lesson. We also

---

MODEL IN ACTION 6.1

People Find

DESCRIPTION

This is one of our favorites. In this activity the teacher prepares a handout that lists a number of characteristics, likes, or abilities. Students have 2 to 3 minutes to find as many people as they can who are similar to them. Students move from person to person asking questions to see who shares their characteristics. When they find someone who is similar, that person signs their sheet and they move on to the next person. Examples of characteristics are likes to dance, can eat with chopsticks, likes cold weather, likes to read books, can speak another language, has a pet dog or cat, has a sister or brother, favorite color is red.

EQUIPMENT

Sheet listing characteristics.

VARIATIONS

- Play music during the activity.
- Have students come up with the characteristics to list on the sheet.
- Include blanks on the sheet for students to fill in other similarities.
- Create a not-similar list.

use the "What?", "So what?", "Now what?" method of structuring the awareness talk. This technique assists us in drawing meaning from the activity in the relationship time; it also models for students how they may direct the awareness talk as we eventually move to the side and allow them to lead this portion of the lesson (developmental stages 2 and 3). For example, in developmental stage 1, we might ask these questions:

- "What were some of the things you found out about each other that are similar?"
- "What things did you find out about each other that are different?"

On the basis of responses from the students, we lead them to extend their thinking by asking questions such as the following:

- "So what might be some things you learned about others that you might want to try?"
- "What are some qualities you might adopt for this lesson that you learned from your peers?"

Lesson Focus

Themes identified during the awareness talk set the stage for teachable moments throughout the remainder of the lesson focus. Selection of pedagogical strategies that provide opportunities for students to make a cognitive or affective connection between the tasks and the themes supports a TPSR-based classroom. Although in developmental stage 1 it is often beneficial to maintain a somewhat teacher-centered approach (command or direct style), we must also provide students with opportunities to work toward

---

MODEL IN ACTION 6.2

Let's Breathe

DESCRIPTION

These exercises help students learn the correct ways to breathe and thus support learning more complex poses.

Balloon Breath

This activity helps students begin to think about how their breath moves through and about their bodies. Students begin in a cross-legged seated position. They are cued to pretend they are blowing up a balloon in the body: "Ready; start blowing up the balloon and feel it move from your belly, to your ribs, to the top of your chest. Now slowly let the air out of the balloon by exhaling slowly and feel the air move from your chest down to your ribs and finally your belly." Have students place their hands on their body as the air moves through: inhale—belly, ribs, chest; exhale—chest, ribs, belly. Have students go through the exercise a few times slowly.

Hot Air Balloon Breath

Have students begin in a crouched position, down low. As they inhale, tell them to start filling the balloon by slowly standing up until they are fully upright with arms overhead. Have them hold the hot air balloon up for 3 seconds. Now, as they exhale, tell them the balloon is deflating; slowly they return to the crouching position. Hold for 3 seconds. Repeat.

Wave Breath

Have students lie in a supine position with their legs straight out and arms by their sides. They then place a small beanbag just below their belly button. They are to place their hand over their mouth or hold their mouth shut tightly so that they breathe only through the nose. On the inhale, they breathe into the belly and watch the beanbag rise. On the exhale, they let the belly relax and watch the beanbag gently descend. Repeat.

EQUIPMENT

Floor mats, beanbags (for Wave Breath).

VARIATIONS

Have students do breathing activities to music.

Adapted, by permission, from N.E. Tummers, 2009, *Teaching yoga for life* (Champaign, IL: Human Kinetics), 85-86.

skill development in developmental stage 3. The style you choose will be influenced by your teaching philosophy, the learning styles of your students, and the context in which the lesson is presented. Here we provide an example of a lesson focus on yoga activities using two different styles of teaching.

Table 6.1 presents considerations for teaching the Let's Breathe (Model in Action 6.2) activity through two teaching styles and shows how they connect to the TPSR model. The command style is more teacher centered, and the practice/task style progresses a little toward the divergent end of the teaching spectrum.

Command (Direct) Style

Presenting the breathing activities through a command style allows you to direct the students through the progression of tasks. This encourages them to perform the task in the same way at the same time and allows you to check student performance. For each breathing activity, provide a demonstration and identify cues:

1. Breathing in, feel your belly rise.
2. Follow the air up into your ribs, to your chest.
3. As you exhale, follow the air back down from your chest to your ribs and belly.

The teacher starts and stops the students for each activity, demonstrating and establishing cues. Throughout each, the teacher moves about the space providing feedback.

Practice/Task Style

To use the practice/task style of teaching, create stations around the gymnasium for the three breathing exercises noted above. Each station includes task sheets or task cards. Instruct the students through each activity, providing critical cues and checking for understanding. After students see each facet of each activity, they can begin. They move through the stations in any order and are instructed to complete the repetitions for each activity as noted earlier. Students can repeat stations, but ask them to chal-

Table 6.1   Developmental Stage 1 Instructional Strategies for Yoga

Instructional style	Teaching considerations	Links to TPSR
Command (direct)	• Students perform task together on teacher's cue. • Students progress through activity together. • Teacher is in position to see all students. • Teacher controls pacing of all facets of the activity.	• Students can demonstrate self-control and respect (Level I) for the teacher (e.g., following directions, staying in control) and for peers (e.g., not interfering with their practice). • Students can demonstrate participation with effort (Level II) by staying engaged throughout the activities.
Practice/Task	• Students make decisions about order of tasks to be completed, pace of practice, starting and stopping on a particular task. • Students work individually. • Teacher provides objectives of lesson. • Teacher provides feedback to students.	• Students can demonstrate self-control and respect (Level I) for the teacher (e.g., following directions, staying in control) and for peers (e.g., not interfering with their participation). • Students can demonstrate participation with effort (Level II) by staying engaged throughout the breathing activities. • Students can begin to demonstrate self-direction (Level III) by progressively challenging themselves throughout the activities (e.g., time themselves, count errors made). • Students learn to be accountable for their own practice decisions and goal setting (Level III).

lenge themselves by completing each station before repeating. The teacher moves about the gymnasium providing feedback.

Group Meeting

Group meetings during the first developmental stage are facilitated by the teacher but provide an opportunity for students to have a voice in the learning process. This is the time for students to have input on how the lesson went, how their peers did, and even how the teacher did, all in relation toward working on Level I goals. Questions concerning how the activities challenged the students and questions about how they felt participating in the lesson when the teacher used a given teaching style are good beginning points. Students can also be asked how they felt the class as a whole or they as partners or in a small group did. Lastly, you can ask how *you* did and ask if there are things you might work on for next session. As Don Hellison notes, this facet of the lesson will be foreign to students initially as youth are not often asked to provide feedback to each other, much less to and about the teacher. Keep with it, and over time students will feel more comfortable verbalizing their thoughts as this becomes a consistent part of the class.

Don suggests that teachers initially lay down some ground rules; they can do this also in collaboration with the students. These are examples of group meeting ground rules:

- No blaming others—accept responsibility for yourself.
- Include everyone in the discussion.
- Be respectful of yourself and others (full-value contract).
- Use each other's names.
- Do not talk over each other.
- Wait for classmates to finish their comments.

These are only a few examples; we encourage teachers to solicit input from their classes about what the ground rules should include.

Another especially relevant issue concerning group meetings is time. If you do not have sufficient time to check in with all students, ask for responses on how things went from just a few. A common practice in many TPSR-based programs is to have the students keep a journal. They can do this for homework and turn in their comments the next day. This way you keep track of how things are going and get timely input from the class.

Reflection

Reflection time should flow fairly seamlessly from the group meeting time. Group meeting time focuses on student evaluation of the lesson, and reflection time focuses on evaluation of the students' roles as learners and support. Thus, questions can move from how the activities or style of teaching challenged or engaged the students to a focus on how they participated as independent learners, demonstrated respect, showed self-direction, and cooperated during the lesson. During developmental stage 1, the teacher directs the discussion. For example, you might ask the following questions:

- "During the breathing activities today, did you demonstrate Level I characteristics?"
- "Did you show stick-to-itiveness during the Wave Breath activity to see your beanbag rise?"

Students can respond to the questions verbally in small groups or with a partner. In groups they can use the thumbometer (thumbs up, sideways, or down) to respond. The teacher notes where most of the students are (e.g., more thumbs up than down) so as to facilitate activities toward the higher levels (III through V). As Don notes in his book, it is important to acknowledge that kids have bad days, too, which means we should support them and encourage honest self-evaluation. We also want to underscore not blaming others for our behavior.

Lastly, the reflection time is when we can begin to encourage students to think about how they can demonstrate the levels outside of the class or program. Asking students where in their out-of-class or out-of-program lives they could demonstrate a given level of responsibility allows them to begin to conceptualize this transition. It can also be helpful to ask students to share one thing they learned from the activity and about themselves relative to the TPSR model as a way to begin to scaffold between in-class goals and transfer out of class.

Developmental Stage 2

Once students are consistently demonstrating Level I and II behaviors, you should transition to the second developmental stage. This means providing opportunities for students to work collaboratively with their peers with little teacher guidance (Level III, self-direction). During this stage you begin to call upon students to take a role in the learning process.

As you will see in this section, you begin to relinquish some of the control of the class to students during awareness talks and group meetings. As this occurs, some students may begin to demonstrate a desire to take leadership roles (Level IV), but most will continue to need some guidance in keeping self-directed without individual supervision.

Relationship Time

People Find (Model in Action 6.1) can be easily modified to provide students with the opportunity to continue to demonstrate respect (Level I) and participate with effort (Level II) while working collaboratively with their classmates without direct supervision from the teacher (Level III). Instead of centering on characteristics, this activity could use different types of warm-up exercises. Students first find a partner who likes to do a particular exercise; the partners then do the exercise together for a count of 10, sign each other's sheets, and find a new partner. We call this variation Exersign. You can also include various yoga breathing activities as a way to warm up for the day's lesson.

Awareness Talk

During the second developmental stage, you begin to share the responsibility for the awareness talks. You identify the theme, ask one or more students to guide the questioning, and draw the connection to the lesson focus. Commonly used themes during developmental stage 2 include self-control, self-direction, goal setting, and problem solving.

Using students to help guide the awareness talk is key in the development of youth leaders (Level IV). Following the activity, you can use student leaders to "debrief" so as to draw the attention of the learners to the cognitive and affective attributes of an activity. Have the students think about themes that arose as they did the activity during relationship time to help them connect to discussion during the awareness talk. Again, we encourage students to follow the model used by the teacher to ask "What?", "So what?", and "Now what?" questions.

"What?" Questions

- "What did you need to be successful in this activity?"
- "What did you learn about your classmates?"

"So What?" Questions

- "What strategies did you use or see others use that helped you complete each exercise?"

- "How did you show support for your partner during the activities?"

"Now What?" Questions

- "What are a few things you can think about when trying to cooperate with someone?"
- "How can you tell that someone might want you to help them out with something even if they don't ask for help?"

Lesson Focus

The opportunities for self-direction take center stage during developmental stage 2. Again, activities should transition from individuals performing within the context of the group to individuals positively interacting with partners and small groups in self-guided learning experiences. For this segment of the lesson, we introduce balance poses as presented by Tummers (2009).

Table 6.2 presents considerations for teaching the Balance Poses (Model in Action 6.3) activity through two teaching styles and shows how they connect to the TPSR model.

Being mindful of the activities used during this stage provides you with opportunities to alter your teaching style and encourage greater student responsibility. This allows for students to begin leading the group meeting segment of the lesson and speaking as to how the lesson activities address the theme(s) identified during the awareness talk.

Convergent Discovery Style

Presenting Balance Poses through the convergent discovery style of teaching allows student groups to discover the solution to the task through problem solving and trial and error. This encourages them to work together during the task and provide feedback to their peers throughout, thus facilitating student leaders. You can provide prompts or ask questions that assist students in their reflection on what works best to solve the problem presented.

Explicit learning cues are not presented. Instead, use questioning to assist students in understanding how their execution arrives at success. Move about the gymnasium and question the students who are working together. Questions might include the following:

- "From the mountain pose, what might you do to position yourself like an airplane supported on one foot?" (lighthouse pose)
- "From the mountain pose, what might you do to position yourself like a human arrow?" (tree pose)

Balance Poses

DESCRIPTION

Learning to balance is key to many sport and physical activities beyond yoga. For all poses, students are reminded to think of their breathing: inhale—belly, ribs, chest; exhale—chest, ribs, belly.

Arrow

Begin in the mountain pose with feet hip-width apart, arms extended yet relaxed at sides. Head is forward, knees are slightly bent or relaxed. Keep core muscles strong. From this position, step forward slightly with one leg and bend forward at the hips, bringing the chest over the front leg with arms stretched out in front. Hands are clasped together with index fingers forming a steeple. The back leg remains straight. Hold. Switch legs.

Lighthouse

Begin in the mountain pose. From this position, stand on right leg, lift left knee to hip height; arms are straight out to the sides. Hold. Release back to mountain pose and change support leg to left.

Tree

Begin in the mountain pose. Place weight on one leg, and bring the sole of the other foot to rest on the inner calf of the standing leg. Students can keep hands on hips or clasp hands and extend arms above head. Hold. Release back to mountain pose and switch support legs.

Standing Bow

Begin in the mountain pose. Standing on the right leg, bend the left leg at the knee; reach back with the left hand and hold the left ankle, shin, or foot. Reach up to the sky with the right arm. Bend forward at the hip. Hold. Release back to mountain pose and switch support legs.

Standing bow balance pose.

EQUIPMENT

None.

VARIATION

Have students do poses to music.

Adapted, by permission, from N.E. Tummers, 2009, *Teaching yoga for life* (Champaign, IL: Human Kinetics), 136-138.

Table 6.2   Developmental Stage 2 Instructional Strategies for Yoga

Instructional style	Teaching considerations	Links to TPSR
Convergent discovery	• Student solves problem presented by the teacher (cognitive engagement). • Teacher is free to provide suggestions for balance poses. • Style provides opportunity for students to work toward a "best practice" solution. • Provides opportunity for students to voice opinions to peers. • One student can dominate the group. • May lead to some students "checking out" during the task.	• Students can demonstrate respecting the rights of other students as they work through solutions (Level I). • Students demonstrate effort and participation (Level II) as they evaluate correctness of their own and peers' poses. • Students begin to set goals as they reassess throughout the lesson (Level III). • Students learn to deal with agreement or discrepancy between their aspirations and actual performance (Levels II and III).
Reciprocal	• Students work in pairs and are assigned a role (observer, doer). • Students have a list of tasks as well as feedback phrases. • Pairs work at own pace. • Teacher ensures that students are maintaining their roles and intervenes only if there is a safety issue.	• Students can demonstrate self-control (Level I) in relation to peers (e.g., not interfering with their participation). • Students can demonstrate participation with effort (Level II) by staying engaged in the balance poses. • Students can begin to demonstrate self-direction (Level III) by progressively challenging themselves throughout the activities (e.g., increase the time they hold a position). • Students develop patience and tolerance as they work with peers (Level IV).

Refine the questions based on the students' responses until they achieve the desired pose. Students use the questions from the teacher along with feedback from their peers to self-correct their performances. Thus, students work together collaboratively and also emerge as group leaders.

Reciprocal Style

To teach this activity using the reciprocal style, have students in pairs. Give each pair a task sheet that briefly describes the poses (perhaps with photos or illustrations) and provides cues. We also suggest providing a list of possible motivation-type feedback phrases students can use. In addition, the task sheet should list clear role expectations for students; this helps them keep focus. For example, spell out what the observer ought to be observing (performance cues) and what the doers are doing (practicing). Specify the amount of time students should hold each pose (students can count out loud). Once a student

has completed a pose, the partners exchange roles; the doer becomes the observer and the observer becomes the doer. This process is repeated for pose variations.

The teacher's role is to move about the space and assist the observers in accurately observing the doer. You must step in to provide feedback if there is a safety issue. Otherwise, encourage or suggest feedback to the observer only if the observer is not providing feedback.

Group Meeting

The group meeting during the second developmental stage should continue to provide students with an opportunity to have a voice in the learning process but should facilitate their leading more of the discussion. Because you have modeled leading the discussion in developmental stage 1, you can help students assume more responsibility by asking questions such as these:

- "What sorts of questions did I ask you about the lesson?"
- "What questions do you have of your peers from the lesson?"

Another strategy is to have students write their questions or comments on a slip of paper and then exchange with partners and engage in small-group discussions. You can then bring them back to the large group and ask for culminating thoughts from the day's lesson. Don't be disappointed if this developmental stage takes a bit more effort. Be consistent and caring and be a good model for your students, and they will begin to assume more responsibility.

Reflection

Key to this stage is that students begin to lead more of the discussion. You can cue students to questions that address the particular levels they are working at for this stage (Level III) and begin to scaffold to goals for the next levels (IV and V). Examples include the following:

- "How did you feel you and your partner worked independent of teacher direction?"
- "What might you improve on?"
- "As we move toward more independence, what goals can you set to show more leadership in class?"

Students can begin to generate these types of questions once you have modeled them. We encourage you to note the many examples in *Teaching Personal and Social Responsibility Through Physical Activity, Third Edition*, of different ways to engage students in reflection time. Methods such as exit slips, journaling, and tapping in (students tap on a poster showing the levels to indicate where they are) can be quite effective and keep this part of the lesson fresh.

Developmental Stage 3

Transitioning students to developmental stage 3 within the confines of physical education settings can be difficult. At this stage students should routinely demonstrate behaviors consistent with Levels I through III and actively seek out opportunities to lead. Students are increasingly provided with opportunities to lead their peers in skill development, awareness talks, and group meeting settings. These opportunities for caring and leadership take center stage during developmental stage 3. Accordingly, relationship time activities should transition from individuals positively interacting with partners and small groups to collaborative learning experiences led by student leaders with the support of the teacher.

Relationship Time

As students begin to work within developmental stage 3, you can provide for them to lead the activities during this segment of the lesson. You can have volunteers or predetermined leaders identified so that they can be ready with a pose for Model in Action 6.4. In addition, the activity within this stage should include increasing amounts of problem solving as well as communication and working together.

The activity provides students with opportunities to problem solve and work together, as well as to lead segments of the activity. These opportunities facilitate multiple teachable moments for students during the activities. In addition, the students you have designated to lead the activity get a chance to provide guidance and cue their peers on behaviors that support this stage.

Awareness Talk

During the third developmental stage, the teacher releases the responsibility for the awareness talks to student leaders. The student leaders identify the theme, guide the questioning, and draw the connection to the lesson focus. Commonly used themes during developmental stage 3 include self-direction, leadership, and transfer.

Since you have been consistent in modeling this aspect of the lesson throughout the developmental stages and have allowed for more and more student leadership, it is highly likely that students will follow the familiar "What?", "So what?", "Now what?" format. You then truly become a guide on the side. The teacher's nonverbal behavior can really be important here. Remain involved by demonstrating active listening, nodding your head, and making eye contact with whoever is speaking. This models to the students behaviors that they too can maintain in the process.

Lesson Focus

Developmental stage 3 activities should offer students the opportunity for leadership experiences and also provide strategies for encouraging transfer to other aspects of the curriculum. Model in Action 6.5 can give students opportunities to exhibit behaviors consistent with responsibility Levels I through IV.

Teaching strategies for developmental stage 3 include providing students with opportunities to emphasize previous levels but, more importantly,

MODEL IN ACTION 6.4

Simon Sez Pose

DESCRIPTION

For this activity, students are in groups of about 8 to 10. The activity is like traditional Simon Says except that the students use yoga poses they have learned throughout the lesson or unit. In addition, instead of a student's being eliminated when he does a pose without the cue "Simon Sez," he becomes the new caller. Students hold poses for a count of 5 seconds before a new pose is called.

The Simon Sez caller does a downward dog pose.

EQUIPMENT

None.

VARIATIONS

- In groups of two or three, students work together to create their own unique yoga pose, which can be totally new or a combination of other poses. Students name the pose and show it to the class.
- Have students do poses to music.
- Incorporate major categories (e.g., breathing, balance, and standing).

focus on Levels IV (caring and leadership) and V (outside the gymnasium). Table 6.3 presents considerations for teaching the Moving Yoga activity through two teaching styles and shows how they connect to the TPSR model.

Divergent Discovery Style

Presenting the various poses that may be used via the divergent discovery approach can engage students in multiple domains—cognitive, affective, and psychomotor. Through questioning or the presentation of a problem, you can have students diverge on solutions

for successfully completing the task. For this task, you can simply cue students to increasingly challenge themselves by focusing on stringing poses together first within a category and then across categories to create their own moving yoga poses. You are willing to accept an array of solutions to the task and to assist via questions that challenge students to think toward solutions.

Self-Check Style

With use of the self-check style, you create a task sheet that includes the learning cues and descriptions of

Moving Yoga

DESCRIPTION

Moving Yoga links various poses to movement. This activity is a terrific way to encourage students to become creative and achieve new poses. Poses can be grouped in a variety of ways that move from seated to standing to balancing (see Tummers 2009 for more examples and descriptions).

Warm-Up Poses

- **Cobra:** Begin in the prone position, bringing the legs together so they form a shape like a long tail. Place hands at the chest line under the shoulders, fingers pointed forward with a bend in the elbows. Gently lift chest off floor.

- **Downward-facing dog:** Begin on all fours and make a table by keeping the back flat, then lift up on the legs; hands are flat on the floor with fingers spread apart. Balance on the balls of the feet, which are about hip-width apart. Relax the head and keep focus toward the knees.

- **Yoga jumping jack:** Begin lying flat on the back. Pay attention to breathing (belly, ribs, chest); on an inhale, raise arms overhead, touching the back of the hands to the floor, while separating and moving legs out to the sides. This is just like a jumping jack except that it is done on the floor. Exhale and return to original position, arms by the sides and legs together.

Adapted, by permission, from N.E. Tummers, 2009, *Teaching yoga for life* (Champaign, IL: Human Kinetics), 108-111, 116.

Balance Poses

We use the same poses presented earlier to underscore the power of scaffolding new activities with previously taught activities. This helps students learn through repetition and also extends the tasks by adding something new.

- **Arrow:** Begin in the mountain pose with feet hip-width apart, arms extended yet relaxed at sides. Head is forward, knees are slightly bent or relaxed. Keep core muscles strong. From this position, step forward slightly with one front leg and bend forward at the hips, bringing the chest over the front leg with arms stretched out in front. Hands are clasped together with index fingers forming a steeple. The back leg remains straight. Hold. Switch legs.

- **Lighthouse:** Begin in the mountain pose. From this position, stand on right leg, lift left knee to hip height; arms are straight out to the sides. Hold. Release back to mountain pose and change support leg to left.

- **Tree:** Begin in the mountain pose. Place weight on one leg, and bring the sole of the other foot to rest on the inner calf of the standing leg. Students can keep hands on hips or clasp hands and extend arms above the head. Hold. Release back to mountain pose and switch support legs.

- **Standing bow:** Begin in the mountain pose. Standing on the right leg, bend the left leg at the knee, reach back with the left hand, and hold the left ankle, shin, or foot. Reach up to the sky with the right arm. Bend forward at the hip. Hold. Release back to mountain pose and switch support legs.

Adapted, by permission, from N.E. Tummers, 2009, *Teaching yoga for life* (Champaign, IL: Human Kinetics), 136-138.

Standing Poses

- **Chair:** Begin in the mountain pose with feet hip-width apart, arms extended yet relaxed at sides. Head is forward, knees are slightly bent or relaxed. Keep core muscles strong; keep knees and feet pointed ahead. Gently begin to sit down as if you had a chair; keep knees bent and gluteals down, keeping weight over the heels. Reach arms overhead and look at your hands. Hold. Return to mountain pose.

(continued)

(continued)

- **Horse:** In the mountain pose, lift left knee up to a right-angle height while simultaneously lifting right arm up with elbow at right angle. Hold. Switch support legs and arms.
- **Standing wide-angle fold:** Begin in the mountain pose. Then jump feet out to the sides, planting feet wide, with toes and head pointing forward. Reach to the sky and gently bend forward. Place palms or your fingertips in line with feet on the floor; knees are slight bent. The hands can also be placed anywhere on the legs if the student is unable to touch the floor. Hold.

Adapted, by permission, from N.E. Tummers, 2009, *Teaching yoga for life* (Champaign, IL: Human Kinetics), 121, 124, 129.

EQUIPMENT
Floor mats.

VARIATION
Have students do poses to music.

Table 6.3 Developmental Stage 3 Instructional Strategies for Yoga

Instructional style	Teaching considerations	Links to TPSR
Divergent discovery	• Student solves problem presented by the teacher (cognitive engagement). • Teacher is free to offer prompts or questions to groups struggling to "solve" the task. • Provides opportunity for groups to solve task in unique ways. • Provides opportunity for students to voice opinions to peers. • May lead to greater variance in performance.	• Students can demonstrate caring (Level IV) by respecting the rights of other students as they engage in activities with their peers. • Students can demonstrate leadership (Level IV) by organizing the group to attempt various moving yoga poses. • Students have opportunity to become cognitively, emotionally, and socially secure in moving beyond knowledge production (Level V). • Students tolerate others' ideas and solutions (Levels I and IV).
Self-check	• Teacher values students' ability to self-evaluate their performance. • Teacher values students' ability to work independently of teacher and peers. • Students have demonstrated competency in the skill.	• Students can demonstrate responsibility outside the gym (Level V) by gaining self-awareness about their proficiency. • Students can demonstrate leadership (Level IV) by maintaining honesty about their performance.

the various poses. You can demonstrate the activity and focus students on their task sheet. Once students are in pairs and have read their sheets, they can begin the activity at their own pace.

Students are responsible for creating their own sequence of moving yoga poses based on combinations of the poses described earlier. They are also responsible for their own feedback based on the criteria for the pose as noted on the task sheets. Your role

is to ask questions relative to the student's process of self-checking or self-assessing.

Group Meeting

As with the awareness talk, this portion of the lesson is mostly student led. You can assist in cueing the students regarding the levels they are working on, as well as remind them of what sorts of questions have been asked in previous classes. Questions that focus on how the lesson was conducted, how the activity met the students' needs or provided challenge, and how the style of teaching engaged them are all examples of program-related discussion questions. You can encourage small-group discussion and then bring everyone back to the larger group. Most importantly, allow students to direct this process while you remain as a support.

Reflection

Allowing students to lead the discussion using the various methods discussed in the chapter or in small groups provides them with the choice and leadership opportunities inherent to this developmental stage. Students might begin to read each other's journals and provide feedback, assist each other in goal setting, or create strategies to transfer the levels to experiences outside of the program. Again, the teacher remains connected to the process as an active listener and support.

Keeping SITE

As discussed in chapter 1, the key to TPSR is keeping SITE of four thematic objectives (student relationships, integration, transfer, and empowerment) throughout your lessons and program. Using the content from this chapter, reflect on the following questions:

Student Relationships

1. What aspects of the variation in teaching styles assisted in enhancing student–teacher relationships? How?
2. What aspects of the variation in teaching styles assisted in enhancing student–student relationships? How?

Integration

1. What are elements within this chapter that facilitate development of personal responsibility in students? How?
2. What are elements within this chapter that facilitate development of social responsibility in students? How?

Transfer

1. What are elements within the chapter that might assist in transfer of TPSR outside of the class but within the school or program? How?
2. What are elements within the chapter that might assist in transfer of TPSR outside of the school or program? How?

Empowerment

1. What elements of your lessons support an empowering pedagogy for students?
2. What pedagogical choices can you make to promote autonomy and a sense of control in your students?

Teaching Personal and Social Responsibility Through

Soccer

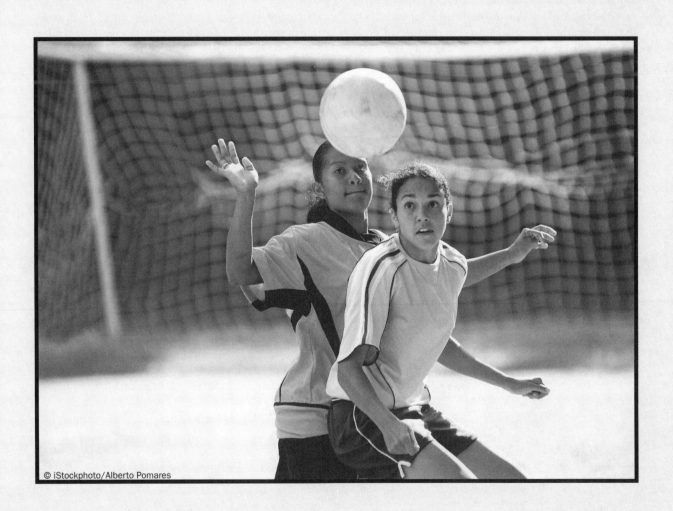

© iStockphoto/Alberto Pomares

Soccer is among the most popular sports and is routinely part of the physical education curriculum across educational settings. *Soccer: Steps to Success, Third Edition,* by Joseph Luxbacher (2005) is the primary resource for content in this chapter. By incorporating developmentally appropriate modifications to equipment and rules, teachers can use soccer with elementary and secondary students alike. Soccer provides an environment for students to demonstrate self-control, effort, self-direction, and caring.

Developmental Stage 1

Soccer offers students the opportunity to develop individual motor and manipulative skills while applying these skills in the context of a team sport that they can play recreationally and competitively throughout their lives. It is through planned interactions that we can target the responsibility attributes and keep SITE of the model. Developmental stage 1 learners are new to the idea of taking personal and social responsibility and benefit from teaching styles and learning experiences that work on developing respect and participating with effort. During this stage the teacher takes the predominant role in leading the awareness talk, choosing developmentally appropriate tasks and challenges, structuring the group meeting, and providing reflection opportunities.

Relationship Time

During this initial developmental stage, many students may need to learn or relearn how to stay in control physically and emotionally while interacting with peers. Starting the lesson with relationship time gives students the opportunity to develop positive interactions with peers and the teacher.

Ups (Model in Action 7.1) provides students with the opportunity to demonstrate respect (Level I) and participate with effort (Level II). You can transition from this activity to the awareness talk by drawing the students' attention to the effort they exerted during the game or behaviors that demonstrated respect.

Awareness Talk

At the initial developmental stage, the teacher is primarily responsible for facilitating the awareness talks. She identifies the theme, guides the questioning, and makes the connection to the lesson focus. Commonly used themes during developmental stage 1 include respect, self-control, participation, effort, and effective communication. Using the Ups activity (Model in Action 7.1), you can highlight attributes during the awareness talk so as to help students transition from a relationship activity to the lesson focus. For example, in developmental stage 1, you might ask the following questions:

MODEL IN ACTION 7.1

Ups

DESCRIPTION

Students are in groups. One student begins play by striking a beach ball up in the air. A second student strikes the ball up, and play continues until the ball hits the ground. The team should count the number of hits they are able to perform for each round. Players are allowed to strike the ball twice in a row, but three hits in a row by the same player is not allowed. Play continues for a set amount of time (3 to 5 minutes), for a set number of trials per round (five to seven), or until a target goal is met (45 hits in a row).

- Round 1: Players count the number of consecutive hits.
- Round 2: Before hitting the ball, the hitter must clap once.
- Round 3: Players clap before hitting and touch the ground after hitting.
- Round 4: Add a new challenge (e.g., spinning in a circle, jumping in the air).

EQUIPMENT

One beach ball per group. The game works well with groups as small as six and as large as 30+.

VARIATIONS

The variations are built into the rounds already described.

- "What were some ways you demonstrated effort during the activity?"
- "How did you respond when there was a debacle (dropped ball)?"

On the basis of the responses from the students, you can guide them to extend their thinking by asking questions such as the following:

- "What can we do to demonstrate respect when a classmate causes an error?"
- "Today we are continuing our soccer unit. What are some things you can do in this unit to demonstrate respect and effort?"
- "As you head into the rest of the lesson, think about your goals. How can you challenge yourself during the lesson?"

Lesson Focus

The use of lesson themes assists students in making a connection between their actions and the responsibility levels. During stage 1 it is a critical role of the teacher to begin the conversation about how individual behavior connects to the theme identified during the awareness talk and to reinforce expectations throughout the lesson focus. You can do this by being mindful when selecting tasks or by using pedagogical strategies that provide opportunities for

students to make a cognitive or affective connection between the tasks and the theme. During the soccer unit, you can make curricular choices based on the attributes you wish to target. Team sports provide opportunities to target a variety of personal and social attributes (respect, effort, self-direction, caring, teamwork, trust, communication), with the understanding that how we present the task can greatly affect the attributes that are targeted and developed.

One way to promote a connection between the lesson and the desired behavior is through modification of the teaching style. At developmental stage 1, it is often beneficial to maintain a somewhat teacher-centered approach while introducing opportunities to demonstrate respect and participate with effort. In this section we discuss how to use the command and reciprocal styles of teaching to present soccer activities while making connections to the themes pertaining to responsibility levels. The style you choose is influenced by your teaching philosophy, the learning styles of your students, and the context in which the lesson is presented.

The Slalom Dribble activity (Model in Action 7.2) is an example of a commonly used soccer drill that can be modified to draw the attention of the learner to the responsibility levels.

The characteristics of the students (e.g., psychomotor and cognitive developmental levels, motivation, and responsibility level) influence how we present

---

MODEL IN ACTION 7.2

Slalom Dribble

DESCRIPTION

This drill gives students the opportunity to practice dribbling a soccer ball through cones and can be modified to meet the developmental needs of students from the control through proficient levels. Position six to eight cones 1 to 2 yards (about 1 to 2 meters) apart to form a line. Working individually or in pairs, students take turns dribbling the soccer ball around the cones and back as quickly as possible (see the accompanying figure). Have students work on proper dribbling technique (keeping the ball close) and correct footwork. Hitting the cones or losing control of the ball is considered a dribbling error.

EQUIPMENT

Open playing area; six to eight cones and one soccer ball per group or per pair of partners.

(continued)

(continued)

VARIATIONS

- Increase difficulty by placing the cones closer together.
- Have partners perform 10 trials through the cones (five in each direction) as quickly as possible.
- For each cone a student passes without touching, score 1 point.
- Use as a warm-up once students have practiced the skill.

Adapted, by permission, from J. Luxbacher, 2005, *Soccer: Steps to success*, 3rd ed. Champaign, IL: Human Kinetics), 3.

Students dribble around cones in the Slalom Dribble drill.

skill practice. The teaching style used and the amount of control released to the students influence which responsibility attribute the activity addresses. We can use Slalom Dribble with students at any developmental level by modifying how we present the activity and deciding who has the primary responsibility for the learning experience.

Table 7.1 presents considerations for teaching Slalom Dribble through two teaching styles and shows how they connect to the TPSR model.

Command (Direct) Style

Presenting Slalom Dribble through use of a command style allows you to observe the students throughout skill practice. This encourages them to perform the task in the same way at the same time and allows you to check student performance. Setting up multiple courses means less waiting time for students.

Set up multiple slalom courses (one course for every two students is recommended), demonstrate the task, and identify cues (i.e., inside/outside of foot, keeping ball close, head up). Position groups around the gym.

There are a number of ways to assess students during skill practice. The example below shows a three-question rubric that could be used by the teacher or provided to the students at later developmental stages for peer assessment.

Table 7.1 Developmental Stage 1 Instructional Strategies for Soccer

Instructional style	Teaching considerations	Links to TPSR
Command (direct)	• All students perform task together. • Teacher is in position to see all students. • Provides order for new tasks and high-risk activities. • Class progresses together. • Limits opportunity for student voice. • Does not accommodate student differences. • Limits opportunity for students to demonstrate self-direction. • Limits student–student interaction.	• Students can demonstrate respect (Level I) for the teacher (e.g., following directions, staying in control) and for peers (e.g., not interfering with their practice). • Students can demonstrate participation with effort (Level II) by staying engaged while their partner takes a turn. • Students can begin to demonstrate self-direction (Level III) by progressively challenging themselves throughout the Slalom Dribble activity (e.g., speed at which they travel through the cones).
Reciprocal	• Students work in pairs and are assigned specific roles (observer, dribbler). • Students have task sheets and a list of feedback phrases. • Partners work at own pace and rotate positions. • Teacher ensures that students are maintaining their roles and intervenes only if there is a safety issue.	• Students can demonstrate respect (Level I) for the teacher (e.g., following directions, staying in control) and for peers (e.g., not interfering with their practice). • Students can demonstrate participation with effort (Level II). • Students can begin to demonstrate self-direction (Level III) by progressively challenging themselves throughout the activities (e.g., increasing speed, decreasing number of errors). • Students develop leadership as they maintain their role as observers and provide feedback to peers (Level IV).

1. Dribbler uses the inside and outside of the foot to control the ball (Y/N).
2. Head is up during dribbling (Y/N).
3. Ball stays close to the dribbler (Y/N).

Reciprocal Style

With use of the reciprocal style, students are in pairs, with one student performing the task and the other observing the performance. Provide task sheets that briefly describe the activity and note clear role expectations for students to help them keep their focus. For example, spell out what the observer should be observing (performance cues) and what the doer should be doing (practicing). Specify a time or number of trials for each facet of the activity. Once the performer has completed the task, the students switch roles—the observer becomes the dribbler, and the dribbler becomes the observer. This process is repeated for each drill variation.

The teacher's role is to move about the space and assist the observers as they attempt to observe the doer accurately. You must step in to provide feedback if a safety issue arises. Otherwise, encourage or suggest feedback to the observer only if feedback is not occurring.

The reciprocal style of teaching with Level I students requires that students have a level of competency in the skill that allows them to perform the skill with little supervision from the teacher. At this stage you may want to control how students are paired and the pacing of practice. Using the reciprocal style during this activity with students at the third developmental stage would mean releasing this responsibility to the students.

Group Meeting

With students in the first developmental stage, the group meeting is facilitated by the teacher. The teacher guides students through a reflection on the lesson experiences and how they relate to the responsibility levels. Be mindful that the purpose of the group meeting is to provide students with a voice in the learning process; your interpretation of what occurred throughout the lesson should not dominate. This aspect of the lesson need not take a great deal of time but is essential for connecting the responsibility attributes of the activities to student learning. During this stage you may need to reinforce ground rules for group meeting discussions. These are examples of group meeting ground rules:

- No blaming others—accept responsibility for yourself.
- Include everyone in the discussion.
- Be respectful of yourself and others (full-value contract).
- Use each other's names.
- Do not talk over each other.
- Wait for classmates to finish their comments.

At the beginning of the year, allow the students to generate a behavior contract to guide group meeting discussions. Post and reinforce this contract throughout the year.

Students at developmental stage 1 may benefit from discussion techniques that allow them to provide input quickly and safely (e.g., buzz words, show of hands, thumbometer). For example, after Slalom Dribble (Model in Action 7.2), you might ask students to rate their performance using a show of hands (hands up if they kept the ball under control while dribbling, hands up if they kept their head up while dribbling, and hands up if they observed their partner and provided appropriate feedback). On the basis of the students' responses, you could ask for examples of actions that illustrate their ratings (e.g., keeping the ball close to your feet is a way of demonstrating you are in control of the ball). You could then link these discussion points back to the theme ("Our theme today focused on control, and I noticed a lot of good examples of students staying in control while dribbling the soccer ball").

Reflection

The reflection time is dedicated to individual self-reflection on the learning experience. It can link to the responsibility levels (e.g., "In what ways did you demonstrate respect during the lesson today?") or get students to think about ways to transfer what they learned in the lesson to other aspects of their lives (e.g., "Today our theme was control; what happens when we lose control?" "Can you think of a time when you lost control? What was the result?"; "What would you do differently if faced with the same situation again?"). Questions can move from how the activities or style of teaching challenged or engaged students to a focus on how they participated as independent learners, demonstrated respect, showed self-direction, and cooperated. During developmental stage 1, the teacher directs the discussion and generally targets Level I and II behaviors. This can be accomplished through a variety of formats (e.g., student drawings, journal assignments, rubrics) in class or outside of class time. For the Slalom Dribble activity, this could include asking students to

- use the thumbometer to rate their behavior across the responsibility levels (e.g., "How well did you demonstrate respect today?") or
- rate their performance with regard to effort (3, pushed myself; 2, tried hard; 1, took it easy).

Developmental Stage 2

When the students are able to demonstrate Level I and II behaviors consistently, we begin to release some control of the lesson to the students. This is the hallmark of developmental stage 2. During this stage we want to ask students to show an ability to work independently (Level III) and give them opportunities to demonstrate leadership and caring (Level IV) during the lesson. Within a soccer curriculum, this would mean providing opportunities for students to work collaboratively with their peers with little teacher guidance. It is during this stage that students experiment with leadership roles, and by relinquishing some of the control of the class to students we can foster this development.

Relationship Time

The role of the relationship time remains consistent across the developmental stages—to provide an opportunity for students to develop a sense of belonging in the classroom through the development of student–student and student–teacher relationships. At the second developmental stage we begin using relationship time activities that allow students to self-regulate, start and stop independently, and make choices as to whom they work with. These opportunities transition relationship time activities from individuals performing within the context of the group to individuals positively interacting with partners and in small groups in self-guided learning experiences.

The Back to Back activity (Model in Action 7.3) gives students an opportunity to continue to demonstrate respect (Level I) and participate with effort (Level II) while working collaboratively with a partner (Level III). Transition from this activity to the awareness talk by drawing the students' attention to the level of effort and self-control you observed during the activity. "How did you communicate with your partner? I liked to hear partners asking specific questions when they were drawing. It was also nice to see everyone focused on the task and working independently." With comments like these, you can bring about an awareness of the concept of participating with effort, self-regulating behavior, and working collaboratively with peers.

Awareness Talk

At the second developmental stage you should begin to ask students to take more responsibility for the learning experience. The awareness talk is one way for students to participate in the lesson. For this transition to work best, identify the theme, select one or more students to guide the questioning, and help the group draw connections to the lesson focus. Commonly used themes during developmental stage 2 include self-control, self-direction, communication, collaboration, goal setting, and problem solving.

Here we use Back to Back to illustrate how an awareness talk can transition students from a relationship activity to the lesson focus. These are examples of questions you might provide to the student leaders:

- "What did you need from your partner during this activity?"
- "How did you break down the picture and provide instructions to your partner?"
- "What strategies did you notice helped the artist during this activity?"
- "What other strategies could the describer use to help the artist?"

By providing the student leaders with a selection of questions, you maintain the direction of the conversation while giving them a chance to comfortably explore taking a leadership role in class. Help guide the discussion by adding probing questions to follow up on student responses. Use these questions to point toward the theme selected for the lesson.

MODEL IN ACTION 7.3

Back to Back

DESCRIPTION

Working in pairs, students attempt to redraw an image. One student (the describer) selects an image card, does not show it to anyone else, and sits back-to-back with his partner (the artist). The object of this game is for the describer to give the artist the necessary instructions to redraw the image shown on the card. The describer should not look at the artist's work during the activity. When they are finished, the students can compare the images and discuss strategies for the next round. They then switch roles.

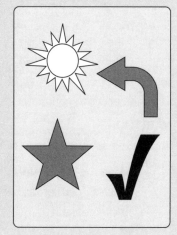

EQUIPMENT

Paper and pencils for each pair of students, image cards (see the accompanying figure for an example). The images can range from simple geometric shapes to complex images with text boxes. They should be challenging enough to promote communication between partners but not so complicated that they can't be drawn in 2 to 4 minutes.

VARIATION

Provide the artists with a blank piece of paper and ask them to come up with an image of their own that represents the theme of the day.

Lesson Focus

During the second developmental stage, we continue to transition from a teacher-centered teaching style to student-centered approaches. Students benefit from opportunities to demonstrate self-regulation and leadership behaviors. Simply by changing the way you present the tasks, you can use soccer activities to promote student responsibility and foster self-direction and leadership and caring behaviors consistent with TPSR Levels III and IV. The Kicking and Shooting Drill (Model in Action 7.4) uses foundational skills for soccer. Students can perform skill practice individually, with partners, or in small groups. Consider the psychomotor development level of your students when selecting appropriate tasks to work on passing and catching. The Kicking and Shooting Drill is an example of an activity you can use with students across a variety of responsibility levels.

The Kicking and Shooting Drill provides you with the flexibility to maintain control of the activity (i.e., all students show ready position, all students kick at the same time) or release some of the control to the students (i.e., students self-pace their practice, self- or peer assess during the practice).

Table 7.2 presents considerations for teaching the Kicking and Shooting Drill through two teaching styles and shows how they connect to the TPSR model. With use of a teacher-centered (i.e., inclusion) teaching style, the activity primarily reinforces responsibility Levels I and II. By releasing some of the control during the skill practice, you can begin to integrate responsibility Level III and IV behaviors. However, by using a more student-centered approach (e.g., self-check), you can foster self-direction and leadership behavior in students.

Inclusion Style

Presenting the Kicking and Shooting Drill using an inclusion style allows you to maintain some structured practice across a variety of tasks. One way to accomplish this is to create stations around the gymnasium that include each facet of the activity. Stations include a variety of levels of challenge from which students can select. Instruct the students through each task, providing critical cues and checking for understanding. Once students have seen each facet, they may begin the practice. Students can move through the stations in any order and are instructed to complete a specified number of repetitions for each task. Students can repeat stations, but ask them to challenge themselves.

Move about the gymnasium providing feedback.

- **Task 1:** Instep kick to target (distance to target: 12 feet [3.7 meters], 15 feet [4.5 meters], 18 feet [5.5 meters]; size of target: 6 feet [2 meters], 4 feet [1.2 meters], 2 feet [.6 meters])
- **Task 2:** Outside kick to target (distance to target: 6 feet, 8 feet [2.4 meters], 12 feet; size of target: 6 feet, 4 feet, 2 feet)

MODEL IN ACTION 7.4

Kicking and Shooting Drill

DESCRIPTION

This drill can work on instep, outside, and drive kicking techniques. Students practice kicking through a target goal (two cones placed 2 yards [approximately 2 meters] apart). They position themselves in front of their target at a distance of 12 to 15 feet (3.7 to 4.5 meters). Position the cones near a wall for individual practice, or place students in pairs.

EQUIPMENT

One ball and two cones per student or per pair.

VARIATIONS

To add a level of challenge to this activity, try some of the following:

- Move the cones closer together.
- Move the kicker farther back.
- Add a goalie.

- **Task 3:** Drive kick to target (distance to target: 15 feet, 18 feet, 20 feet [6 meters]; size of target: 6 feet, 4 feet, 2 feet)
- **Task 4:** Kick to partner through goal (cones in the middle of the area) (distance between partners: 15 feet, 18 feet, 20 feet; target size: 6 feet, 4 feet, 2 feet)
- **Task 5:** Kick to partner through goal (cones in the middle of the area) past a goalie (distance between partners: 15 feet, 18 feet, 20 feet; goal size: 18 feet, 15 feet, 12 feet)

Self-Check Style

To use a self-check style of teaching, create a task sheet that includes the learning cues and description of the task or drill. You can ask a student to demonstrate the drills and focus students on their task sheet. After reading the task sheets, students begin the activity at their own pace.

Following each kick, students recheck the criteria noted on the task sheet relative to their execution of the kick. Students are responsible for their own feedback based on the criteria for the skill. The teacher's role is to ask questions about the student's process of self-checking or self-assessing.

Group Meeting

During developmental stage 2, the teacher shifts much of the responsibility for the facilitation of the group meeting to the students; however, you should be prepared to redirect responses and initiate guided questioning. Use techniques that allow students to quickly and safely respond to questions. For example, to conduct a buzz word discussion of the Kicking and Shooting Drill, you could ask each student to respond to a question (e.g., "What aspect of the task did you have control over?") with a simple answer (e.g., "type of kick," "distance"). You can link these responses back to the theme and set the stage for the reflection on how the theme can be transferred beyond the classroom experience.

Table 7.2 Developmental Stage 2 Instructional Strategies for Soccer

Instructional style	Teaching considerations	Links to TPSR
Inclusion	• Students make decisions about how each task is to be completed, pace of practice, level of challenge for each task. • Students work individually or in partners. • Teacher provides objectives of lesson. • Teacher provides feedback to students.	• Students can demonstrate self-control and respect (Level I) for the teacher (e.g., following directions, staying in control) and for peers (e.g., not interfering with their practice). • Students can demonstrate participation with effort (Level II) by staying engaged throughout the kicking and shooting tasks. • Students can begin to demonstrate self-direction (Level III) by progressively challenging themselves throughout the activities (e.g., progressing though variations). • Students learn to be accountable for their own practice decisions and goal setting (Level III).
Self-check	• Teacher values students' ability to self-evaluate their performance. • Teacher values students' ability to work independently of teacher and peers. • Students have demonstrated competency in the skill.	• Students can demonstrate caring (Level IV) by respecting the rights of other students. • Students can demonstrate transfer outside the gym (Level V) by gaining self-awareness about their proficiency. • Students demonstrate leadership (Level IV) by maintaining honesty about their performance.

Reflection

During developmental stage 2, reflection time is an opportunity for students to self-reflect on their actions and what they observed in others throughout the lesson. Self-reflection can be elicited through a variety of formats (e.g., student drawings, journal assignments, rubrics) in class or outside of class time. Consider using a two-part reflection in which students have questions to reflect upon (e.g., "How did getting to choose your own challenge help motivate you today?") during class and write their responses during their next class (classroom teacher partnership) or after school (homework). This provides time for students to informally reflect on the experience before speaking for the experience. For the Kicking and Shooting Drill, consider asking students to

- describe why they selected the level of challenge they did and whether it was appropriate,
- describe how they challenged themselves in today's lesson, or
- rate their performance with regard to self-regulation (3, picked tasks that were challenging today; 2, selected tasks that I was comfortable with; 1, selected tasks that were inappropriate for my skill level—too hard or too easy).

Developmental Stage 3

Transitioning students to developmental stage 3 within the confines of physical education settings can be difficult. At this stage students should routinely demonstrate behaviors consistent with Levels I through III and actively seek out opportunities to lead. Students are increasingly provided with opportunities to lead their peers in skill development, awareness talks, and group meeting settings. These opportunities for caring and leadership take center stage during developmental stage 3.

Relationship Time

Relationship time activities during developmental stage 3 should transition from individuals positively interacting with partners and small groups to collaborative learning experiences led by student leaders with the support of the teacher. This setting allows

---

MODEL IN ACTION 7.5

The Path

DESCRIPTION

Students work in groups of 10 to 12 and attempt to find a safe path (created beforehand by the teacher but unknown to the participants) across the playing area (see the accompanying figure). Students enter the grid by stepping into a box. If they are correct they can continue; if they are incorrect, they must leave the grid and allow the next player an attempt. The goal is for the group, working together, to determine the correct path through the grid. Only one player may be on the grid at a time, and players must not step on the same box twice. They can move only between adjacent boxes. Allow groups 5 to 7 minutes to find the path. You can create multiple patterns and have them ready for groups that finish a pattern earlier than the other groups.

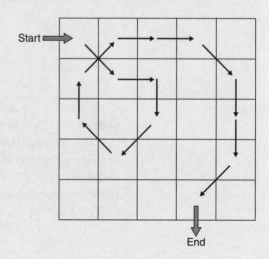

EQUIPMENT

Five-by-five grid on the floor. You can form the grid by taping on a large mat, drawing on a sheet, or using 25 poly spots.

VARIATIONS

- Allow one student to serve as the guide, indicating whether a move is correct or incorrect. The guide should not provide hints or show the pattern to other students during the activity.
- Place letters on the spots so the correct path spells out a "secret message." In this case students would be allowed to step on a spot more than once.

students to experiment with leadership opportunities within the safety of small-group and partner activities. Consider providing students with greater autonomy in selecting and self-pacing relationship activities as they develop these leadership skills.

The Path (Model in Action 7.5) activity allows student groups to work collaboratively during the relationship time activity. Each group can select a leader to acquire the necessary equipment. The teacher is free to move between groups and discuss strategies during game play.

Awareness Talk

During the third developmental stage, student leaders identify the theme, guide the questioning, and draw the connection to the lesson focus. Commonly used themes during developmental stage 3 include self-direction, leadership, and transfer. To illustrate an awareness talk for this stage, let's consider The Path activity.

In speaking for The Path activity, the student leaders would generalize the lessons learned from the activity to the theme and subsequent activities. These are examples of statements they might use:

- "I liked how my group talked through each step and offered suggestions while others were trying to solve the path. Did other groups talk through what moves to make?"

- "In our group we used the planning time to establish an order. How did other groups decide their order?"

By speaking for the experience, the student leaders can generalize what occurred in the activity.

Lesson Focus

Developmental stage 3 activities should provide students with the opportunity for leadership experiences and provide strategies for encouraging transfer to other aspects of the curriculum. Through Passing 4v2 (Model in Action 7.6) offers students opportunities to exhibit behaviors consistent with responsibility Levels I through IV. The activity allows flexibility in the way in which the teacher presents the task to the students.

Altering the teaching style allows you to use this drill with students in any of the three developmental stages. Table 7.3 presents considerations for teaching

---

MODEL IN ACTION 7.6

Through Passing 4v2

DESCRIPTION

Use this drill to develop strategies for supporting teammates during offense. Students work in groups of six, with two playing defense and four playing offense (see the accompanying figure). For each group, use four cones to set up a 10-yard by 10-yard (9- by 9-meter) playing area. The offense tries to complete 12 consecutive passes, and the defense tries to disrupt the passes. Both offensive and defensive players should focus on moving the ball to support their teammates. Apart from maintaining possession of the ball, the offense should attempt to pass the ball through the defenders. Award 1 point for a successful pass between adjacent offensive players and 3 points for each pass that travels through the middle. After the offense completes 12 consecutive passes or the defense disrupts three passes (whichever comes first), the students rotate positions. A disrupted pass is one in which the defender stops the ball or deflects the ball away from the intended target.

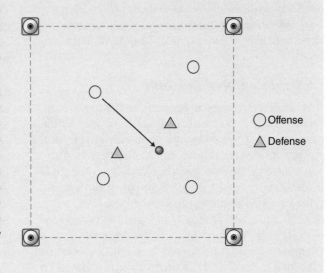

○ Offense
△ Defense

(continued)

(continued)

EQUIPMENT

One ball and four cones per group of six students.

A student considers her options during the Through Passing drill.

VARIATIONS

• Have students play with one-touch passing.

• Increase playing area and encourage offense to move without the ball.

the Through Passing 4v2 activity and demonstrates how alterations in the reciprocal teaching style can elicit leadership and communication skills in students.

Student-Centered Teaching

It is often a challenge to move students to developmental stage 3 within the confines of traditional physical education and youth sport settings. Physical education especially presents a challenge because you work with populations that have diverse motivations toward course content. If you are fortunate and skilled enough to guide your group to this level, much of your time will be spent using student-centered teaching styles. In the next section we present one example of student-centered teaching that can be modified to fit other styles on the spectrum based on the content, your students' learning style, and your preferred teaching style.

Reciprocal Style

To use a reciprocal style, you would have groups of eight. The two additional students serve as offensive and defensive observers. Provide task sheets that briefly describe the game and cues for the observers. The sheet should also list clear role expectations for students to help them stay focused. For example, spell out what the observer ought to be observing (movement of the ball, kicking to an open space) and what the doers are doing (passing through or defending). Provide a time or number of passes for the activity. Once students have finished, they rotate their roles: Offense becomes observers and defenders, and observers and defenders become offense.

The teacher's role is to move about the space and assist the observers in observing the doers accurately. You must step in to provide feedback if there is a safety issue. Otherwise, encourage or suggest feedback to the observer only if feedback is not occurring.

Table 7.3 Developmental Stage 3 Instructional Strategies for Soccer

Instructional style	Teaching considerations	Links to TPSR
Reciprocal	• Students work in groups of eight and have specific roles (four offensive players, two defenders, offense observer, defense observer). • Students have task sheets and a list of feedback phrases. • Groups work at own pace and rotate positions. • Teacher ensures that students are maintaining their roles and intervenes only if there is a safety issue.	• Students can demonstrate respect (Level I) for the teacher (e.g., following directions, staying in control) and for peers (e.g., not interfering with their practice). • Students can demonstrate participation with effort (Level II). • Students can begin to demonstrate self-direction (Level III) by progressively challenging themselves throughout the activities (e.g., increasing speed, decreasing number of errors). • Students develop leadership as they maintain their role as observers and provide feedback to peers (Level IV). • Students begin to develop empathy, social manners, and trust through interacting with peers (Level IV).

At this developmental stage, you should be able to release the learning groups to perform the lesson tasks with limited guidance. Students consistently demonstrate the ability to work independently and provide appropriate feedback to their peers. Use group leaders to gather equipment, set up learning experiences, and assign roles to peers.

Group Meeting

During this developmental stage, students should be able to lead the group meetings. While shifting much of the responsibility to the students during developmental stage 3, you should continue to make available techniques that promote peer-to-peer responses. Students will begin higher-level questioning that guides peers toward the integration and transfer of what has been learned in the activities to experiences beyond the classroom. For example, for Through Passing 4v2, a student leader can initiate a group reflection on what happened by asking "How did the defenders support each other during this drill?" and follow up with "What are other ways we support our teammates during soccer?" You can assist by cueing the students regarding the levels they are working on, as well as by reminding them of the kinds of questions that were asked in previous classes. Questions can address how the activity was conducted, how students contributed to the group success, how observing and providing feedback influenced learn-

ing of the task, or how the style of teaching engaged the participants.

Reflection

As with the group meeting, students who reach developmental stage 3 will begin to use higher-order questions during their reflections. These reflections should continue to be an opportunity for students to self-reflect on their actions and what they observed in others throughout the lesson while they explore ways they can transfer the responsibility attributes they are developing in physical education to life beyond the gym. To accomplish this you can use a variety of formats in class or outside of class time. Students might begin to read each other's journals and provide feedback; they might also assist each other in goal setting or creating strategies to transfer the levels outside of the program. Again, the teacher remains connected to the process as an active listener and supporter.

Keeping SITE

As discussed in chapter 1, the key to TPSR is keeping SITE of four thematic objectives (student relationships, integration, transfer, and empowerment) throughout your lessons and program. Using the content from this chapter, reflect on the following questions:

Student Relationships

1. What aspects of the variation in teaching styles assisted in enhancing student–teacher relationships? How?

2. What aspects of the variation in teaching styles assisted in enhancing student–student relationships? How?

Integration

1. What are elements within this chapter that facilitate development of personal responsibility in students? How?

2. What are elements within this chapter that facilitate development of social responsibility in students? How?

Transfer

1. What elements within the chapter might assist in transfer of TPSR outside of the class but within the school or program? How?

2. What elements within the chapter might assist in transfer of TPSR outside of the school or program? How?

Empowerment

1. What elements of your lessons support an empowering pedagogy for students?

2. What pedagogical choices can you make to promote autonomy and a sense of control in your students?

Teaching Personal and Social Responsibility Through

Basketball

Basketball was possibly the first activity used by Don Hellison as he sought to work with youth in a more meaningful way. Basketball is also a mainstay in most physical education curricula. The fact that most youth have played or are familiar with the sport can have both positive and negative aspects. Trash talking and grandstanding can quickly become dominant behaviors on the court. Important to the use of TPSR is to structure the learning environment in a way that capitalizes on youth expertise in the skills and also facilitates opportunities for them to assist others. *Basketball: Steps to Success, Third Edition*, by Hal Wissel (2012) is the primary resource for content in this chapter.

Developmental Stage 1

As we discussed in the beginning of this book, students in the first developmental stage are often working on exhibiting Level I (respecting self and others) and II (participating with effort and self-direction)

behaviors consistently. During this stage the teacher takes the predominant role in leading the awareness talk, choosing developmentally appropriate tasks and challenges, structuring the group meeting, and providing reflection opportunities. As the lessons progress, the teacher is mindful to provide students with opportunities to begin to transition to developmental stage 2 (Level III, self-direction).

Relationship Time

We advocate using icebreaker games throughout the learning process to facilitate a more coordinated effort to build connections between the teacher and students. They provide an opportunity for students and teachers to interact, develop relationships, and have fun. Icebreakers can vary in length, but all serve the purpose of creating an environment that fosters acceptance and interaction. When working with developmental stage 1 learners, consider selecting activities that focus on individual traits (communi-

---

MODEL IN ACTION 8.1

Juggler's Carry

DESCRIPTION

This activity is a fun way to start a series of basketball lessons and get the students interacting—and even laughing a little. Begin with an area about the size of a basketball court (smaller is fine). Place two balls (any size) at the baseline. This will be both the starting and finishing line. Place two more balls at midcourt (see the accompanying figure). Students are in groups of five to seven and are connected in that they hold hands and stand side by side. The task is to transfer the four balls across the midcourt line and back to the finish line. The group begins by picking up a ball and making their way to midcourt; they then pick up another ball. They return to the baseline, picking up the third ball, and then to midcourt to pick up the fourth ball and return to the baseline with all four balls. The group must communicate about who is picking up the ball and how it will be transported. No ball can touch the floor during transport; if it does, the group starts over. Team members cannot touch the ball with their hands and must remain connected. The task is completed when all four balls are past the start line.

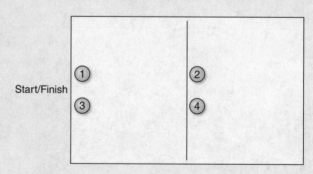

EQUIPMENT

Four balls per group of five to seven students.

VARIATION

Place obstacles in the way, such as poly spots, cones, or a rope that students must step over.

cation, cooperation, self-control, respect, and effort) within the context of group interactions.

Juggler's Carry (Model in Action 8.1) provides students with the opportunity to demonstrate respect, self-control, and cooperation (Level I) as well as to participate with effort (Level II). Because the group must figure out how to move while they are connected and how to grasp the balls without using their hands, this activity is an excellent way to underscore communication and working together. It is likely that groups will have to "reset" themselves by starting over, which can lead to conflict. This bit of conflict can allow for the students to consider their goals for the lesson as they undertake the awareness talk.

Awareness Talk

During the first developmental stage, the teacher takes the primary role in the awareness talks. She identifies the theme, guides the questioning, and makes the connection to teachable moments in the lesson focus. Commonly used themes during developmental stage 1 include respect, self-control, participation, effort, and effective communication. This is the reason we like to use icebreakers such as Juggler's Carry; it provides connections from the activity to the remainder of the lesson. Teachers can use "What?", "So what?", and "Now what?" questions to draw meaning, such as the following:

- "The icebreaker today was really about working together as a unit. What were some of the things your teammates did that helped your group find success?"
- "In addition to cooperating, what other things were helpful to the group's success?"
- "What things were not helpful?"
- "Think about some goals you can set for yourself to help you be a good teammate during today's lesson. Think about what worked and did not work during the icebreaker activity."

Lesson Focus

The theme identified during the awareness talk can set the stage for teachable moments throughout the lesson focus. You can select tasks or use teaching strategies that provide opportunities for students to make a cognitive or affective connection between the tasks and the theme. The teaching style you use can assist in creating a space for those teachable moments to occur. Although in developmental stage 1 it is often beneficial to maintain a somewhat teacher-centered approach, we must also provide students with

opportunities to work toward skill development in developmental stage 2. The style you choose will be influenced by your teaching philosophy, the learning styles of your students, and the context in which the lesson is presented. Here we provide an example of a lesson focus on a basketball skill using two different styles of teaching.

Table 8.1 presents considerations for teaching the Ball Handling and Dribbling activity (Model in Action 8.2) through two teaching styles and shows how they connect to the TPSR model. The practice/task style moves slightly away from completely convergent, and the reciprocal style is more student centered or divergent.

These instructional styles provide students with the opportunity to directly demonstrate personal and social responsibility; they also give teachers opportunities to reinforce respect, effort, caring, and leadership consistent with the TPSR philosophy.

Icebreaker activities can facilitate stronger connections between students and teachers during the lesson focus.

MODEL IN ACTION 8.2

Ball Handling and Dribbling

DESCRIPTION

This activity is used to improve ball handling and dribbling skills. Students complete each of the following drills.

- **One leg:** With feet shoulder-width apart, students rotate the ball around one leg for a count of 10, then reverse directions. Complete the same on the opposite leg.
- **Two legs:** With feet together, students pass the ball around their legs for a count of 10 and then reverse the direction.
- **Figure eight:** With feet shoulder-width apart (ready position), students move the ball around each leg in a figure-eight motion. Do for a count of 10 and then reverse the direction.
- **Around the waist:** With feet in ready position, students pass the ball around their waist for a count of 10, then reverse.
- **Around the head:** Same as the preceding drill, only around the head. Reverse direction at the count of 10.

After ball handling, students work on dribbling skills. This five-part drill works on each critical element of the dribble as well as challenges the student's nondominant hand. Give the following instructions:

- **Crossover:** From the ready position, dribble below the knees, changing from the left hand to the right hand. Be sure to keep your nondribbling hand up for protection and change the position of your feet depending on which hand you are using to dribble. For example, if the ball is in your right hand, your left hand is up for protection and your left foot is forward. Complete 20 repetitions.
- **Figure eight:** Dribble the ball in a figure eight from back to front through your legs, changing from one hand to the other as the ball goes through your legs. After 20 repetitions, change direction.
- **One knee:** Place one knee on the ground; from that position, dribble the ball starting in front of the knee, then around to one side and under your knee. Change hands and dribble behind your back leg. Dribble in this way for 10 repetitions and then reverse direction or change knees.
- **Sitting:** As you dribble, sit down. Continue dribbling on one side, raising your legs off the floor and dribbling under them. Dribble on each side for 10 repetitions, then reverse.
- **Lying down:** While lying down, dribble on one side for 10 repetitions. Then sit up, dribble around your back, lie back down, and dribble on the other side for 10 repetitions.

EQUIPMENT

Basketballs.

VARIATIONS

- Have students speed up or slow down while handling or dribbling the ball.
- Vary the size of the ball.

Practice/Task Style

To use the practice/task style, you create stations around the gymnasium that include each facet of the Ball Handling and Dribbling activity. Stations offer task sheets or task cards. Task sheets include a brief description of the activity and provide the cues. We also suggest providing a list of possible motivation-type feedback for students to use. Instruct the students through each drill, providing critical cues and checking for understanding. Once students have seen each facet of each drill, they may begin the practice. They can move through the stations in any order and complete the repetitions specified for each activity. Students can repeat stations, but ask them to challenge themselves. Move about the gymnasium providing feedback.

Table 8.1 Developmental Stage 1 Instructional Strategies for Basketball

Instructional style	Teaching considerations	Links to TPSR
Practice/Task	• Students make decisions about order of tasks to be completed, pace of practice, starting and stopping on a particular task. • Students work individually. • Teacher provides objectives of lesson. • Teacher provides feedback to students.	• Students can demonstrate self-control and respect (Level I) for the teacher (e.g., following directions, staying in control) and for peers (e.g., not interfering with their practice). • Students can demonstrate participation with effort (Level II) by staying engaged throughout the ball handling and dribbling activities. • Students can begin to demonstrate self-direction (Level III) by progressively challenging themselves throughout the activities (e.g., time themselves, count errors). • Students learn to be accountable for their own practice decisions and goal setting (Level III).
Reciprocal	• Students work in pairs and have assigned roles (doer, observer). • Students have task sheets and a list of feedback phrases. • Pairs work at own pace. • Teacher ensures that students are maintaining their roles and intervenes only if there is a safety issue.	• Students can demonstrate respect (Level I) for the teacher (e.g., following directions, staying in control) and for peers (e.g., not interfering with their practice). • Students can demonstrate participation with effort (Level II) by staying engaged in the activities. • Students also demonstrate Level II by staying in their assigned roles. • Students begin to develop empathy, social manners, and trust by interacting with peers (Levels I-III).

Reciprocal Style

Reciprocal style is similar to practice/task style in that students go through stations but different in that the students are assigned roles. Task sheets include a brief description of the activity and provide the cues. We also suggest providing a list of possible motivation-type feedback for students to use. The task sheets also note the students' roles, doers and observers. Groups begin when they are ready. They can move from station to station in any way they wish, but all group members must complete the drill before the group moves to the next activity.

The teacher's role is to move about the space and assist the observers in accurately observing the doers. You must step in to provide feedback if there is a safety issue. Otherwise, encourage or suggest feedback to the observer only if feedback is not occurring. Key to this style is for the students to interact with minimal if any input from the teacher.

Group Meeting

Group meetings during the first developmental stage are facilitated by the teacher but provide an opportunity for students to have a voice in the learning process. The discussion can focus on how the lesson went or how the teacher did. Questions about how the activities challenged the students and about how they felt participating in the lesson when the teacher used a given teaching style are good beginning points. Students can also be asked how they felt the class as a whole or just they as partners or in small groups did. Lastly, you can ask how you as the teacher did and if there are things you might work on for next session. This portion of the lesson may feel odd to students since young people are not often asked to provide feedback to each other, much less to and about the teacher. Stay with it; over time, students will feel more comfortable verbalizing their thoughts as this becomes a consistent part of the class.

During this stage you may need to reinforce ground rules for group meeting discussions. These are examples of group meeting ground rules:

- No blaming others—accept responsibility for yourself.
- Include everyone in the discussion.
- Be respectful of yourself and others (full-value contract).
- Use each other's names.
- Do not talk over each other.
- Wait for classmates to finish their comments.

These are only a few examples; we encourage you to solicit input from your classes about other ground rules that might be included.

Another especially relevant issue concerning group meetings is time. If you do not have sufficient time to check in with all students, ask for responses on how things went from just a few. A common practice in many TPSR-based programs is to have the students keep a journal. They can do this as homework and turn in their comments the next day. This way you keep track of how things are going and get timely input from the class.

Reflection

Reflection time should flow fairly seamlessly from the group meeting time. Group meeting time focuses on student evaluation of the lesson, and reflection time focuses on evaluation of their role as learners and support. Thus, questions can move from how the activities or style of teaching challenged or engaged them to a focus on how they participated as independent learners, demonstrated respect, showed self-direction, and cooperated during the lesson. During developmental stage 1, the teacher directs the discussion. As noted in previous chapters, the thumbometer is a simple technique that provides the teacher with quick and individualized information on where the students are in relation to the levels. These are examples of questions you might ask:

- "During the dribble drill today, did you support your partner by giving feedback?"
- "Did you show stick-to-itiveness during the ball handling drill as it got harder?"
- "Did you keep your focus when we used the practice/task style and complete the drill?"

Students respond as a group by pointing their thumbs. The teacher notes where most of the kids are (more thumbs up than down) so as to facilitate

activities toward the higher levels (Levels III through V). As Don notes, it is important to acknowledge that kids have bad days, too. This means that we should support them and encourage honest self-evaluation. We also want to underscore not blaming others for our behavior.

Lastly, the reflection time is when we can begin to encourage students to think about how they can demonstrate the levels outside of the class or program. Asking students where in their out-of-class or out-of-program lives they could demonstrate a given level of responsibility allows them to begin to conceptualize this transition. For some students, reaching a certain level outside of class but still within the school (which is a nice scaffold) might be all that is possible. In any case, we should begin to encourage students to think about responsibility outside the class.

Developmental Stage 2

Once students are consistently demonstrating Level I and II behaviors, you should transition to the second developmental stage. This means providing opportunities for students to work collaboratively with their peers with little teacher guidance (Level III, self-direction). During the second stage you begin to call upon students to take a role in the learning process. As you will see in this section, you begin to relinquish some of the control of the class to students during awareness talks and group meetings. As this occurs, some students may begin to demonstrate a desire to take leadership roles (Level IV), but most will continue to need some guidance in keeping self-directed without individual supervision.

Relationship Time

Juggler's Carry (Model in Action 8.1) gives students the opportunity to continue to demonstrate respect (Level I) and participate with effort (Level II) while working collaboratively with their classmates without direct supervision from the teacher (Level III). Following the same format ("What?", "So what?", "Now what?") but now inviting more student leadership during the process, we can begin to navigate TPSR Level III and to transition to Level IV concepts.

Awareness Talk

During the second developmental stage, the teacher begins to share the responsibility for the awareness talks. He identifies the theme, asks one or more students to guide the questioning, and draws the connection to the lesson focus. Commonly used themes

Students work with peers and with little teacher guidance in the second developmental stage.

during developmental stage 2 include self-control, self-direction, goal setting, and problem solving.

Using students to help guide the awareness talk is key in the development of youth leaders (Level IV). Following the activity, you can use student leaders to "debrief" so as to draw the attention of the learners to the cognitive and affective attributes of an activity. These are examples of questions you might provide the student leader following Juggler's Carry:

"What?" Questions

- "What helped you when talking with your group members to be successful at the activity?"
- "What were your feelings when you failed to keep balls from hitting the ground? How did you feel when you were successful in keeping balls from hitting the ground?"

"So What?" Questions

- "How might your feelings when you failed and succeeded help as you work in groups?"
- "How might you do things differently in this activity to find more success individually and as a member of the group?"

"Now What?" Questions

- "Thinking about the activity and how you felt as you succeeded or failed, how can those feel-

ings help you as you engage in other activities during basketball?"
- "What might you do to help regain focus when you are not succeeding at something?"

By providing the students with a selection of questions, you maintain the direction of the conversation while giving students a chance to comfortably explore what it is like to take a leadership role in class.

Lesson Focus

The opportunities for self-direction take center stage during developmental stage 2. Again, activities should transition from individuals performing within the context of the group to individuals positively interacting with partners and small groups in self-guided learning experiences.

Table 8.2 presents considerations for teaching the Pass and Shoot activity (Model in Action 8.3) through two teaching styles and shows how they connect to the TPSR model. You can alter both styles so as to create challenge and, most importantly, provide students with the opportunity to work individually and in groups as well as pace themselves.

Being mindful of the activities used during this stage provides you with opportunities to alter the teaching style and encourage greater student responsibility. This allows for students to begin leading the

MODEL IN ACTION 8.3

Pass and Shoot

DESCRIPTION

This activity addresses squaring up to the basket following a pass. Mark four or five spots around the key or use existing court markings. One partner stands out of bounds, and one partner begins at the bottom of the key. The out-of-bounds partner passes the ball to the shooter, who catches the ball and shoots. The out-of-bounds partner follows the shot and retrieves the ball, then returns to out of bounds and passes again to the shooter, who now has moved to another spot on the key. Students continue until the shooter has moved around the key and back, then switch.

EQUIPMENT

Floor markers, basketballs.

VARIATIONS

- Vary the size of the ball.
- Vary the distance from the shooter to the basket.
- Have shooters rebound their own ball and pass back out to their partner.

group meeting segment of the lesson and speaking as to how the lesson activities address the theme or themes identified during the awareness talk.

Inclusion Style

To use the inclusion style, you demonstrate the cues for Pass and Shoot and present task sheets that provide a diagram and performance cues. Identify the options available for students in deciding how and where to enter the drill. For example, students can vary distances to the basket and use different types of balls to make the task more difficult. Students can also count missed or made shots, or they can time themselves and see how many shots they can make. These options, chosen by the students for themselves, create additional challenges. Students are placed in pairs and dispersed throughout the teaching area. Allow time for the learners to assess their level though trial and error and begin the drill. After each drill, the learners reassess and set new challenges based on the levels available and the achievement of performance criteria.

Your role is to circulate throughout the learning space and provide feedback only on the decisions of the students. You can ask, for example, "How are you doing at the level you have selected?" On the basis of the students' response, inquire about the decisions made and how successful the students feel they are. With this style it is important not to start out by overtly challenging the decision made initially but to help students in their self-assessments.

Reciprocal Style

To use the reciprocal style for this activity, arrange students in groups of three; the third person becomes the observer. Provide task sheets that briefly describe the activity, the cues, and the participants' roles. We also suggest including a list of possible motivation-type feedback for students to use. Clear role expectations for students on the task sheet will help them keep focus. For example, spell out what the observer ought to be observing (performance cues) and what the doers are doing (practicing). Provide a time or a number of passes for each facet of the activity. Once they are finished, the students rotate their roles. This process is repeated for each drill variation.

Your role is to move about the space and assist the observers in accurately observing the doer. You must step in to provide feedback if there is a safety issue. Otherwise, you encourage or suggest feedback to the observer only if feedback is not occurring.

Group Meeting

The group meeting during the second developmental stage should continue to provide students with an opportunity to have a voice in the learning process but facilitate their leading more of the discussion. Because you have modeled leading the discussion in developmental stage 1, you can help students assume more responsibility by asking questions such as "What sorts of questions did I ask you about the lesson?" and "What questions do you have of

Table 8.2 Developmental Stage 2 Instructional Strategies for Basketball

Instructional style	Teaching considerations	Links to TPSR
Inclusion	• Teacher decides on skill to be practiced and provides possible levels for the task. • Students make individual choices to accommodate their ability (e.g., distance to basket, size of basketball). • Students reassess abilities and make allowances as lesson progresses (e.g., stepping farther from partner, using a different ball). • Students' assessments allow them to rechallenge themselves or set goals (e.g., number of shots to make at a spot before moving on).	• Students can demonstrate respect (Level I) for self as they reassess and rechallenge themselves. • Students demonstrate effort and participation (Level II) as they reassess and rechallenge themselves. • Students set goals and demonstrate self-direction as they reassess throughout the lesson (Level III). • Students practice skills intrinsic to self-reliance (Level III). • Students begin to accept the reality of individual differences in performance abilities (Level IV).
Reciprocal	• Students work in pairs or small groups and are provided a specific role (e.g., shooter, passer, observer). • Students have task sheets and a list of feedback phrases. • Groups work at their own pace. • Teacher ensures that students are maintaining their roles and intervenes only if there is a safety issue.	• Students can demonstrate respect (Level I) for the teacher (e.g., following directions, staying in control) and for peers (e.g., not interfering with their practice). • Students can demonstrate participation with effort (Level II). • Students can begin to demonstrate self-direction (Level III) by progressively challenging themselves throughout the activities (e.g., number of shots made). • Students develop leadership as they maintain their role as observers and provide feedback to peers (Level IV). • Students begin to develop empathy, social manners, and trust by interacting with peers (Level IV).

your peers from the lesson?" Another strategy is to have students write their questions or comments on a slip of paper and then exchange with partners and engage in small-group discussions. You can then bring them back to the large group and ask for culminating thoughts from the day's lesson. Don't be disappointed if it takes a bit more effort during this developmental stage to get things going. Be consistent, be caring, and be a good model, and your students will begin to assume more responsibility.

Reflection

Key to this stage is that students begin to lead more of the discussion. Students can be cued on questions

that address the particular levels they are working at during this stage (Level III) and begin to scaffold to goals for the next levels (IV and V). These are examples of helpful questions:

- "How did you feel you and your partner worked independent of teacher direction?"
- "What might you improve on?"
- "As we move toward more independence, what goals can you set to show more leadership in class?"

Students can begin to generate these types of questions once you have modeled them. We encourage you to note the many examples in *Teaching Personal and Social Responsibility Through Physical Activity, Third Edition,* of different ways to engage students in reflection time. Methods such as exit slips, journaling, and tapping in (students tap on a poster listing the levels to indicate where they are) can be quite effective and keep this part of the lesson fresh.

Developmental Stage 3

Transitioning students to developmental stage 3 within the confines of physical education settings can be difficult. At this stage students should routinely demonstrate behaviors consistent with Levels I through III and actively seek out opportunities to lead. Students are increasingly provided with opportunities to lead their peers in skill development, awareness talks, and group meetings. These opportunities for caring and leadership take center stage during developmental stage 3. Accordingly, relationship time activities should transition from individuals positively interacting with partners and small groups to collaborative learning experiences led by student leaders with teacher support.

Relationship Time

As students begin to work within developmental stage 3, you can provide for them to lead the activities during this segment of the lesson. You can have volunteers or predetermined leaders identified so that students can be ready with an activity. As demonstrated by Where Do I Go? (Model in Action 8.4), the activity in this stage ought to include increasing amounts of problem solving as well as communication and working together.

Awareness Talk

During the third developmental stage, the teacher releases the responsibility of the awareness talks to student leaders. The student leaders identify the theme, guide the questioning, and draw the connection to the lesson focus. Commonly used themes during developmental stage 3 include self-direction, leadership, and transfer. It might be necessary in the initial portion of the activity to cue students to the sorts of things the activity addresses. Use previous lessons as a scaffold. For example, you might say, "In the previous lessons we have focused on what types of qualities? As you engage in Where Do I Go? this morning, think about what sorts of skills we are focusing on and what you might bring to the awareness talk after the activity."

Since you have been consistent in modeling this aspect of the lesson throughout the developmental stages and have allowed for more and more student leadership, it is highly likely that students will follow the "What?", "So what?", "Now what?" format they are familiar with. You then truly become a guide on the side. Your nonverbal behavior can really be important here. Remain involved by demonstrating active listening, nodding your head, and making eye

---

MODEL IN ACTION 8.4

Where Do I Go?

DESCRIPTION

In groups of about six to eight, students form a circle. One member of the group is blindfolded and stands in the center of the circle. One by one, participants provide instructions to the person in the center to direct her in accomplishing a task. The task could be moving to a ball and then placing the ball in a bucket, for example, or stepping through an obstacle course. Students in the circle take turns giving an instruction until the task has been accomplished. Take steps beforehand to ensure that the student who will be blindfolded cannot tell what the task will involve.

EQUIPMENT

Various types of equipment depending on the task (e.g., cones, balls, small buckets, blindfolds).

VARIATIONS

- Challenge the group to a limited number of instructions (for example, one less than the group number).
- Vary the complexity of the tasks to make them easier or harder.

Adapted, by permission, from D.W. Midura and D.R. Glover, 2005, *Essentials of team building principles and practices* (Champaign, IL: Human Kinetics), 58.

contact with whoever is speaking. This models to the students behaviors that they too can maintain in the process.

Lesson Focus

Developmental stage 3 activities should provide students with the opportunity for leadership experiences and provide strategies for encouraging transfer to other aspects of the curriculum. Model in Action 8.5 can offer students opportunities to exhibit behaviors consistent with responsibility Levels I through IV.

Teaching strategies for developmental stage 3 include providing students with opportunities to emphasize previous levels but, more importantly, focus on Levels IV (caring and leadership) and V (outside the gymnasium).

Table 8.3 presents considerations for teaching Pass and Shoot With Defense through the divergent discovery teaching style. The activity is an extension of Pass and Shoot (Model in Action 8.3), and thus you can note alterations between the styles as presented.

Student-Centered Teaching

It is often a challenge to move students to developmental stage 3 within the confines of traditional physical education and youth sport settings. Physical education especially presents a challenge because you work with populations that have diverse motiva-

tions toward course content. If you are fortunate and skilled enough to guide your group to this level, much of your time will be spent using student-centered teaching styles. In the next section we present one example of student-centered teaching that can be modified to fit other styles on the spectrum based on the content, your students' learning style, and your preferred teaching style.

Divergent Discovery Style

Presenting Pass and Shoot With Defense via the divergent discovery approach allows you to engage students in multiple domains—cognitive, affective, and psychomotor. Through questioning or the presentation of a problem, you can have students diverge on solutions for successfully completing the task. Shooters are asked to shoot baskets successfully around the key while the shooter, the passer, or both contend with varying degrees of defense. Each group (shooters and defense) assists each other in the strategies students have learned to produce the most effective ways of completing the task. Ask the students to think about these questions:

- What must the passer do to make a successful pass?
- What must the shooter do to make a successful shot?

MODEL IN ACTION 8.5

Pass and Shoot With Defense

DESCRIPTION

In this activity, students work on squaring up to the basket following a pass. Mark four or five spots around the key or use existing court markings. One partner stands out of bounds, and the other partner begins at the bottom of the key. The out-of-bounds partner passes the ball to the shooter, who catches the ball and shoots. The out-of-bounds partner follows the shot, retrieves the ball, and then returns to out of bounds and passes again to the shooter, who now has moved to another spot on the key. The activity continues until the shooter has moved around the key and back; then the students switch roles. The difference between this activity and Pass and Shoot is that two defensive people are added—one for the passer and one for the shooter—to increase difficulty.

EQUIPMENT

Floor markers, basketballs.

VARIATIONS

- Vary the distance from the shooter to the basket.
- Vary the size of the ball.
- Have shooters rebound their own ball and pass it back out.
- Vary the aggressiveness of the defense (light, medium, or tight).

Table 8.3   Developmental Stage 3 Instructional Strategies for Basketball

Instructional style	Teaching considerations	Links to TPSR
Divergent discovery	• Students solve problem presented by the teacher (cognitive engagement). • Teacher is free to offer prompts or questions to groups struggling to solve the task. • Provides opportunity for groups to solve task in unique ways. • Provides opportunity for students to voice opinions to peers. • Can lead to greater variance in performance.	• Students can demonstrate caring (Level IV) by respecting the rights of other students. • Students can demonstrate leadership and caring (Level IV) by organizing the group to try out ideas for completing the activity when contending with defense. • Students tolerate other's ideas and solutions (Levels I and IV).

Group Meeting

As with the awareness talk, this portion of the lesson is mostly student led. Assist in cueing the students regarding the levels they are working on and also remind them of what sorts of questions have been asked in previous classes. Questions that focus on how the lesson was conducted, how the activity met the students' needs or provided challenges, and how the style of teaching engaged the participants are all examples of program-related discussion questions. You can also encourage small-group discussion and then bring everyone back to the larger group. Most important, allow students to direct this process and remain as a support.

Reflection

Allowing students to lead the discussion using the various methods we have discussed or in small groups provides them with the choice and leadership opportunities inherent to this developmental stage. Students might begin to read each other's journals and provide feedback, or assist each other in goal setting or creating strategies to transfer levels to outside of the program. The teacher remains connected to the process as an active listener and support.

Keeping SITE

As discussed in chapter 1, the key to TPSR is keeping SITE of four thematic objectives (student relationships, integration, transfer, and empowerment) throughout your lessons and program. Using the content from this chapter, reflect on the following questions:

Student Relationships

1. What aspects of the variation in teaching styles assisted in enhancing student–teacher relationships? How?
2. What aspects of the variation in teaching styles assisted in enhancing student–student relationships? How?

Integration

1. What are elements within this chapter that facilitate development of personal responsibility in students? How?
2. What are elements within this chapter that facilitate development of social responsibility in students? How?

Transfer

1. What were elements within the chapter that might assist in transfer of TPSR outside of the class but within the school or program? How?
2. What were elements within the chapter that might assist in transfer of TPSR outside of the school or program? How?

Empowerment

1. What elements of your lessons support an empowering pedagogy for students?
2. What pedagogical choices can you make to promote autonomy and a sense of control in your students?

Teaching Personal and Social Responsibility Through

Team Handball

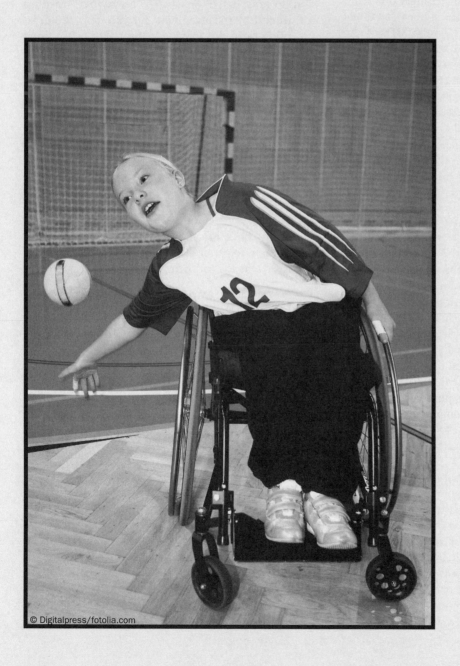

© Digitalpress/fotolia.com

Team handball, also known as European handball, is making its way into physical education classrooms across the country. *Team Handball: Steps to Success* by Clanton and Dwight (1997) is the primary resource for content in this chapter. Modifications to equipment and rules allow participation by elementary and secondary students alike. Team handball provides an environment in which students can demonstrate self-control, effort, self-direction, and caring.

Developmental Stage 1

Team handball offers students the opportunity to develop individual motor and manipulative skills while applying these skills in the context of a team sport. It is through this interaction that we can target the responsibility attributes and keep SITE of the TPSR model. By recognizing that students in the first developmental stage are often working on exhibiting behaviors consistent with TPSR responsibility Levels I and II, teachers can make curricular choices to foster developing respect and participating with effort. During this stage the teacher takes the predominant role in leading the awareness talk, choosing developmentally appropriate tasks and challenges, structuring the group meeting, and providing reflection opportunities.

Relationship Time

Relationship time provides the opportunity for teachers to target learning in the affective domain. As such, it allows opportunities for the development of student–teacher and student–student relationships. During this initial developmental stage, many students may need to learn or relearn how to stay in control physically and emotionally while interacting with peers. Deinhibitor games, introduced in the adventure unit, can serve as a medium for promoting positive interaction during this phase of the lesson. When working with developmental stage 1 learners, continue to select activities that focus on individual traits (self-control, respect, and effort) within the context of group interactions.

The Rock, Paper, Scissors Olympics activity (Model in Action 9.1) gives students an opportunity to demonstrate respect (Level I) and participate with effort (Level II). The game can give rise to conflict but also conflict resolution and compromise. Transition from this activity to the awareness talk by drawing the students' attention to the effort you observed during the game or behaviors that demonstrated respect. With these comments you can bring out an awareness of the concept of respect. Similarly, you could link the

effort you noticed as students moved during the game to Level II behavior.

Awareness Talk

During the first developmental stage, the teacher takes the primary role in the awareness talks. She identifies the theme, guides the questioning, and makes the connection to the lesson focus. Commonly used themes during developmental stage 1 include respect, self-control, participation, effort, and effective communication. Using Rock, Paper, Scissors Olympics, you can highlight attributes during the awareness talk that will serve as a transition for students from a relationship activity to the lesson focus. Using the "What?", "So what?", "Now what?" method of structuring the awareness talk can help you draw meaning from the activity in the relationship time; it also models for students how they may lead the awareness talk once you have transferred control for this part of the lesson to them (developmental stages 2 and 3). For example, in developmental stage 1, you might ask questions like these:

- "What were some ways you demonstrated effort during the activity?"
- "How did you respond when you won or lost a round during the Rock, Paper, Scissors Olympics activity?"

On the basis of the students' responses, you can guide them to extend their thinking by asking questions such as the following:

- "What can we do to demonstrate respect when we are the winner or loser in an activity?"
- "What might be a couple of things you know about yourself that you want to try to stop doing?"
- "Today we are continuing our team handball unit. What are some things you can do within this unit to demonstrate respect and effort?"
- "As you head into the rest of the lesson, what are some goals you can take forward from today's lesson? Challenge yourself a bit!"

Selecting relationship activities that can be used to stimulate discussion during the awareness talk provides a medium for linking concrete experiences to the lesson that follows. The shared experience of the group during the activities and subsequent reflection can make students aware of the theme of the lesson and give you teachable moments from which to guide the discussion. As we move through the developmental stages, student awareness talk leaders

Rock, Paper, Scissors Olympics

DESCRIPTION

The game begins with all the students, in pairs, in the middle of the playing area. Partners play Rock, Paper, Scissors for the best two out of three. The winner moves to the silver medal round; the losing player moves to the bronze medal round. Play continues for 3 to 5 minutes. Rotation pattern is as follows (see also the accompanying figure):

- Win in the middle—go to silver
- Win at silver—go to gold
  Lose at silver—go to bronze
- Win at gold—stay at gold
  Lose at gold—return to middle
- Lose in the middle—go to bronze
- Win at bronze—go to silver
  Lose at bronze—go out of medal (O of M)
- Win at O of M—return to middle
  Lose at O of M—stay at O of M

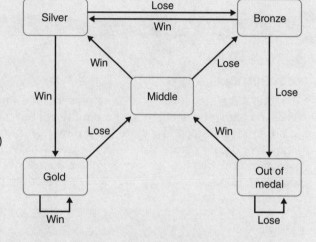

EQUIPMENT

Four cones, preferably different colors, to mark the different areas.

VARIATION

Have partners stand back-to-back and recite "rock, paper, scissors," then jump and turn around when they shoot. This increases the physical activity requirement and prevents confusion about when to shoot.

---

can also benefit from having had an experience that can help guide the awareness talk.

Lesson Focus

The theme identified during the awareness talk often sets the stage for what will occur during the lesson focus. You can select tasks or use pedagogical strategies that give students opportunities to make a cognitive or affective connection between the tasks and the theme. During the team handball unit, you can make curricular choices based on the attributes you wish to target. Team sports allow us to target a variety of personal and social attributes (respect, effort, self-direction, caring, teamwork, trust, communication) with the understanding that how we present the task can greatly affect the attributes that are targeted and developed.

The teaching style we use can also influence how the students perceive the task. At developmental stage 1, it is often beneficial to maintain a somewhat teacher-centered approach. To meet the students' developmental needs, select challenges that provide

opportunities for them to demonstrate respect (Level I) and participating with effort (Level II) while using a style that transitions them to working independently with their peers (Level III). The examples that follow illustrate use of the command or task style to present team handball activities across the personal and social attribute themes. The style you choose will be influenced by your teaching philosophy, the learning styles of your students, and the context in which the lesson is presented.

Sequencing learning experiences to match the developmental level of learners is essential for creating a positive learning environment. The activities presented in this chapter were selected to illustrate team handball tasks and skills that allow students to demonstrate developmental stage 1 behaviors. By modifying the manner of presentation, you can use these activities with any developmental stage. It is important to recognize that a highly skilled class may be functioning at developmental stage 1 while another class that is less highly skilled may be able to take greater responsibility for the learning process. By modifying how the information is presented and practiced, you can target the appropriate responsibility level and developmental stage.

Here we use the Circle Drill activity (Model in Action 9.2) to demonstrate how a team handball activity can connect to the levels of responsibility discussed throughout this book.

The psychomotor and cognitive developmental levels of your students will influence how you pres-

ent skill practice. Likewise, the stage of responsibility students are in should affect your curricular choices. The teaching style you use and the level of control students are responsible for will change as your students move across the responsibility and developmental levels. You can use Circle Drill with students at any developmental level by modifying how you present the activity and determining who has the primary

---

MODEL IN ACTION 9.2

Circle Drill

DESCRIPTION

This drill gives students a chance to practice throwing and catching and can be modified to meet the developmental needs of students from the control through proficient levels. Working in groups of five or six, students stand in a circle (approximately 30 feet [9 meters] in diameter). Students use either an overhand pass across the circle or a lateral flip pass (e.g., pass to the side accomplished by elbow extension and wrist flexion) to one of the students next to them. Have students work on proper catching technique (e.g., presenting a two-hand target for the passer to throw to) and correct footwork.

Students perform Circle Drill with modified equipment.

EQUIPMENT

Open playing area, one handball per group of five or six students.

VARIATION

After passing the ball, the thrower follows the ball to the position it was thrown to (i.e., player A throws to player D and runs to player D's position as player D throws to another student). Players can begin to catch and throw on the move, guide receivers with throws, and further develop footwork as they catch and switch direction.

Adapted, by permission, from R. Canton and M.P. Dwight, 1997, *Team handball: Steps to success* (Champaign, IL: Human Kinetics), 19.

responsibility for the learning experience. Table 9.1 presents considerations for teaching the Circle Drill activity through two teaching styles and shows how they connect to the TPSR model.

These instructional styles give students a chance to directly demonstrate personal and social responsibility; they also provide teachers with teachable moments for reinforcing respect, effort, caring, and leadership consistent with TPSR philosophy.

Command (Direct) Style

Presenting Circle Drill using a command style allows the teacher to direct the students through the progression of tasks. This encourages them to perform the task in the same way at the same time and allows the teacher to check student performance. The following lists suggest what this might look like.

To organize the Circle Drill, the teacher establishes groups (five or more students per group) and has one group provide a demonstration of the task and identify cues (i.e., two-hand target, absorb force, shift feet). Groups are positioned around the gym. The teacher directs the groups through a variety of skill challenges:

1. Overhand pass across circle
2. Lateral flip pass around circle
3. Combination of passes
4. Group goal—50 balls successfully passed and received
5. Throw and follow variation, overhead pass
6. Throw and follow variation, combination of passes

There are a number of ways to assess students during skill practice. The example below shows a three-question rubric that could be used by the

Table 9.1 Developmental Stage 1 Instructional Strategies for Team Handball

Instructional style	Teaching considerations	Links to TPSR
Command (direct)	• All students perform task together. • Teacher is in position to see all students. • Provides order for new tasks and high-risk activities. • Class progresses together. • Limits opportunity for student voice. • Does not accommodate student differences. • Limits opportunity for students to demonstrate self-direction. • Limits student–student interaction.	• Students can demonstrate respect (Level I) for the teacher (e.g., following directions, staying in control) and for peers (e.g., not interfering with their participation). • Students can demonstrate participation with effort (Level II) by staying engaged in Circle Drill. • Students can begin to demonstrate self-direction (Level III) by progressively challenging themselves.
Practice/Task	• Students make decisions about order of tasks to be completed, pace of activity, starting and stopping on a particular task. • Teacher provides objectives of lesson. • Teacher provides feedback to students.	• Students can demonstrate self-control and respect (Level I) for the teacher (e.g., following directions, staying in control) and for peers (e.g., not interfering with their participation). • Students can demonstrate participation with effort (Level II) by staying engaged throughout the ball passing and catching tasks. • Students can begin to demonstrate self-direction (Level III) by progressively challenging themselves throughout the activities (e.g., time themselves, count errors). • Students learn to be accountable for their own practice decisions and goal setting (Level III).

teacher or provided to the students at later developmental stages for peer assessment.

1. Catcher presents a two-hand target to the thrower. (Y/N)
2. Lateral flip pass: Thrower faces forward, passes laterally. (Y/N)
3. Overhand pass: Thrower faces and throws to target across circle. (Y/N)

Practice/Task Style

Alternatively, you can teach Circle Drill by creating tasks for each group to complete. This strategy gives the group an opportunity to self-pace practice; it also allows you to work with individual groups who need additional help or more or a challenge.

- Overhand pass across circle 50 times
- Lateral flip pass around circle 50 times
- Fifty passes, alternating wrist and overhand passes
- Timed—how fast can you complete 50 passes?
- Throw and follow variation using a combination of passes

Ask a group to demonstrate each Circle Drill station, providing critical cues and checking for understanding. Once students have seen each facet of each drill or activity, they may begin to practice in their groups. Groups could be guided through (e.g., teacher identifies the order of completion) or allowed to self-select the order they complete the stations. For example, one group may decide they need additional practice at the lateral flip and could choose to redo that station. Allow groups to repeat stations, but ask them to challenge themselves ("Can you complete the 50 passes with two, one, or no drops?"; "Can you better your time?"). Move about the gymnasium providing feedback.

Group Meeting

Group meetings in the first developmental stage are facilitated by the teacher but provide an opportunity for students to have a voice in the learning process. This gives the teacher a chance to make connections between the activities presented during the lesson and the theme; in addition, students can voice how they or their peers met the responsibility expectations of TPSR. This aspect of the lesson need not take a great deal of time, but it is essential for connecting the responsibility attributes of the activities to student learning. Although the teacher takes the primary role in facilitating the group meeting, student voices should be encouraged.

During this stage you may need to reinforce ground rules for group meeting discussions. These might include the following:

- No blaming others—accept responsibility for yourself.
- Include everyone in the discussion.
- Be respectful of yourself and others (full-value contract).
- Use each other's names.
- Do not talk over each other.
- Wait for classmates to finish their comments.

These are only a few examples; we encourage you to solicit input from your classes about other ground rules that might be included.

Use techniques that allow students to provide input quickly and safely (e.g., buzz words, show of hands). As another example, during Circle Drill (Model in Action 9.2) you might ask students to rate their performance using the thumbometer (thumbs up if they indicated they were ready to receive passes by showing the thrower a two-handed target, thumbs sideways if they got their hands up when the ball was passed, and thumbs down if they forgot to use two hands to catch the ball). On the basis of the responses you can then ask for specific examples that illustrate the students' ratings. Students can also be asked to speak to positive aspects of performance that they noticed in their peers, for example:

- "I was amazed at how Michael was able to get the ball right to my target every time—I never had to move my feet to catch the ball."
- "I appreciated how Danielle reminded me to use two hands and absorb the force of the ball."

You can then link these discussions back to the theme ("Our theme today focused on collaboration; I noticed a lot of good examples of groups working together today during the tasks") or set the stage for the reflection portion of the lesson.

Reflection

Reflection time should flow fairly seamlessly from the group meeting time. Group meeting time focuses on student evaluation of the lesson, and reflection time focuses on evaluation of their role as learners and support. Thus, questions can move from how the activities or style of teaching challenged or engaged them to a focus on how they participated as independent learners, demonstrated respect, showed self-direction, and cooperated during the lesson.

During developmental stage 1, the teacher directs the discussion and generally targets Level I and II behaviors. For the Circle Drill activity, you could ask students to

- use the thumbometer to rate their behavior across the responsibility levels (e.g., "How well did you demonstrate respect today?") or
- rate their performance with regard to effort (3, pushed myself; 2, tried hard; 1, took it easy).

Reflection can be accomplished through a variety of formats (e.g., student drawings, journal assignments, rubrics) both in or outside of class time. At the elementary level, consider partnering with the classroom teacher to create a writing assignment linked to physical education experiences in which students can reflect on their learning experiences and the TPSR levels. In doing so, you extend student learning beyond the time constraints of physical education and may facilitate the transfer of personal and social responsibility attributes beyond the gymnasium.

Developmental Stage 2

Teachers should consider transitioning learning experiences to developmental stage 2 once students are consistently demonstrating Level I and II behaviors.

Within the team handball curriculum this would mean providing opportunities for students to work collaboratively with their peers with little teacher guidance (Level III, self-direction). It is during this stage that student leaders emerge, allowing teachers to relinquish some of the control of the class to students during awareness talks and group meetings.

Relationship Time

The transition to developmental stage 2 occurs once students have consistently demonstrated an ability to perform with respect (Level I) and to participate with effort (Level II). At this point, you should begin to offer students opportunities to demonstrate self-directed learning behaviors (Level III) through planned activities and a gradual transition to student-centered teaching approaches. These opportunities for self-direction take center stage during developmental stage 2, and relationship time activities should transition from individuals performing within the context of the group to individuals positively interacting with partners and small groups in self-guided learning experiences.

The Meteor Ball activity (Model in Action 9.3) gives students an opportunity to continue to demonstrate respect (Level I) and participate with effort (Level II) while working collaboratively with their

---

MODEL IN ACTION 9.3

Meteor Ball

DESCRIPTION

The object of this game is to eliminate other players by hitting them in the foot or lower leg with the yarn ball. During round 1, players who have been hit and so are "out" move outside the playing area. Set a time limit on the round and proclaim any players still in the game as winners of round 1. In round 2, create teams using the colors of the yarn balls. During this round, players attempt to knock out other teams by hitting players in the foot or lower leg with the yarn ball. Once hit, players take a knee in the location where they were hit. A teammate still in the game can tap them on the shoulder to bring them back into play. Give teams 1 minute to strategize before starting the round. Set a time limit for the round and proclaim the team with the most players remaining the winner of round 2.

EQUIPMENT

Four cones for boundaries and one yarn ball per student.

VARIATIONS

The variations are endless with games like this. These are examples of variations:

- During round 1, have students perform a task (e.g., eight jumping jacks) to return to game play.
- During round 2, allow students who have taken a knee to get themselves back into the game by tagging an active player from another team.
- Add a partner round; partners must stay connected (holding hands) during the round.

team in round 2 (Level III). Transition from this activity to the awareness talk by drawing the students' attention to the level of effort and self-control you observed during the activity: "Whose heart is racing? I am impressed with the level of effort I noticed during this activity. It was also nice to see during round 2 how you worked with your team to get players back in the game when they were knocked out." With comments like these you can bring out an awareness of the concepts of participating with effort, self-regulating behavior, and working collaboratively with peers.

Awareness Talk

During the second developmental stage, the teacher begins to share the responsibility for the awareness talks. He identifies the theme, asks one or more students to guide the questioning, and draws the connection to the lesson focus. Commonly used themes during developmental stage 2 include self-control, self-direction, collaboration, goal setting, and problem solving. Here we use Meteor Ball to illustrate awareness talk techniques that can move students from a relationship activity to the lesson focus.

Using students to help guide the awareness talk is key in the development of youth leaders (Level IV). Following the activity you can use student leaders to debrief so as to draw the attention of the learners to the cognitive and affective attributes of an activity. These are examples of questions you might provide the student leader after the Meteor Ball activity:

- "What did you need to be successful in this activity?"
- "What did you do to help your team during round 2?"
- "What strategies were used by players who made it to the end of the round?"
- "How did you collaborate with your teammates during round 2?"

By providing the students with a selection of questions, you maintain the direction of the conversation while allowing students to comfortably explore taking leadership roles in class. Help guide the discussion by adding follow-up questions after students have responded. Use these questions to point to the theme you have selected for the lesson.

Lesson Focus

Stage 2 lessons should shift further from a teacher-centered to a student-centered teaching style. To use the team handball skill and task progressions to promote student responsibility and foster self-direction, leadership, and caring behaviors consistent with TPSR Levels III and IV, simply change the way you present the tasks and adjust the responsibility for the learning process to the level the students are prepared to take on. As the students continue to demonstrate behaviors consistent with responsibility Levels I and II, you should integrate opportunities for self-direction and leadership roles into lesson experiences. Passing and catching are foundational in a variety of sports and are essential elements of team handball. Students can perform skill practice individually (wall passing, ball drop), with partners (hand tug-of-war, partner passing), or in small groups (four-corner drill, endline handball). Consider the psychomotor development level of your students when selecting tasks to work on passing and catching. The Wall Passing activity (Model in Action 9.4) is an example of an activity that can be used with students across a variety of responsibility levels.

The Wall Passing activity gives you the flexibility to maintain control of the practice (i.e., all students show ready position, all students pass and rebound at the same time) or to release some control to the students (i.e., students self-pace practice, self- or peer assess during practice). With use of a teacher-centered (i.e., task) style, the activity primarily reinforces responsibility Levels I and II. By releasing some of the control during the skill practice you can begin to integrate Level III and IV behaviors. However, if you use a more student-centered approach (e.g., self-check), you can foster self-direction and leadership behavior. This allows you to make connections to Levels III and IV in the debrief of the activity as you reflect on concrete examples of behaviors you observed during the group trials. In doing this you can link the behavior (e.g., self-direction) to subsequent tasks and to experiences beyond the classroom, thus providing an opportunity for transferring what has been learned.

Table 9.2 presents considerations for teaching Wall Passing through two teaching styles and shows how they connect to the TPSR model.

Practice/Task Style

By presenting Wall Passing through a task style of teaching, you can maintain some structured skill practice across a variety of tasks. Create stations around the gymnasium that include each facet of Wall Passing, as well as task sheets or cards. Instruct the students through each drill, providing critical cues and checking for understanding. Once students have seen each facet of each activity, they may begin

MODEL IN ACTION 9.4

Wall Passing

DESCRIPTION

This drill can address both overhand and wrist passing technique. Students practice passing to targets on the wall (taped 1-meter-square [3-foot-square] targets or hula hoops hung at shoulder height) and catching the ball after it rebounds and bounces once. Students position themselves in front of their target at a distance of 12 to 15 feet (around 4 meters). (They should use a side-facing position from 8 to 10 feet [2.4 to 3 meters] for wrist passing.) Students should work on catching the ball with two hands, transitioning feet and body to the ready position, and passing to the target again.

EQUIPMENT

Handball and wall target for each student.

VARIATIONS

The following variations add a level of challenge to this activity:

- Have students take three steps before passing to the target.
- Have them receive a pass from a partner, make an overhand pass to the wall, get the rebound, and wrist pass to their partner.

Adapted, by permission, from R. Canton and M.P. Dwight, 1997, *Team handball: Steps to success* (Champaign, IL: Human Kinetics), 18.

Teachers using a practice/task style of teaching the Wall Passing drill will move around the gym to assess students and provide feedback.

the practice. They can move through the stations in any order and complete the specified repetitions for each activity. They can repeat stations, but ask them to challenge themselves. Move about the gymnasium providing feedback.

- **Station 1:** Overhand pass to target (distance to target: 12 feet, 15 feet, 18 feet [3.7 meters, 4.5 meters, 5.5 meters])
- **Station 2:** Wrist pass to target (distance to target: 6 feet, 8 feet, 12 feet [2 meters, 2.4 meters, 3.7 meters])
- **Station 3:** Three-step approach: overhand pass, rebound, wrist pass
- **Station 4:** Receive pass from partner, overhand pass to wall, rebound, wrist pass to partner
- **Station 5:** Partner pass, overhand
- **Station 6:** Partner pass, wrist

Self-Check Style

Alternatively, you can use the self-check style with students at this stage of development. For Wall Passing, you would create a task sheet that includes the learning cues and a description of the task. You can ask a student to demonstrate the activity and focus the other learners on their task sheets. Once students have read their task sheets, they can begin the activity at their own pace. After each pass, students recheck

Table 9.2 Developmental Stage 2 Instructional Strategies for Team Handball

Instructional style	Teaching considerations	Links to TPSR
Practice/Task	• Students make decisions about order of tasks to be completed, pace of practice, starting and stopping on a particular task. • Students work individually. • Teacher provides objectives of lesson. • Teacher provides feedback to students.	• Students can demonstrate self-control and respect (Level I) for the teacher (e.g., following directions, staying in control) and for peers (e.g., not interfering with their participation). • Students can demonstrate participation with effort (Level II) by staying engaged throughout the wall passing and catching tasks. • Students can begin to demonstrate self-direction (Level III) by progressively challenging themselves throughout the activities (e.g., progressing though variations). • Students learn to be accountable for their own practice decisions and goal setting (Level III).
Self-check	• Teacher values students' ability to self-evaluate their performance. • Teacher values students' ability to work independently of teacher and peers. • Students have demonstrated competency in the skill.	• Students can demonstrate caring (Level IV) by respecting the rights of other students. • Students can demonstrate transfer outside the gym (Level V) by gaining self-awareness about their proficiency. • Students demonstrate leadership (Level IV) by maintaining honesty about their performance.

the criteria on the task sheet to compare to their own execution. Students are responsible for their own feedback based on the criteria for the skill. The teacher's role is to ask questions about the student's process of self-checking or self-assessing.

Group Meeting

The group meeting during the second developmental stage should continue to provide students with an opportunity to have a voice in the learning process. This aspect of the lesson may warrant a greater time commitment during developmental stage 2 than during developmental stage 1, as students will take a more active role. During developmental stage 2, you shift much of the responsibility for facilitating the meeting to the students, but you should be prepared to redirect responses and initiate guided questioning. Use techniques that allow students to quickly and safely elicit peer responses (e.g., deck of questions). You can link these discussions back to the

theme ("Our theme today focused on goal setting; I heard a lot of good examples of how you set goals and evaluated or adjusted them as you practiced the Wall Passing tasks") and set the stage for reflection on how the theme can be transferred beyond the classroom experience.

Reflection

The reflection time at this stage is an opportunity for students to self-reflect on their actions and what they observed in others throughout the lesson. During developmental stage 2, the focus is typically on a self-reflection around Level III and IV behaviors. This can be accomplished through a variety of formats (e.g., student drawings, journal assignments, rubrics) in class or outside of class time. Consider using a two-part reflection in which students identify questions to reflect upon (e.g., Why is goal setting useful when practicing a new skill? What actions did I or my peers use to demonstrate self-directed learning?) during class and write the response to the questions during their next class (classroom teacher partnership) or after school (homework). This provides time for students to informally reflect on the experience before speaking for the experience. For the Wall Passing activity, consider asking students to

- draw a three-picture comic strip showing their progress in Wall Passing,
- describe how they used SMART goals in today's lesson, or
- rate their performance with regard to goal setting (3, set SMART goals; 2, set goals that were appropriate for today's lesson; 1, set unrealistic goals [too hard or too easy]).

SMART goals are specific, measurable, attainable, realistic, and timely goals that are individualized. A SMART goal

1. identifies a specific (e.g., run the 100-meter dash in 11.5 seconds) as opposed to a generic outcome (e.g., I want to run my best time);
2. is one that can be easily measured, usually quantitatively (e.g., time, distance, weight);
3. is one that is attainable while being realistic for the individual (e.g., dunking a basketball is attainable but probably not realistic for a 2nd-grade student); and
4. sets a timeline, usually under 6 months, that will serve as a motivating factor for the goal setter.

SMART goals are also revisited and adjusted often.

Developmental Stage 3

Transitioning students to developmental stage 3 within the confines of physical education settings can be difficult. At this stage students should routinely demonstrate behaviors consistent with Levels I through III and actively seek out opportunities to lead. They are increasingly given opportunities to lead their peers in skill development, awareness talks, and group meetings. These opportunities for caring and leadership take center stage during developmental stage 3.

Relationship Time

Relationship time activities during stage 3 should transition from individuals positively interacting with partners and small groups to collaborative learning experiences led by student leaders with the support of the teacher. This setting allows students to experiment with leadership opportunities within the safety of small-group and partner activities. Consider giving them greater autonomy in selecting and self-pacing relationship activities as they develop these leadership skills.

The Paper Tower activity (Model in Action 9.5) allows student groups to work independently during relationship time. Each group can select a group leader to acquire the necessary equipment. The teacher is free to move between groups and discuss strategies during game play. Consider printing words or phrases on the paper that relate to the lesson theme or the responsibility levels.

MODEL IN ACTION 9.5

Paper Tower

DESCRIPTION

Students work in groups of three or four to construct a tower with 10 pieces of paper. The goal is to create the highest tower using only the pieces of paper. Students may fold or rip the paper. Allow groups to strategize for 2 to 3 minutes and then build the tower in a 5- to 7-minute period.

EQUIPMENT

10 pieces of paper per group.

VARIATION

Allow groups to partner with other groups to construct a community tower. Provide students with different weights of paper (printer, construction, card stock).

Awareness Talk

At the third developmental stage, the teacher releases the responsibility for the awareness talks to student leaders. The student leaders identify the theme, guide the questioning, and draw the connection to the lesson focus. Commonly used themes during developmental stage 3 include self-direction, leadership, and transfer. To illustrate a developmental stage 3 awareness talk, let's consider the Paper Tower activity (Model in Action 9.5).

In speaking for the Paper Tower activity, the student leaders would generalize the lessons learned from the activity to the theme and to subsequent activities. Examples of statements and questions they might present include the following:

- "I was impressed with how Michael explained his plan to our group and then took a leadership role as we constructed the tower. How did your group decide what each person would do?"

- "In our group we used the planning time to hear everyone's idea and then voted on which one to try first. How did other groups decide what they would build?"

By speaking for the experience, the student leaders can generalize what occurred in the activity.

Student leaders can also use the debrief format discussed in chapter 4 to draw the attention of their peers to the cognitive and affective attributes of an activity. These are examples of questions they might use following the Paper Tower activity:

- "What did you need to be successful in this activity?"
- "In what ways did your group work together?"
- "Why was communication important during this activity?"
- "How can working as a team make groups more successful in activities?"

Lesson Focus

The Crossing 2v1 activity (Model in Action 9.6) demonstrates ways to promote student leadership and provide strategies for encouraging transfer to other aspects of the curriculum. This activity gives students an opportunity to demonstrate responsibility Levels I through IV. Teachers have flexibility regarding the way they present the task to the students. Altering the teaching style allows you to use this drill with students at any of the three developmental stages.

Table 9.3 presents considerations for teaching the Crossing 2v1 activity using the reciprocal teaching style, which can elicit leadership and communication skills in students.

At this developmental stage, students have demonstrated the ability to work independently while putting forth effort and showing respect to their peers. By properly selecting and sequencing activities, you can provide opportunities for the development of leadership skills. These skills can be carried over to the group meeting segment of the lesson, increasing the contribution of students to the learning process.

Student-Centered Teaching

It is often a challenge to move students to developmental stage 3 within the confines of traditional physical education and youth sport settings. Physical education especially presents a challenge because you work with populations that have diverse motivations toward course content. If you are fortunate and skilled enough to guide your group to this level, much of your time will be spent using student-centered teaching styles. In the next section we present one example of student-centered teaching that can be modified to fit other styles on the spectrum based on the content, your students' learning style, and your preferred teaching style.

Reciprocal Style

During developmental stage 3, you should use a student-centered style to present much of the instruction. For the Crossing 2v1 drill, you can use a reciprocal style to provide students with the opportunity to develop leadership skills. In this case you would use groups of four. Provide task sheets that briefly describe the drill and list cues. In addition, the sheets should list clear participant roles and expectations to help the students keep focus. For example, spell out what the observer ought to be observing (performance cues) and what the doers are doing (practicing). Provide a time or number of shots for each facet of the activity. Once they have finished, the students rotate their roles—center back becomes an observer, observer becomes the defender, and so on. This process is repeated for each drill variation.

Your role is to move about the space and assist the observers in accurately observing the doer. You must step in to provide feedback if there is a safety issue. Otherwise, encourage or suggest feedback to the observer only if feedback is not occurring.

MODEL IN ACTION 9.6

Crossing 2v1

DESCRIPTION

This drill is used to develop strategies for supporting teammates during offense. Grouping students in threes, assign one student to be the defender, one to be the center back, and one to be the left back. The activity proceeds as follows (see also the accompanying figure):

1. The ball begins with the left back, who passes to the center back (pass 1).

2. The center back makes an offensive move to the left, and the defender steps up to block the center back's progress. At the same time the center back makes his move, the left back moves toward the center, running behind the center back.

3. The center back passes to the left back (pass 2), who shoots on goal.

4. The defender cuts off the attacking center back; he should not attempt to block the shot on goal but rather force the pass to the left back, who should be allowed to take the shot.

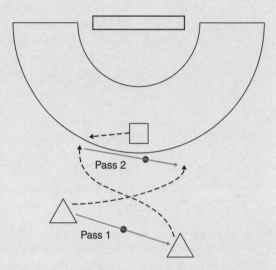

EQUIPMENT

One handball per group of three students.

VARIATIONS

- Add a goalie; offense gets 1 point for proper execution of the skill and an additional point if a goal is scored.

- Allow the center back to fake the pass to the left back and take the shot if the defender is out of position.

Adapted, by permission, from R. Canton and M.P. Dwight, 1997, *Team handball: Steps to success* (Champaign, IL: Human Kinetics), 111.

Group Meeting

The group meeting during the final developmental stage should provide students with an opportunity to lead the reflection on the learning experiences. While shifting much of the responsibility to the students during developmental stage 3, you should continue to make available techniques that promote peer-to-peer responses (e.g., deck of questions). Students will begin to use higher-level questioning that guides peers toward the integration and transfer of what they have learned in the activities to experiences beyond the classroom. For example, for the Crossing 2v1 activity (Model in Action 9.6), a student leader can begin a group reflection on the lesson activities by asking "How did the left back support the center back during this drill?" and then following up with "What are other ways we support our teammates during team handball?" You can assist by cueing the students regarding the levels they are working on, as well as reminding them of what sorts of questions have been asked in previous classes. Questions can address how the lesson was conducted, how students contributed to the group success, how observing and providing feedback influenced learning of the task, or how the style of teaching engaged the participants.

Reflection

The reflection time at this stage continues to be an opportunity for students to self-reflect on their

Table 9.3   Developmental Stage 3 Instructional Strategies for Team Handball

Instructional style	Teaching considerations	Links to TPSR
Reciprocal	• Students work in groups of four and are given specific roles (center back, left back, defender, observer). • Students have task sheets as well as a list of feedback phrases. • Groups work at own pace and rotate positions. • Teacher ensures that students are maintaining their roles and intervenes only if there is a safety issue.	• Students can demonstrate respect (Level I) for the teacher (e.g., following directions, staying in control) and for peers (e.g., not interfering with their participation). • Students can demonstrate participation with effort (Level II). • Students can begin to demonstrate self-direction (Level III) by progressively challenging themselves throughout the activities (e.g., speed, type of shot). • Students develop leadership as they maintain their role as observers and provide feedback to peers (Level IV). • Students begin to develop empathy, social manners, and trust by interacting with peers (Level IV).

actions and what they observed in others throughout the lesson. During developmental stage 3, the focus is typically on how students can transfer the responsibility attributes they are developing in physical education to life beyond the gym. This can be accomplished through a variety of formats in class or outside of class time. Students might begin to read each other's journals and provide feedback; they might assist each other in goal setting or creating strategies to transfer the levels outside of the program. Again, the teacher remains connected to the process as an active listener and support.

Keeping SITE

As discussed in chapter 1, the key to TPSR is keeping SITE of four thematic objectives (student relationships, integration, transfer, and empowerment) throughout your lessons and program. Using the content from this chapter, reflect on the following questions:

Student Relationships

1. What aspects of the variation in teaching styles assisted in enhancing student–teacher relationships? How?

2. What aspects of the variation in teaching styles assisted in enhancing student–student relationships? How?

Integration

1. What are elements within this chapter that facilitate development of personal responsibility in students? How?

2. What are elements within this chapter that facilitate development of social responsibility in students? How?

Transfer

1. What were elements within the chapter that might assist in transfer of TPSR outside of the class but within the school or program? How?

2. What were elements within the chapter that might assist in transfer of TPSR outside of the school or program? How?

Empowerment

1. What elements of your lessons support an empowering pedagogy for students?

2. What pedagogical choices can you make to promote autonomy and a sense of control in your students?

Teaching Personal and Social Responsibility Through

Golf

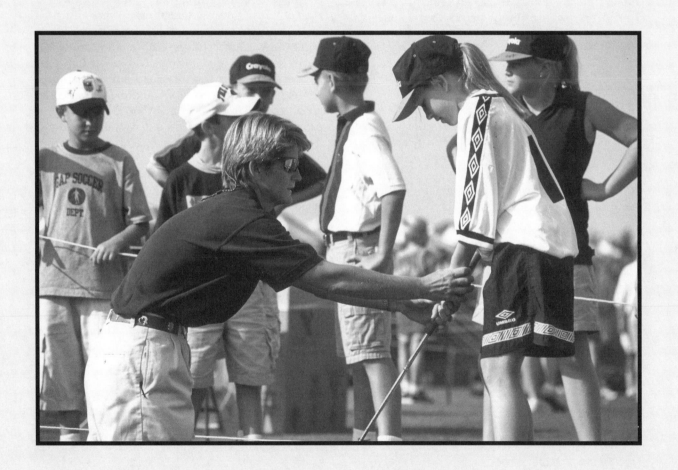

Individual and dual sports are often overlooked in physical education and after-school settings. Golf has gained popularity in recent years, and with efforts like the PGA's First Tee program, more physical education programs are using golf in their curriculum across grade levels. Golf has long been associated with self-control, responsibility, and fair play and thus offers a natural link to the TPSR model. *Golf: Steps to Success* served as the primary source for the content of this chapter (Schempp & Mattsson 2005). If you work with elementary-aged students, we encourage you to explore The First Tee program for ideas on bringing golf into your physical education curriculum (www.thefirsttee.org). This program promotes "Nine Core Values" that are easy to align with the TPSR model: honesty, integrity, sportsmanship, respect, confidence, responsibility, perseverance, courtesy, and judgment.

Developmental Stage 1

In the first developmental stage, students are often working on exhibiting Level I (respecting self and others) and II (participating with effort) behaviors consistently. Any time we place implements (golf clubs, tennis rackets, lacrosse sticks) in the hands of students, these behaviors are essential for maintaining a safe learning environment. During this stage the teacher takes the predominant role in leading the awareness talk, choosing developmentally appropriate tasks and challenges, structuring the group meeting, and providing reflection opportunities. As students gain an understanding of their roles in the lesson, you can give them opportunities to begin to transition to developmental stage 2 (Level III, self-direction). You can modify the examples in this section to meet the needs of students at any developmental stage by altering the way you present them.

Relationship Time

With developmental stage 1 learners, activities should focus on individual traits (communication, cooperation, self-control, respect, and effort) within the context of group interactions. In providing this focus, you give students an opportunity to explore social interactions and develop relationships. Icebreaker activities used during relationship time serve to engage students and offer teachable moments in subsequent awareness talks. You can use a variety of activities during relationship time as long as they provide an opportunity for student–student and student–teacher interactions that foster communication and acceptance.

The Fitness Stations activity (Model in Action 10.1) is appropriate for students in any developmental stage. By structuring relationship time activities to

---

MODEL IN ACTION 10.1

Fitness Stations

DESCRIPTION

Many teachers use a set warm-up throughout the year to establish a protocol for starting the lesson. You can select fitness activities that encourage student–student interaction and teacher engagement. Create a series of 8 to 10 fitness-related stations around the space to encourage student interaction. For example, one station could ask students to perform high-five push-ups (students move around the area in the push-up position giving high-fives to other students), one can ask students to perform sit-and-throw sit-ups (the student with the ball performs a sit-up and throws the ball to her partner, who catches the ball and performs a sit-up), and a third station could ask students to conduct a three-question interview while in a wall-sit position. Have students record their results in a fitness journal or on a class score sheet.

EQUIPMENT

Various pieces of fitness-related equipment (jump ropes, stopwatches, exercise mats).

VARIATIONS

- Allow students to change partners at each station.
- Have students self-select stations.
- Incorporate heart rate monitoring.
- Incorporate music.

provide students with the opportunity to demonstrate respect for others (Level I) and self-control (Level II), as well as to begin to work toward self-direction (Level III), you set the stage for the lesson. During this initial developmental stage, you may want to control the order of the stations and the time spent at each station and also preselect partners. The activity is simple and is easy to modify to reinforce what is being taught in the unit of instruction.

Awareness Talk

As part of the introduction to the responsibility model, or for classes that struggle to demonstrate behaviors consistent with responsibility Levels I and II, you should lead the awareness talks. In doing so you will model appropriate questioning, reinforce awareness talk protocols, and guide the students' responses. During the awareness talk you identify the theme, guide the questioning, and make the connection to the lesson focus. Commonly used themes during this stage include respect, self-control, participation, effort, and effective communication. With the Fitness Stations activity, you can highlight attributes that will serve as a link from a relationship activity to the lesson focus. These are examples of questions you might ask at this stage:

- "What were some ways you demonstrated respect during the activity?"
- "How did you respond when you were asked to do an exercise with another student?"

On the basis of responses from the students, you can guide them to extend their thinking by asking questions such as these:

- "What can we do to demonstrate respect when a classmate asks to participate in activities with us?"
- "Today we are continuing our golf unit. What are some things you can do within this unit to demonstrate respect and effort?"
- "Can you think of ways you can demonstrate respect during the rest of the lesson?"

Lesson Focus

To illustrate how subtle changes in the way we teach can influence student responses, we will use the Putting Ladder Drill (Model in Action 10.2) throughout this chapter. In doing so, we hope to illustrate that the student responsibility characteristics do not influence the content we teach but rather the pedagogical strategies we use to teach the content. At the initial developmental stage, students have not consistently

demonstrated the ability to show respect and participate with effort. As a result, much of the control of the lesson remains in the hands of the teacher. As students progress through the developmental stage, they should have increased opportunities to work in self-directed learning experiences.

Table 10.1 presents considerations for teaching the Putting Ladder Drill using the command (direct) teaching style and shows how it connects to the TPSR model.

Teacher-Centered Teaching

As you begin to implement the TPSR model into your curriculum, there may be a need to maintain more control over the learning environment. This allows you to teach what is expected during the lesson, have students model appropriate behavior, and reinforce that behavior prior to asking them to do this independently. The following is an example of how we can utilize a teacher-centered style of teaching (command) to structure a lesson to guide students that are new to the TPSR model.

Moving from practice to game play.

© sonya etchison/fotolia.com

MODEL IN ACTION 10.2

Putting Ladder Drill

DESCRIPTION

Putting is an essential skill in golf and can easily be integrated into a variety of physical education settings (indoors, outdoors, hallways). This drill works on students' control in putting a golf ball. Place five markers (golf clubs, cones, poly spots) in a ladder formation in front of the putter. The first marker should be 10 feet [3 meters] from the putter, and subsequent markers should be placed at 3-foot intervals (10 feet, 13 feet [4 meters], 16 feet [5 meters], 19 feet [about 6 meters], and 22 feet [about 7 meters]). See the accompanying figure. Students practice putting the golf ball to a zone created by the markers: zone A, between the 10- and 13-foot markers; zone B, between 13 and 16 feet; zone C, between 16 and 19 feet; and zone D, between 19 and 22 feet. The focus should be on distance control and not a specific target. Additionally, you want the student to "swing as a unit" when putting: Shoulders, arms, wrists, and club all move in unison during the putting motion.

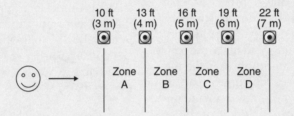

EQUIPMENT

One putter, five markers, and 10 golf balls for each student (students can share equipment if equipment or space is limited).

VARIATIONS

- Decrease the zone distance (to 2 feet [.6 meters]).
- Add an incline or decline.
- Set a target in each zone.

Adapted, by permission, from P.G. Schempp and P. Mattsson, 2005, *Golf: Steps to success* (Champaign, IL: Human Kinetics), 10.

Command (Direct) Style

By presenting the Putting Ladder Drill using a command style, you can direct the students through the progression of tasks. This will encourage them to perform the task in the same way at the same time and allow you to check student performance. Create several ladders and position the students at them. Provide a demonstration of the drill and identify cues:

1. Ready position
2. Practice your stroke
3. Club face square to putting line
4. Swing as unit
5. Club face square after the hit
6. Follow-through equals backswing

Identify the target zone before each putt. Throughout the activity you move about the space providing feedback. Give each student 10 golf balls and have all students retrieve their balls after the 10th hit.

By using the command style of teaching, you maintain control over the class. This becomes particularly important if students are struggling to maintain control or respect or to put forth effort during class. Responsibility lessons can be gleaned from these learning experiences if you take time to pinpoint actions and behaviors observed throughout the lesson.

Group Meeting

During the group meeting, you "connect the dots" with the students between attitudes and behaviors observed during the lesson and the responsibility

Table 10.1 Developmental Stage 1 Instructional Strategies for Golf

Instructional style	Teaching considerations	Links to TPSR
Command (direct)	• Students perform task together on teacher's cues. • Students progress through activity together. • Teacher is in position to see all students. • Teacher controls pacing of all facets of the activity.	• Students can demonstrate self-control and respect (Level I) for the teacher (e.g., following directions, staying in control) and for peers (e.g., not interfering with their practice). • Students can demonstrate participation with effort (Level II) by staying engaged throughout the Putting Ladder Drill activity. • Students can begin to demonstrate self-direction (Level III) by progressively challenging themselves throughout the activity (e.g., hitting to specific zones).

model. The teacher facilitates much of the group meeting during the first developmental stage, but there should be opportunities for students to have a voice in this review of the learning experiences. This is the time for students to give input on how the lesson went, how their peers did, and even how the teacher did—all in relation to the lesson theme and responsibility level expectations. Questions about how the activities challenged the students and questions regarding how they felt participating in the lesson when the teacher used a given teaching style are good beginning points. Students at developmental stage 1 may benefit from discussion techniques (detailed in the introduction to part II) that allow them to provide input quickly and safely (e.g., buzz words, show of hands, thumbometer).

Reflection

Reflection time provides an opportunity for each student to reflect on his role in the learning process. Thus, questions can move from how the activities or style of teaching challenged or engaged students to a focus on how they participated as independent learners, demonstrated respect, showed self-direction, and cooperated during the lesson. During developmental stage 1, the teacher guides this discussion. You might ask questions like "During the Putting Ladder Drill today, did you demonstrate respect while your peers were putting?" and "How did you show effort while doing the putting trials?" Students can respond to the questions verbally in small groups or with a partner.

Developmental Stage 2

As students consistently demonstrate Level I and II behaviors, you should transition to developmental

stage 2. Students should have opportunities to work collaboratively with their peers with little teacher guidance (Level III, self-direction). At this stage you begin to call upon students to take a greater role in the learning process. Throughout this stage, you begin to relinquish some of the control of the class to students during awareness talks and group meetings. As this occurs, students may begin to demonstrate a desire to take leadership roles (Level IV); however, many will continue to need some guidance in keeping self-directed without individual supervision.

Relationship Time

Relationship time with students at the second developmental level should provide opportunities for students to explore working in self-directed activities and taking on leadership roles in the classroom. Activities like the Big Ten Warm-Up (Model in Action 10.3) can allow them to lead short bouts of exercise while adhering to the guiding philosophy of relationship time—that is, provision of opportunities for students to positively interact with one another and the teacher.

Awareness Talk

Give students the opportunity to lead awareness talks when they consistently demonstrate respect and participate with effort during class. With younger students and those new to speaking in front of their peers, create a list of questions that connect the relationship time activities to the rest of the lesson. You will need to stay engaged in the discussion to help redirect student responses and reinforce awareness talk protocols. As students gain experience with the format, they will begin generating their own questions and following up on peer responses. This will

Big Ten Warm-Up

DESCRIPTION

Students take turns identifying and leading a warm-up activity for a count of 10 (10 seconds or 10 repetitions). All students perform the activity with the peer leader. You can post a list of activities related to the unit of instruction or fitness concept or allow students to self-select activities based on a common theme (e.g., cardio, stretches).

EQUIPMENT

Make equipment available based on the theme or posted activity list.

VARIATIONS

- Allow students to opt out of leading.
- Create groups of 8 to 10 students.

not happen overnight, but we have seen third- and fourth-grade students effectively lead awareness talks in physical education and recreation settings.

The Big Ten Warm-Up provides an opportunity to discuss respect, participating with effort, and self-directed learning concepts. One technique is to create a list of questions for a student leader that relate to how respect, effort, and self-directed learning concepts were integrated in the lesson, such as these:

- "What are ways the Big Ten Warm-Up touches on responsibility levels?"
- "How did you demonstrate respect during the activities?"

By providing students with a selection of questions, you maintain the direction of the conversation while giving them a chance to comfortably explore taking leadership roles in class.

Lesson Focus

Creating opportunities for students to work independently and demonstrate self-direction should be the focus during the second developmental stage. We can achieve this focus by modifying the way we set up learning experiences, shifting toward a student-centered approach. To illustrate, we look again at the Putting Ladder Drill activity (Model in Action 10.2) from two teaching perspectives. Both teaching approaches begin to shift the responsibility for learning to the students by providing opportunities for self-direction and collaboration with peers. This example illustrates that adding a responsibility-based focus to physical education curricula does not influ-

ence the content we teach but rather the pedagogical strategies we use to teach the content.

Table 10.2 presents considerations for teaching the Putting Ladder Drill activity through the practice/task and inclusion styles and shows how they connect to the TPSR model.

By presenting the drills through these teaching styles, you give students a chance to demonstrate behaviors consistent with responsibility Levels III and IV. These styles are flexible enough that you can either maintain the control or release a significant amount of the control for the lesson. If the students' responsibility level is such that they can handle self-directed activities, allow them to make more of the decisions (e.g., choosing which station to work at, how long they spend at each station, which peer they practice with, and the level of challenge). If students are relatively new to the skill and are still developing the ability to work independently, you can limit the number of decisions they make.

Practice/Task Style

A practice/task-style lesson routinely uses stations for practice of skills and tasks. As such the ladder drill could be one of the putting stations used during a lesson. Stations could change the distance between zones, have students putt up an incline or down a decline to zones, or use specific targets in each zone.

The teacher instructs the students through each drill, providing critical cues and checking for understanding. Once students have seen each facet of each ladder drill station, they may begin the practice. Students can move through the stations in any order and are instructed to complete the specified number of

Table 10.2 Developmental Stage 2 Instructional Strategies for Golf

Instructional style	Teaching considerations	Links to TPSR
Practice/Task	• Students make decisions about order of tasks to be completed, pace of practice, starting and stopping on a particular task. • Teacher provides objectives of lesson. • Teacher provides feedback to students.	• Students can demonstrate self-control and respect (Level I) for the teacher (e.g., following directions, staying in control) and for peers (e.g., not interfering with their participation). • Students can demonstrate participation with effort (Level II) by staying engaged throughout Putting Ladder Drill. • Students can begin to demonstrate self-direction (Level III) by progressively challenging themselves throughout the activities (e.g., distance between the ladders' rungs, specific targets within hitting zones). • Students learn to be accountable for their own practice decisions and goal setting (Level III).
Inclusion	• Students make individual choices to accommodate their ability (distance between ladder rungs, terrain—flat surface, uphill, downhill). • Students are reassessing abilities and making allowances as lesson progresses (e.g., change size of ladder zones, hit on different terrains). • Students' assessment allows them to rechallenge themselves or set goals (e.g., number of consecutive hits in the right zone). • Teacher decides on skill to be practiced and provides possible levels in the task.	• Students can demonstrate respect (Level I) for self and peers. • Students practice honesty in selecting appropriate level of entry (Level I). • Students demonstrate effort and participation (Level II) as they reassess and rechallenge themselves. • Students set goals and demonstrate self-evaluation as they reassess throughout the lesson (Level III). • Students learn to deal with agreement or discrepancy between their aspirations and actual performance (Levels II and III).

repetitions for each. Students can repeat stations, but ask them to challenge themselves (for example, "Can you putt four out of five balls to the correct ladder zone?"). The teacher moves about the gymnasium providing feedback.

Inclusion Style

Alternatively, the inclusion style can be used to provide opportunities for students to demonstrate self-direction. The teacher initially demonstrates the skill correctly while identifying the cues learners need to focus on while performing the Putting Ladder Drill activity and identifies the options available for students in deciding how and where they enter. Chal-

lenges might include varying the distance between markers and using different types of terrain if the activity is being conducted outside. The teacher hands out task sheets that provide a diagram of the activity as well as performance cues.

Students are then dispersed throughout the teaching area. The learners are allowed time to assess their level though trial and error and begin the drill. Each time, the learner reassesses and sets new challenges based on the levels available and the achievement of performance criteria.

The teacher's role is to circulate throughout the learning space and provide feedback only on the decisions of the students. You can ask, "How are you

A teacher provides individualized feedback during the practice session.

doing at the level you have selected?" The students' responses will help you inquire about the decisions made and how successful the students feel they are. With this style it is important not to start out by overtly challenging decisions made by students but to assist them in accomplishing the level of challenge they selected.

Group Meeting

Providing time for students to reflect on what they have learned and how their actions affect the learning environment is central to the TPSR model. During the second developmental stage, the group meetings continue to offer students the opportunity to voice their reflections while introducing them to leadership experiences. You can use a variety of techniques to elicit student responses and encourage student-guided group meetings.

A strategy that we like to use to debrief a learning experience is post-a-question. This method of debrief allows students to work as partners to discuss and reflect on the lesson and develop a question for the group meeting. Once the partners have developed their question, they post it on the wall or on the floor near the group meeting leader. The leader then debriefs the whole class based on the questions. For students who are new to having a voice in the lesson, this method offers an opportunity to share their thoughts without having to speak in front of the entire class. For students with experience sharing their thoughts with others, it allows them to communicate with their partner and open their discussion to the entire class. Consider asking one or two students to share with the class their response to each discussion question. At first, you may need to develop and post a list of generic questions for students to use. Once they become familiar with this method, they can be asked to quickly generate a question (90 seconds) and move to the group discussion phase.

Reflection

You can extend the group meeting by asking students to write a response to their partner's question in a journal entry. Their response should begin to reflect how they can take lessons learned in class and transfer them to other areas. As with the group meeting, a number of techniques can be used to promote reflection. We encourage you to note the many examples in *Teaching Personal and Social Responsibility Through Physical Activity, Third Edition,* of different ways to engage students in reflection time. The key in this stage is for students to begin to reflect on how they can transfer what they have learned in the physical education setting to life beyond the gym walls. Students can be cued on questions that address the particular levels they are working on for this stage (Level III) and begin to scaffold to goals for the next levels (IV and V).

Developmental Stage 3

Moving a class of students to the third developmental stage can be difficult given the realities that physical educators face in most schools, including large class sizes, heterogeneous groups of students (skills, motivation, and so on), and limited contact days. However, individual students within each class often rise to your expectations when afforded the opportunity. At this stage students should routinely demonstrate behaviors consistent with Levels I through III and should actively seek out leadership opportunities. These opportunities for caring and leadership take center stage during developmental stage 3. Caring and leadership qualities can manifest themselves during all aspects of the lesson as students explore ways to engage in the learning process.

Relationship Time

Relationship time during the third developmental stage should be run almost entirely by students. Student leaders can be responsible for setup, instruction, and facilitation of the relationship time tasks. For example, many teachers use a warm-up routine that is performed throughout the year. Consider allowing students to lead, or even better create, relationship time activities. Seek volunteers to set up the activities, a volunteer to review instructions and expectations, and a leader to facilitate transitions. You can be an active participant in these activities or work individually with students. You can also use this time to identify an awareness talk leader and discuss the lesson theme.

Awareness Talk

Student leaders should be comfortable with identifying the theme, guiding the questioning, and drawing connections to the lesson by the time they reach the third developmental stage. Commonly used themes during developmental stage 3 include self-direction, leadership, and transfer. In speaking for the relationship time activities, the student leaders would generalize the lessons learned from the activities to the theme and to subsequent activities. These are examples of statements they might use:

- "I liked that everyone quickly moved to a station and began performing the task. How did you decide on which activity you would start with?"
- "Did your partner provide you with feedback on your performance during the task?"

- "Today we will be working in partner groups and independently as we continue to work on putting in golf. Analyzing performance and providing meaningful feedback are essential parts of today's lesson."

In speaking for the experience, the student leaders can generalize what occurred in the activity. The teacher's nonverbal behavior can really be important here. Remain involved by demonstrating active listening, nodding your head, and making eye contact with whoever is speaking. This models to students behaviors that they too can maintain in the process.

Lesson Focus

Developmental stage 3 activities should give students an opportunity for leadership experiences and provide strategies for encouraging transfer to other aspects of the curriculum. The Putting Ladder Drill (Model in Action 10.2) allows students to exhibit behaviors consistent with responsibility Levels I through IV. Teaching strategies for developmental stage 3 include providing students with opportunities to emphasize previous levels but, more importantly, focus on Levels IV (caring and leadership) and V (outside the gymnasium). We can elicit these behaviors by modifying the way we present the task.

Table 10.3 presents considerations for teaching the Putting Ladder Drill activity through the reciprocal and self-check styles. These provide students with an opportunity to evaluate performance (of their partner or themselves) and thus opportunities to demonstrate developmental stage 3 behaviors.

In the Putting Ladder Drill activity, students can demonstrate responsibility Levels I through IV. Using a reciprocal approach provides opportunities for students to collaboratively develop putting accuracy. The use of a self-check style allows them to self-assess in the context of group play. At this developmental stage, students have demonstrated the ability to work independently while putting forth effort and showing respect to their peers. These skills can be carried over to the group meeting segment of the lesson, increasing the contribution of students in the learning process.

We used the Putting Ladder Drill throughout this chapter to illustrate that integrating TPSR into physical education does affect what is taught. However, by modifying the way in which information is presented and reflected upon, we can greatly influence student learning across all three learning domains. Meeting the developmental needs of the students with regard to responsibility is as important as meeting skill-related developmental needs. Teaching with personal

Table 10.3 Developmental Stage 3 Instructional Strategies for Golf

Instructional style	Teaching considerations	Links to TPSR
Reciprocal	• Students work in groups of three and have specific roles (putter, scorer, observer). • Students have task sheets and lists of feedback phrases. • Groups work at own pace and rotate positions. • Teacher ensures that students are maintaining their roles and intervenes only if there is a safety issue.	• Students can demonstrate respect (Level I) for the teacher (e.g., following directions, staying in control) and for peers (e.g., not interfering with their participation). • Students can demonstrate participation with effort (Level II). • Students can begin to demonstrate self-direction (Level III) by progressively challenging themselves throughout the activities (e.g., specific targets in a ladder zone). • Students develop leadership as they maintain their role as observers and provide feedback to peers (Level IV). • Students begin to develop empathy, social manners, and trust by interacting with peers (Level IV).
Self-check	• Teacher values students' ability to self-evaluate their performance. • Teacher values students' ability to work independently of teacher and peers. • Students have demonstrated competency in the skill.	• Students can demonstrate caring (Level IV) by respecting the rights of other students. • Students can demonstrate transfer outside the gym (Level V) by gaining self-awareness about their proficiency. • Students demonstrate leadership (Level IV) by maintaining honesty about their performance.

and social responsibility as a foundation therefore can be integrated into any subject matter with any age group you work with.

Reciprocal Style

To present this drill through the reciprocal style, you would create groups of three. Hand out task sheets that briefly describe the drill and list the performance cues. The sheets should also clearly define the participant roles and expectations to help students keep focus. For example, spell out what the observer ought to be observing (performance cues) and what the doers are doing (putting). Specify a time or a number of putts for each round of the activity. Once they have finished a round, the students rotate their roles: The putter becomes the observer, the observer becomes the scorer, and the scorer becomes the putter. The process is repeated for each drill variation.

The teacher's role is to move about the space and assist the observers in accurately observing the doer.

You must step in to provide feedback only if there is a safety issue. Otherwise, encourage or suggest feedback to the observer only if feedback is not occurring.

Self-Check Style

For a self-check lesson, you would hand out task sheets that briefly describe the drill and list the performance cues. Students work independently to complete the task by performing the drill, scoring their results, and reflecting on their performance. You can ask a student to demonstrate the activity and focus students on their task sheet. Once students have read their task sheets, they can begin the activity at their own pace.

After each round (10 putts), students recheck the criteria listed on the task sheet relative to their execution of putting. Students are responsible for their own feedback based on the criteria for the skill. The teacher's role is to ask questions related to the student's process of self-checking or self-assessing.

Group Meeting

This portion of the lesson, as with the awareness talk, is mostly student led during the third developmental stage. Student leaders can facilitate discussions based on the levels the students are working on, how the lesson was conducted, how the activity met the students' needs or provided challenge, and how the style of teaching engaged them. For example, during the Putting Ladder Drill activity, a student leader can initiate a group reflection on the lesson activities by asking questions like these:

- "What feedback did you provide your partner with during this drill?"
- "What type of feedback did you find most helpful?"
- "How did your putting strategies change based on the feedback you received?"

The teacher can assist by cueing the students regarding the levels they are working on, as well as remind them of what sorts of questions have been asked in previous classes.

Reflection

As students demonstrate developmental stage 3 behaviors, we should have an expectation that they will be able to use higher-order questions during their reflections. This is dependent, in part, on the age of the students. We have worked with fourth-grade students who could demonstrate behaviors consistent with developmental stage 3 but cognitively struggled with abstract questions or attempts to transfer concepts beyond concrete experiences in the lesson. Reflections should continue to serve as an opportunity for students to self-reflect on their actions and what they observed in others throughout the lesson while exploring ways they can transfer the responsibility attributes they are developing in physical education to life beyond the gym. Again, the teacher remains connected to the process as an active listener and support.

Keeping SITE

As discussed in chapter 1, the key to TPSR is keeping SITE of four thematic objectives (student relationships, integration, transfer, and empowerment) throughout your lessons and program. Using the content from this chapter, reflect on the following questions:

Student Relationships

1. What aspects of the variation in teaching styles assisted in enhancing student–teacher relationships? How?
2. What aspects of the variation in teaching styles assisted in enhancing student–student relationships? How?

Integration

1. What are elements within this chapter that facilitate development of personal responsibility in students? How?
2. What are elements within this chapter that facilitate development of social responsibility in students? How?

Transfer

1. What were elements within the chapter that might assist in transfer of TPSR outside of the class but within the school or program? How?
2. What were elements within the chapter that might assist in transfer of TPSR outside of the school or program? How?

Empowerment

1. What elements of your lessons support an empowering pedagogy for students?
2. What pedagogical choices can you make to promote autonomy and a sense of control in your students?

Teaching Personal and Social Responsibility Through

Tennis

Like golf, tennis has gained in popularity in recent years. In 2006 the United States Tennis Association (USTA) introduced the Quick Start tennis program, designed to provide modified equipment and rules to make tennis developmentally appropriate for all ages. The USTA has also provided training and equipment to physical education teachers across the country. This has brought about renewed interest in racket sports for students from early elementary through high school.

Racket sports provide a natural link to the TPSR philosophy because students use equipment that has the potential to cause harm to others. Self-control is vital for student safety, but teachers can also easily use racket sports to give students opportunities to develop beyond Level I. Racket sports provide opportunities for students to learn through the practice/task, reciprocal, self-check, and inclusion teaching styles. Throughout this chapter we introduce strategies for integrating the responsibility model into instruction through tennis. *Tennis: Steps to Success, Third Edition*, by Jim Brown (2004) served as the primary source of content for the chapter. These strategies could easily be applied to other racket or paddle sports (badminton, Speedminton, pickleball).

Developmental Stage 1

In the first developmental stage, students are often working on consistently exhibiting Level I (respect-ing self and others) and Level II (participating with effort) behaviors. During this stage the teacher takes the predominant role in leading the awareness talk, choosing developmentally appropriate tasks and challenges, structuring the group meeting, and providing reflection opportunities. As students gain an understanding of their roles in the lesson, you can give them opportunities to begin to transition to developmental stage 2 (Level III, self-direction). You can modify the examples in this section to meet the needs of students at any developmental stage by altering how you present them.

Relationship Time

When working with developmental stage 1 learners, consider selecting activities that focus on individual traits (communication, cooperation, self-control, respect, and effort) within the context of group interactions. In so doing you will provide opportunities for students to explore social interactions and develop relationships. We continue to present icebreaker activities during relationship time as we believe that these activities engage students and offer teachable moments during subsequent awareness talks. You can use a variety of activities during relationship time as long as they provide opportunities for student–student and student–teacher interactions that foster acceptance and communication.

The Exersign activity (Model in Action 11.1) gives students the opportunity to demonstrate respect for

MODEL IN ACTION 11.1

Exersign

DESCRIPTION

We use this activity with a variety of content. In Exersign, the teacher prepares a handout that lists exercises and repetitions (10 push-ups, 12 jumping jacks, and so on) with space next to each for a signature. Students are given 5 to 7 minutes to find a peer and complete an exercise with that person. When they both complete the exercise, each student signs the other's sheet and seeks another exercise buddy. Depending on the size of the group, limit the number of times students can do an activity with the same partner (the goal of relationship time activities is interaction, so people shouldn't be partnering with the same buddy for all tasks). Students move from person to person to find their next partner and can complete the exercises in any order. Include enough activities that most students will not complete the list in the allotted time.

EQUIPMENT

Sheets listing exercises and repetitions, pens or pencils.

VARIATIONS

- Include music.
- Include blank spots on the list for students to fill in self-selected exercises.
- Add tasks that review skills learned in previous lessons (e.g., in the tennis unit, hitting 20 self-rallies).

others (Level I) and self-control (Level II) and to begin to work toward self-direction (Level III). The activity is simple and is easy to modify to reinforce what is being taught in the unit of instruction.

Awareness Talk

At the initial developmental stage, the awareness talk is primarily facilitated by the teacher. The teacher identifies the theme, guides the questioning, and makes the connection to the lesson focus. Commonly used themes during developmental stage 1 include respect, self-control, participation, effort, and effective communication. Using Exersign, you can highlight attributes during the awareness talk that will serve as a link from a relationship activity to the lesson focus. For example, at this stage you might ask the following questions:

- "What were some ways you demonstrated respect during the activity?"
- "How did you respond when you were asked to do an exercise with another student?"

On the basis of the students' responses, you can guide them to extend their thinking by asking questions like these:

- "What can we do to demonstrate respect when a classmate asks to participate in activities with us?"
- "Today we are continuing our tennis unit. What are some things you can do within this unit to demonstrate respect and effort?"

- "What are some ways you can demonstrate respect as we head into the rest of the lesson?"

Lesson Focus

Themes identified during the awareness talk set the stage for teachable moments throughout the lesson focus. By selecting pedagogical strategies that provide opportunities for students to make a cognitive or affective connection between the lesson activities and the responsibility themes, you create an environment that supports TPSR-based learning. During developmental stage 1, it is often beneficial to maintain a somewhat teacher-centered approach (command/direct style), but you must also provide students with opportunities to work toward developmental stage 2 attributes (self-directed learning, caring). The teaching style you choose will be influenced by your teaching philosophy, the learning styles of your students, and the context in which the lesson is presented. Here we provide an example of a lesson focus using forehand swing activities and two different styles of teaching.

Table 11.1 presents considerations for teaching the Drop and Hit Forehand activity (Model in Action 11.2) through two different teaching styles: the command (direct) style, which is more teacher centered, and the practice/task style, which provides opportunities for student-directed learning experiences.

Command (Direct) Style

Presenting Drop and Hit Forehand through a command style allows you to direct the students through

---

MODEL IN ACTION 11.2

Drop and Hit Forehand

DESCRIPTION

There are a variety of strategies for practicing the forehand swing in tennis. This drill works on hitting a forehand from a self-dropped ball. Standing on the baseline, the student drops a tennis ball (slightly in front and to the forehand side) and attempts to hit it using a forehand swing. The objective is to have the ball land in the opposite singles court. Students should be adequately spaced to provide a safe swinging radius.

EQUIPMENT

One tennis racket and 10 balls for each student (students can share equipment if equipment or space is limited).

VARIATION

Students can hit the ball against a flat wall that has a painted (or taped) line indicating where the net would be. As skill level increases, have students hit the rebounded ball back to the wall for consecutive forehands.

Adapted, by permission, from J. Brown, 2004, *Tennis: Steps to success*, 3rd ed. (Champaign, IL: Human Kinetics), 16.

Table 11.1   Developmental Stage 1 Instructional Strategies for Tennis

Instructional style	Teaching considerations	Links to TPSR
Command (direct)	• Students perform task together on teacher's cue. • Students progress through activity together. • Teacher is in position to see all students. • Teacher controls pacing of all facets of the activity.	• Students can demonstrate self-control and respect (Level I) for the teacher (e.g., following directions, staying in control) and for peers (e.g., not interfering with their participation). • Students can demonstrate participation with effort (Level II) by staying engaged throughout the Drop and Hit Forehand activity. • Students can begin to demonstrate self-direction (Level III) by progressively challenging themselves throughout the activity (e.g., hitting to specific zones in the opposite court).
Practice/Task	• Students make decisions about order of tasks to be completed, pace of practice, starting and stopping on a particular task. • Students work individually. • Teacher provides objectives of lesson. • Teacher provides feedback to students.	• Students can demonstrate self-control and respect (Level I) for the teacher (e.g., following directions, staying in control) and for peers (e.g., not interfering with their play). • Students can demonstrate participation with effort (Level II) by staying engaged throughout the activity. • Students can begin to demonstrate self-direction (Level III) by progressively challenging themselves throughout the activities (e.g., count errors made, hit to a specific zone). • Students learn to be accountable for their own practice decisions and goal setting (Level III).

the progression of tasks. This encourages students to perform the task in the same way at the same time and allows you to check student performance. Provide a demonstration of the drill and identify cues:

1. Stand in ready position before the ball drops; face target in an athletic stance.
2. Stand in "square" stance as racket is drawn back; leg on hitting side steps back; body is perpendicular to target.
3. The racket moves back and up in a smooth backswing.
4. "Load" the forward swing by shifting weight to the front foot.
5. Hit through ball by hitting early and maintaining forward path of racket.
6. Follow through and return to ready position.

The teacher starts and stops the students for each swing (ready position, drop, hit, recover). Throughout the activity the teacher moves about the space providing feedback. Students each have 10 tennis balls and retrieve their balls after the 10th hit.

Practice/Task Style

Create stations around the gymnasium that present aspects of the activity. Each station includes a task sheet or card. Instruct the students through each drill, providing critical cues and checking for understanding. Once students have seen each facet of each drill, they may begin the practice. They can move through the stations in any order and complete the number of repetitions specified on the task sheet. Students can repeat stations, but ask them to challenge themselves. These are examples of possible stations:

"Load" the forward swing.
© Galina Barskaya/fotolia.com

- Drop and catch (forehand swing without a racket, student catches the ball)
- Drop and hit with hand
- Drop and hit to wall target
- Drop and hit forehand over net
- Drop and hit forehand to targets

The teacher moves about the gymnasium providing feedback.

Group Meeting

The teacher facilitates much of the group meeting during the first developmental stage, but there should be opportunities for students to have a voice in this review of the learning experiences. This is the time for students to give input on how the lesson went, how their peers did, and even how the teacher did, all in relation to the lesson theme and responsibility level expectations. Questions about how the activities challenged the students and questions regarding how they felt participating when the teacher used a given teaching style are good beginning points. Students at developmental stage 1 may benefit from discussion techniques that allow them to provide input quickly and safely (e.g., buzz words, show of hands, thumbometer). For example, after Drop and Hit Forehand, you might ask students to rate their performance using the thumbometer (thumbs up if

they were successful at hitting the ball into the opposite court most of the time, thumbs sideways if they got the ball over some of the time, and thumbs down if they didn't get very many over). On the basis of the responses, you can ask for examples of elements that contributed to their ratings (e.g., using proper form). You can then link these discussions back to the theme ("Our theme today focused on control; what role does control play in being successful at hitting a forehand shot in tennis?").

Reflection

While the group meeting focuses on students' evaluation of the lesson, reflection time focuses on evaluation of their role as learners and supporters of learning in the class context. Thus, questions can move from how the activities or style of teaching challenged or engaged them to a focus on how they participated as independent learners, demonstrated respect, showed self-direction, and cooperated during the lesson. During developmental stage 1, the teacher guides this discussion. These are examples of questions you might ask:

- "During the Drop and Hit Forehand activity today, did you demonstrate Level I characteristics?"
- "How did you show effort while doing the forehand swing stations?"

Students can respond to the questions verbally in small groups or with a partner.

Developmental Stage 2

Students demonstrate that they are ready to transition to the second developmental stage when they consistently exhibit responsibility Level I and II behaviors. This transition is characterized by greater opportunities for students to work collaboratively with their peers with little teacher guidance (Level III, self-direction). During the second stage the teacher begins to call upon students to take a role in the learning process. Initially this will occur during the awareness talk and group meeting aspects of the lesson; later it will likely be a part of all aspects of the lesson. As with motor skill development, progression through the responsibility levels differs from one person to another; while some students at developmental stage 2 may begin to demonstrate a desire to take leadership roles (Level IV), most will continue to need some guidance in keeping self-directed without individual supervision.

Relationship Time

The Math 1-2-3 activity (Model in Action 11.3) is a way to integrate math concepts with physical activity and provides students with the opportunity to continue to demonstrate respect (Level I) and participate with effort (Level II) while working on communication and negotiation skills. Have students practice each variation (addition, multiplication, exponents) and then allow them to negotiate with new partners to determine the number of digits and which concept to use.

Awareness Talk

During the second developmental stage, the students begin to share the responsibility for the awareness talk with the teacher. The teacher can identify the theme, prepare a list of questions, ask one or more students to guide the questioning, and make connections between the student responses and the lesson focus. Commonly used themes during developmental stage 2 include self-control, self-direction, communication, cooperation, goal setting, and problem solving.

The Math 1-2-3 activity provides an opportunity to discuss respect, conflict resolution, communication, and negotiation concepts. For example, if you want the discussion to center on working together, you could give the student leader a list of questions like these:

- "How did you and your partner decide on which math concept to use?"
- "If you disagreed, how did you decide on which method to use?"
- "What are other ways we can resolve differences when working in groups?"

MODEL IN ACTION 11.3

Math 1-2-3

DESCRIPTION

Working as partners, students stand back-to-back. One the count of 3, they jump up and spin around to face each other, holding out one, two, or three fingers. The first student to add up the digits correctly receives a point. Have each pair of students play the best two out of three and then find new partners.

EQUIPMENT

None.

VARIATIONS

- Allow students to use zero to five fingers.
- Use multiplication instead of addition.
- Use exponents (big number raised to the smaller number; for example, if player A shows 2 and player B shows 3, the answer would be 3 raised to the second power, or 9).
- Allow students to negotiate which variation they will use.

Lesson Focus

Creating opportunities for students to work independently and demonstrate self-direction should be the focus during the second developmental stage. You can accomplish this by modifying the way you set up learning experiences, shifting toward a student-centered approach. To illustrate, we consider teaching the Defend Your Turf activity (Model in Action 11.4) using two different approaches. Both approaches provide opportunities for students to demonstrate self-direction (Level III) while working collaboratively with peers. The drill is one of several that can help students develop volleying skills during a net or wall unit.

Table 11.2 presents considerations for teaching the Defend Your Turf activity through two teaching styles and shows how they connect to the TPSR model.

By presenting the drills through these teaching styles, you provide an opportunity for the student to demonstrate behaviors consistent with responsibility Levels III and IV. These teaching styles require some level of competency in the skill. It may be that the students' responsibility level is such that they can handle self-directed activities but their skill level does not support self-monitoring of performance (error detection and correction). In this case, provide detailed task sheets that focus on a single aspect of skill performance and use a peer observer (reciprocal style). You can directly interact with students by using teach–practice–teach episodes, stopping independent skill practice to pinpoint performances that meet your expectations, and providing specific feedback.

Self-Check Style

Use of a self-check style of teaching can provide students with the opportunity to demonstrate self-direction during this drill. Create a task sheet that briefly describes the activity and lists the learning cues. You can ask a student to demonstrate the activity

---

MODEL IN ACTION 11.4

Defend Your Turf

DESCRIPTION

Working in partners, students practice returning volleys. One student (the volleyer) stands in the service court 8 to 10 feet (2.4 to 3 meters) from the net. The partner (the hitter) hits a tennis ball into play, and the volleyer attempts to return the ball into play to the hitter's side of the court. Have each student perform the hitter role for 10 consecutive hits and then have the partners switch roles. The ball can be hit to the forehand or backhand of the volleyer or to one side only.

EQUIPMENT

Two tennis rackets, 10 tennis balls, tennis court.

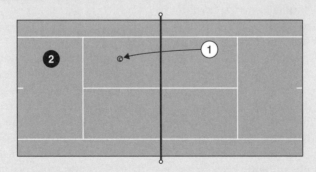

VARIATION

Short-court game: Both players defend their zones by hitting or volleying the ball over the net to their partner's zone. The ball must land within the service court, and no overhead smashes are allowed. The ball is "served" underhand to start the rally.

Adapted, by permission, from J. Brown, 2004, *Tennis: Steps to success*, 3rd ed. (Champaign, IL: Human Kinetics), 59.

Table 11.2   Developmental Stage 2 Instructional Strategies for Tennis

Instructional style	Teaching considerations	Links to TPSR
Self-check	• Teacher values students' ability to self-evaluate their performance. • Teacher values students' ability to work independently of teacher and peers. • Students have demonstrated competency in the skill.	• Students can demonstrate effort (Level II) while working through the assigned tasks. • Students can demonstrate self-direction (Level III) by working independently on the tasks. • Students can demonstrate self-direction (Level III) by self-assessing and reflecting on performance after each task.
Reciprocal	• Students work in groups of three and have specific roles (two doers, one observer). • Students have task sheets and a list of feedback phrases. • Group works at own pace. • Teacher ensures that students are maintaining their roles and intervenes only if there is a safety issue.	• Students can demonstrate respect (Level I) for peers (e.g., not interfering with their participation). • Students can demonstrate participation with effort (Level II) by staying engaged in the volley drills. • Students can begin to demonstrate self-direction (Level III) by progressively challenging themselves throughout the activities (e.g., forehand and backhand volleys, targeting a specific zone with their returns). • Students develop patience and tolerance as they work with peers (Level IV).

and focus students on their task sheets. Once students have read their task sheets, they can begin the activity at their own pace.

Following each set of 10 hits, students recheck the criteria noted on the task sheet relative to their execution of the volley shot. Students are responsible for their own feedback based on the criteria for the skill. The teacher's role is to ask questions related to the student's process of self-checking or self-assessing.

Reciprocal Style

Shifting to a reciprocal style for this activity, you would create groups of three. Provide task sheets that briefly describe the activity and list the cues. In addition, the sheet should clearly note the participant roles and expectations to help students keep focus. For example, spell out what the observer ought to be observing (performance cues) and what the doers are doing (hitting and volleying). Specify a time or number of shots for each facet of the activity. Once a round is completed, the students rotate their roles; the hitter becomes the observer, the observer becomes the volleyer, and the volleyer becomes the hitter.

The teacher's role is to move about the space and assist the observers in accurately observing the doer. You must step in to provide feedback if there is a safety issue. Otherwise, encourage or suggest feedback to the observer only if feedback is not occurring.

Group Meeting

For many students, talking in front of their peers can be intimidating. These students may still lend unique insights to discussions of skill performance and application of the responsibility model in the lesson activities. A strategy that we like to use to debrief a learning experience is Questions in the Round (Model in Action 11.5). This method of debrief allows students to work in pairs to discuss and reflect on the lesson. For students who are new to having a voice in the lesson, this gives them an opportunity to share their thoughts without having to speak in front of the entire class. Every student has an opportunity to communicate, but you save time by not having everyone share with the entire class. Consider asking one or two students to share with

MODEL IN ACTION 11.5

Questions in the Round

DESCRIPTION

Create two circles of students (see the figure), with students in the inner and outer circles facing each other. The group meeting leader (teacher or student) poses a question to the group, and students discuss their answer with the student facing them. The inner circle rotates two positions clockwise for the next question. This creates new pairings.

EQUIPMENT

Circle floor marking (center court).

VARIATIONS

- Provide students in the inner circle with a list of questions they can pose.
- Have students, after rotating, review their responses to the previous question with their new partner before asking a new question.

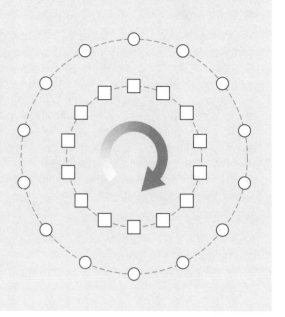

the class their response to a question. In another version of Questions in the Round, when students rotate, they share the response of their first partner with their new partner and discuss with the new partner the same question in greater detail. At the end of the activity you can bring everyone back to the large group and ask for culminating thoughts about the day's lesson.

Reflection

There are a number of strategies for promoting reflection in students. We encourage you to note the many examples in *Teaching Personal and Social Responsibility Through Physical Activity, Third Edition,* of different ways to engage students in reflection time. The key to this stage is for students to begin to reflect on how to transfer lessons learned in the physical education setting to life beyond the gym walls. Students can be cued to questions that address the particular levels the students are working on for this stage (Level III) and begin to scaffold to goals for the next levels (IV and V). You might ask, for example, "As we move toward more self-directed learning, what goals can you set to show more leadership in class?" and "What are ways we can demonstrate self-direction at home?" Students can begin to generate these types of questions once you have modeled them.

Developmental Stage 3

Transitioning students to developmental stage 3 within the confines of physical education settings can be difficult. At this stage students should routinely demonstrate behaviors consistent with Levels I to III and actively seek out leadership opportunities. These opportunities for caring and leadership take center stage during developmental stage 3. Caring and leadership can manifest themselves during all aspects of the lesson as students explore ways to engage in the learning process.

Relationship Time

Relationship time during the third developmental stage should be almost entirely run by students. Student leaders can be responsible for setup, instruction, and facilitation of the relationship time tasks. For example, many teachers use a warm-up routine that is performed throughout the year. Consider allowing students to lead, or even better create, the warm-up or other relationship time activities.

The Create-a-Game activity meets the objectives of relationship time by providing opportunities for students to interact with each other constructively; it also meets the developmental stage 3 needs by providing opportunities for students to be self-directed and to develop leadership skills.

Create-a-Game

DESCRIPTION

Ask students, working in groups of four, to create a warm-up game that they will present to their peers. The game can focus on the lesson content (i.e., tennis) or other skills or concepts (fitness). Create task sheets on which groups can fill in the name of the game, the type of activity (individual, partner, teams), the rules or scoring, and the organization (boundaries, team configuration, equipment needs). Use the relationship time in one lesson for creating the game, and have students present the games during subsequent relationship times.

EQUIPMENT

Task sheets, various pieces of equipment based on criteria you have established.

These students created a game in which they transfer a tennis ball from racket to racket.

Awareness Talk

Student leaders should be comfortable with identifying the theme, guiding the questioning, and drawing connections to the lesson by the time they reach the third developmental stage. Commonly used themes during developmental stage 3 include self-direction, leadership, and transfer. To illustrate a developmental stage 3 awareness talk, let's consider Create-a-Game (Model in Action 11.6).

In speaking for the Create-a-Game activity, the student leaders would generalize the lessons learned from the activity to the theme and subsequent activities. These are examples of statements and questions they might offer:

- "I liked how my group talked through each step and offered game ideas. How did your group decide on the game you would create?"
- "In our group we selected our five pieces of equipment first and then tried to come up with a unique game that used the equipment. How did other groups decide where to begin?"

In speaking for the experience, the student leaders can generalize what occurred in the activity. Nonverbal behavior on the part of the teacher can be really be important here. Remain involved by demonstrating active listening, nodding your head, and making eye contact with whoever is speaking. This models to the students behaviors that they too can maintain in the process.

Lesson Focus

Developmental stage 3 activities should provide students with the opportunity for leadership experiences and encourage transfer to other aspects of the curriculum. The Two Up, Two Back activity (Model in Action 11.7), a volley drill, offers students opportunities to exhibit behaviors consistent with responsibility Levels I through IV.

Two Up, Two Back

DESCRIPTION

The volley in tennis can be an effective way to control the point. It is used particularly in doubles. For this drill, team A players (players 1 and 2) take positions near the net, and team B players (players 3 and 4) start at the baseline (see the accompanying figure). One player from team B begins play by hitting the ball to the player on team A who is in the opposite serving court. The ball is volleyed back and play continues. To allow for opportunities for volley practice, the first two hits of the rally should be playable. The third hit is the first opportunity to score a point for the team. For example:

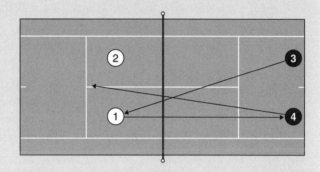

- First hit: Player 3 hits the ball to player 1.
- Second hit: Player 1 volleys the ball to player 4.
- Third hit: Player 4 attempts to hit the ball past team A.

If either the first or second shot is hit out of play, service is rotated but no point is awarded. Play to 10 points, alternating the serve with each point.

EQUIPMENT

Four rackets and one tennis ball for each group of four players (each group plays on their own tennis court).

VARIATIONS

- Increase the number of hits before a point is awarded to increase volley practice and increase difficulty.
- Have players rotate positions after each shot (player 3 moves to 4, 4 to 1, 1 to 2, and 2 to 3).
- Award points individually rather than to teams.

Adapted, by permission, from J. Brown, 2004, *Tennis: Steps to success*, 3rd ed. (Champaign, IL: Human Kinetics), 127.

Teaching strategies for developmental stage 3 include providing students with opportunities to emphasize previous levels but, more importantly, focus on Levels IV (caring and leadership) and V (outside the gymnasium). We can elicit these behaviors by modifying the way we present the task.

Table 11.3 presents considerations for teaching Two Up, Two Back through two different styles. You can use a command style, but this minimizes the opportunity for students to demonstrate developmental stage 3 behaviors. Instead, presenting the task through a divergent discovery style or a self-check style provides opportunities for self-directed learning and leadership.

Two Up, Two Back (Model in Action 11.7) provides students with the opportunity to demonstrate responsibility Levels I through IV. Using a guided discovery approach gives students a chance to collaboratively develop tactical awareness for the volley and passing shots. Self-checking enables them to self-assess

in the context of group play. At this developmental stage, students have demonstrated the ability to work independently while putting forth effort and showing respect to their peers. At this point we hope you can begin to think of ways to modify the learning environment to promote leadership skills in your students. These skills can be carried over to the group meeting segment of the lesson, increasing the contribution of students to the learning process.

Divergent Discovery Style

Presenting Two Up, Two Back using a divergent discovery approach allows you to engage students in both the cognitive and psychomotor domains. Through questioning or the presentation of a problem, you can have students diverge on solutions for successfully completing the task. With this task you can allow groups of students to diverge on a solution that meets the task requirements.

Table 11.3 Developmental Stage 3 Instructional Strategies for Tennis

Instructional style	Teaching considerations	Links to TPSR
Divergent discovery	• Students solve problem presented by the teacher (cognitive engagement). • Teacher is free to offer prompts or questions to groups struggling to "solve" the task. • Provides opportunity for groups to solve task in unique ways. • Provides opportunity for students to voice opinions to peers. • May lead to greater variance in performance.	• Students can demonstrate caring (Level IV) by working with their peers to solve the problem. • Students can demonstrate leadership and caring (Level IV) by organizing the group to try out strategies for scoring points.
Self-check	• Teacher values students' ability to self-evaluate their performance. • Teacher values students' ability to work independently of teacher and peers. • Students have demonstrated competency in the skill.	• Students can demonstrate caring (Level IV) by respecting the rights of other students. • Students can demonstrate transfer outside the gym (Level V) by gaining self-awareness about their proficiency. • Students demonstrate leadership (Level IV) by maintaining honesty about their performance.

Teacher: "Each group will play a modified doubles game. One team starts at the net and the other at the baseline. The team at the baseline begins play, and team locations switch after each point. The first two hits of each round should be easily returnable by the other team. Points can be scored only after two successful hits have been completed. Rotate service each point and play to 10 points."

After each round of 10 points, have students reflect on the following questions:

- How can you support your partner during a point (think about your movement and positioning on the court)?
- What strategies did the volleying team use to score points?
- What strategies did the baseline team use to score points?
- How can we use one hit to set up our next shot?

Self-Check Style

Shifting to a self-check style provides additional opportunities for students to demonstrate self-direction and leadership behaviors. Create a task sheet that briefly describes the activity and provides learning cues. You can ask a group to demonstrate the activity drills and focus students on their task sheet. Once groups have read their sheets, they can begin the activity at their own pace.

Following each game (to 10 points), students recheck the criteria noted on the task sheet relative to their execution of the volley. Students are responsible for their own feedback based on the criteria for the given skill. The teacher's role is to ask questions related to the student's process of self-checking or self-assessing.

Group Meeting

As with the awareness talk, this portion of the lesson is mostly student led. You can assist by cueing students regarding the levels they are working on, as well as reminding them of what sorts of questions have been asked in previous classes. Questions about how the lesson was conducted, how the activity met the students' needs or provided challenge, and how the style of teaching engaged them are all examples of program-related discussion questions.

During the Two Up, Two Back activity, a student leader can initiate a group reflection on the lesson activities by asking questions like these:

- "How did you support your partner during this drill?"
- "What are other ways we support our doubles partner during tennis?"
- "How can we use a shot to set up our partner for the next shot?"

Reflection

We should expect students at this developmental stage to be able to pose higher-order questions during their reflections. Reflections should continue to serve as an opportunity for students to self-reflect on their actions and what they observed in others throughout the lesson while exploring ways they can transfer the responsibility attributes they are developing in physical education to life beyond the gym. This can be accomplished through a variety of formats in class or outside of class time. Students can read each other's journals and provide feedback, assist each other in goal setting, or create strategies to transfer the levels to environments outside of the program. Again, the teacher remains connected to the process as an active listener and support.

Keeping SITE

As discussed in chapter 1, the key to TPSR is keeping SITE of four thematic objectives (student relationships, integration, transfer, and empowerment) throughout your lessons and program. Using the content from this chapter, reflect on the following questions:

Student Relationships

1. What aspects of the variation in teaching styles assisted in enhancing student–teacher relationships? How?
2. What aspects of the variation in teaching styles assisted in enhancing student–student relationships? How?

Integration

1. What are elements within this chapter that facilitate development of personal responsibility in students? How?
2. What are elements within this chapter that facilitate development of social responsibility in students? How?

Transfer

1. What were elements within the chapter that might assist in transfer of TPSR outside of the class but within the school or program? How?
2. What were elements within the chapter that might assist in transfer of TPSR outside of the school or program? How?

Empowerment

1. What elements of your lessons support an empowering pedagogy for students?
2. What pedagogical choices can you make to promote autonomy and a sense of control in your students?

Teaching Personal and Social Responsibility Through

Fitness

Fitness for Life by Corbin and Lindsey (2007) served as the primary reference for this chapter. Possibly of all the types of activity discussed in part II of this book (other than adventure), fitness lends itself most readily to integration of TPSR. The very nature of a unit or program on fitness suggests the evolution of self-regulation, goal setting, and personal responsibility with regard to one's health. In this, the last chapter of part II, we provide examples of developing a lesson around fitness concepts using TPSR principles.

Developmental Stage 1

As we have discussed throughout this book, students in the first developmental stage are often working on exhibiting Level I (respecting self and others) and Level II (participating with effort or stick-to-itiveness) behaviors consistently. During this stage the teacher takes the predominant role in leading the awareness talk, choosing developmentally appropriate tasks and challenges, structuring the group meeting, and providing reflection opportunities. As the lessons progress, the teacher is mindful to provide students with opportunities to begin to transition to developmental stage 2 (Level III, self-direction).

Relationship Time

We advocate the use of icebreaker activities throughout the learning process in a variety of sport or physical activities to facilitate a more coordinated effort to build connections between the teacher and students. Icebreaker games provide an opportunity for students and teachers to interact, develop relationships, and have fun. Icebreakers can vary in length, but they all serve the purpose of creating an environment that fosters acceptance and interaction. When working with developmental stage 1 learners, consider selecting activities that focus on individual traits (communication, cooperation, self-control, respect, and effort) within the context of group interactions.

The Sport Moves activity (Model in Action 12.1) provides students with the opportunity to demonstrate respect for others (Level I) and self-control (Level II) and to begin to work toward self-direction (Level III). The game is simple and does not necessarily invite situations in which conflict may arise; it does support discussions that connect well with kids' recognition of self, others, and the group.

Awareness Talk

With students in the first developmental stage, the teacher takes the primary role during the awareness talks. She identifies the theme, guides the questioning, and makes the connection to teachable moments in the lesson focus. Commonly used themes during developmental stage 1 include respect, self-control, participation, effort, and effective communication. We like to use icebreakers for relationship time as it provides a leaping-off point from the activity to the remainder of the lesson. We use the "What?", "So what?", "Now what?" method of structuring the awareness talk as well. This technique helps us

---

MODEL IN ACTION 12.1

Sport Moves

DESCRIPTION

Form a circle of 5 to 10 students and establish a leader. Instruct the students to think about their favorite sport or physical activity or movement, such as in-line skating or basketball jump shots. Ask them to put their hands up when they have thought of something and to keep them up so you know who is ready. Once all the students have their hands up, the game begins. Have the leader start by saying her name, saying what her favorite sport or movement is, and then mimicking it (e.g., pretend to be in-line skating or making a jump shot). Play then moves clockwise around the circle. Each person repeats the others' names and favorites and copies their movements, then says his own name and favorite movement and mimics it. The game proceeds until the last person in the circle is challenged to remember everyone's name and favorite.

EQUIPMENT

None.

VARIATION

Include music.

draw meaning from the activity during the relationship time; it also models for students how they may direct the awareness talk as we eventually move to the side and allow them to lead this portion of the lesson (developmental stages 2 and 3). For example, in developmental stage 1, you might ask the following questions:

- "What were some similar sport or physical activity likes in the group?"
- "What were some different sport or physical activity likes in the group?"

On the basis of the students' responses, you can lead them to extend their thinking by asking questions like these:

- "What are some things you learned about others that you might want to try?"

- "What are some sports or physical activities you might want to try with one of your classmates?"

Lesson Focus

Themes identified during the awareness talk set the stage for teachable moments throughout the lesson focus. Selection of pedagogical strategies that provide opportunities for students to make a cognitive or affective connection between the tasks and the themes supports a TPSR-based classroom. Although in developmental stage 1, it is often beneficial to maintain a somewhat teacher-centered approach (command or direct style), we must also provide students with opportunities to work toward skill development in developmental stage 2. The style you choose will be influenced by your teaching philosophy, the learning styles of your students, and

---

MODEL IN ACTION 12.2

The Basic 10: Flexibility Circuit

DESCRIPTION

Using the flexibility circuit in Corbin and Lindsey's *Fitness for Life,* students perform static stretches such as the back-saver sit and reach, spine twist, sitting stretch, zipper, and calf stretch, holding for the given count. These are the instructions:

- **Back-saver sit and reach:** Sit on the floor with your right knee bent and your left leg straight. Bend your left knee slightly and push your heel to the floor as you contract the hamstring for 3 seconds. Relax. Grasp your ankles with both hands and gently pull your chest toward your knee; hold for a count of 15 seconds. Repeat with left knee bent and right leg straight.

- **Spine twist:** Lie on your back with your knees bent and arms extended at shoulder level. Cross your left leg over your right leg. Keep your shoulders and arms on the floor as you rotate your lower body to the left, touching your right knee to the floor. Stretch and hold the position for 15 seconds. Reverse the positions of the legs (cross right leg over left leg), then rotate to the right and hold the position for 15 seconds.

- **Sitting stretch:** Sit with the soles of your feet together, your elbows or hands resting on your knees. Gently lean your trunk forward and push down on your knees with your arms to stretch the thighs. Hold for 15 seconds.

- **Zipper:** Stand or sit. Lift your right arm over your right shoulder and reach down your spine. With your left hand, press down on your right elbow. Hold for 15 seconds. Repeat with the other arm.

- **Calf stretch:** Step forward with your right leg in a lunge position. Keep both feet pointed straight ahead and your front knee directly over your front foot. Place your hands on your right leg for balance. Keep the left leg straight and the heel on the floor. Adjust the length of your lunge until you feel a good stretch in the left calf and Achilles tendon. Hold for 15 seconds. Repeat with opposite leg.

EQUIPMENT

Floor mats.

Adapted, by permission, from C.B. Corbin and R. Lindsey, 2007, *Fitness for life,* 5th ed. (Champaign, IL: Human Kinetics), 167.

the context in which the lesson is presented. Here we provide an example of a lesson focus on flexibility using two different styles of teaching.

Table 12.1 presents considerations for teaching the Flexibility Circuit activity (Model in Action 12.2) through two teaching styles and shows how they connect to the TPSR model.

Reciprocal Style

To use reciprocal style for teaching this activity, have students get in pairs. One student will be the doer and the other will be the observer. Provide each pair with a flexibility task sheet that briefly describes the stretches (pictures are helpful also) and provides cues. We also suggest providing a list of possible motivating feedback phrases students can use. In addition, the task sheet should list clear role expectations to help students keep focus. For example, spell out what the observer ought to be observing (performance cues) and what the doers are doing (practicing). Once they have completed the stretches, students rotate

their roles; the doer becomes the observer, and the observer becomes the doer.

The teacher's role is to move about the space and assist the observers in accurately observing the doer. You must step in to provide feedback if there is a safety issue. Otherwise, encourage or suggest feedback to the observer only if feedback is not occurring.

Practice/Task Style

With the practice/task style, the teacher creates stations for the stretches around the gymnasium. Instruct the students through each stretch, providing critical cues and checking for understanding. Once students have seen each stretch, they may begin. Students can move through the stations in any order and complete the specified number of repetitions. They can repeat stations, but ask them to challenge themselves. The main difference between practice/task style and reciprocal style is that practice/task style does not use an observer role. The teacher moves about the gymnasium providing feedback.

Table 12.1   Developmental Stage 1 Instructional Strategies for Fitness

Instructional style	Teaching considerations	Links to TPSR
Reciprocal	• Students work in pairs and have specific roles (doer, observer). • Students have task sheets and a list of feedback phrases. • Partners work at own pace. • Teacher ensures that students are maintaining their roles and intervenes only if there is a safety issue.	• Students can demonstrate respect (Level I) for peers (e.g., not interfering with their participation). • Students can demonstrate participation with effort (Level II) by staying engaged with the flexibility circuit. • Students can begin to demonstrate self-direction (Level III) by progressively challenging themselves throughout the activities (e.g., increase the time they hold a position). • Students develop patience and tolerance as they work with peers (Level IV).
Practice/Task	• Students make decisions about order of tasks to be completed, pace, starting and stopping on a particular task. • Students work individually. • Teacher provides objectives of lesson. • Teacher provides feedback to students.	• Students can demonstrate self-control and respect (Level I) for the teacher (e.g., following directions, staying in control) and for peers (e.g., not interfering with their participation). • Students can demonstrate participation with effort (Level II) by staying engaged throughout the exercises. • Students can begin to demonstrate self-direction (Level III) by progressively challenging themselves throughout the activities (e.g., holding stretch for maximum time).

Group Meeting

Group meetings during the first developmental stage are facilitated by the teacher but provide an opportunity for students to have a voice in the learning process. This is the time for students to have input on how the lesson went, how their peers did, and even how the teacher did—all in relation to working on developmental stage 1 goals. Questions concerning how the activities challenged the students and questions about how they felt participating in the lesson when the teacher used a given teaching style are good beginning points. Students can also be asked how they felt the class as a whole or just they as partners or in small groups did. Lastly, you can ask how you did and ask if there are things you might work on for the next session. As Don Hellison notes, this facet of the lesson may be foreign to students initially because youth are not often asked to provide feedback to each other, much less to and about the teacher. Keep with it; over time, students will feel more comfortable verbalizing their thoughts as this becomes a consistent part of the class.

Don suggests that initially the teacher ought to lay down some ground rules; this can be done in collaboration with the students. Ground rules might include the following:

- No blaming others—accept responsibility for yourself.
- Include everyone in the discussion.
- Be respectful of yourself and others (full-value contract).
- Use each other's names.
- Do not talk over each other.
- Wait for classmates to finish their comments.

These are only a few examples; we encourage you to solicit input from the classes about what other rules could be included.

Another especially relevant issue concerning group meetings is time. If you do not have sufficient time to check in with all students, ask for responses on how things went from just a few. A common practice in many TPSR-based programs is to have the students keep a journal. They can do this as homework and turn in their comments the next day. This way you keep track of how things are going and get timely input from the class.

Reflection

Reflection time should flow fairly seamlessly from the group meeting time. Group meeting time focuses on students' evaluation of the lesson, and reflection time focuses on evaluation of their role as learners and support. Thus, questions can move from how the activities or style of teaching challenged or engaged them to a focus on how they participated as independent learners, demonstrated respect, showed self-direction, and cooperated during the lesson. During developmental stage 1, the teacher directs the discussion. You might ask questions such as the following:

- "During the flexibility activities today, did you demonstrate Level I characteristics?"
- "Did you show stick-to-itiveness during the lesson today by completing all activities in the circuit?"

Students can respond to the questions verbally in small groups or with a partner. As a whole group they can use the thumbometer to respond (thumbs up, sideways, or down). The teacher is responsible for noting where most of the kids are (more thumbs up than down) so as to facilitate activities toward the higher levels (III and IV). It is important to acknowledge that kids have bad days, too, and we ought to support them and encourage honest self-evaluation. We also want to underscore not blaming others for our behavior.

Reflection time is when we can begin to encourage students to think about how they can demonstrate the responsibility levels outside of the class or program. Asking students where in their out-of-class or out-of-program lives they could demonstrate a given level allows for them to begin this transition. It can also be helpful to ask students to share one thing they learned from the activity and about themselves relative to the TPSR model as a way to begin to scaffold between in-class goals and transfer out of class.

Developmental Stage 2

Once students are consistently demonstrating Level I and II behaviors, you should transition to the second developmental stage. This means providing opportunities for students to work collaboratively with their peers with little teacher guidance (Level III, self-direction). During the second stage you begin to call upon students to take a role in the learning process. As you will see in this section, the teacher begins to relinquish some of the control of the class to students during awareness talks and group meetings. As this occurs, some students may begin to demonstrate a desire to take leadership roles (Level IV). However, most students will continue to need some guidance in keeping self-directed without individual supervision.

Relationship Time

Sport Moves (Model in Action 12.1) can be easily modified to provide students with the opportunity to continue to demonstrate respect (Level I) and participate with effort (Level II) while working collaboratively with their classmates without direct teacher supervision (Level III). Instead of one large group, students can be in smaller clusters. In one modification of the game, students are challenged to think of sports or physical activities they like that begin with the first letter of their first name. Another idea is to challenge small groups of students to come up with a Sport Moves routine that represents all the group members' interests. The moves can flow from one to another, similar to a floor routine in gymnastics. Better yet, have the groups do their routines to music! With these modifications students can begin to show leadership and higher levels of problem solving and working together.

Awareness Talk

During the second developmental stage, the teacher begins to share the responsibility for the awareness talks. He identifies the theme, asks one or more students to guide the questioning, and draws the connection to the lesson focus. Commonly used themes during developmental stage 2 include self-control, self-direction, goal setting, and problem solving.

Using students to help guide the awareness talk is key in the development of youth leaders (Level IV). After the activity you can use student leaders to "debrief" so as to draw the attention of the learners to the cognitive and affective attributes of an activity. Having the students think about themes that arose as they did the activity during relationship time can help them connect to the discussion during the awareness talk. Encourage students to follow your model and ask "What?", "So what?", and "Now what?" questions.

Lesson Focus

The opportunities for self-direction take center stage during developmental stage 2; activities should transition from individuals performing within the context of the group to individuals positively interacting with partners and small groups in self-guided learning experiences.

Table 12.2 presents considerations for teaching the Muscular Endurance Exercise Circuit activity (Model in Action 12.3) through two teaching styles and shows how they connect to the TPSR model.

Being mindful of the activities used during this stage gives you opportunities to alter the teaching style and encourage greater student responsibility. This allows for students to begin leading the group meeting segment of the lesson and speaking to how the lesson activities address the theme or themes identified during the awareness talk.

Reciprocal Style

With the reciprocal style, students are in pairs; one is the observer and one is the doer. Each has a muscular endurance task sheet that briefly describes the activities and provides learning cues. We also suggest providing a list of possible motivating feedback phrases for students to use. In addition, the sheet should note clear role expectations for students to help them keep focus; spell out what the observer ought to be observing (performance cues) and what the doers are doing (practicing). Also specify a time or number of repetitions for each exercise. Once they have completed all the exercises, the students rotate their roles, the doer becoming the observer and the observer becoming the doer.

The teacher's role is to move about the space and assist the observers in accurately observing the doer. You must step in to provide feedback if there is a safety issue. Otherwise, encourage or suggest feedback to the observer only if feedback is not occurring.

Inclusion Style

With inclusion style, the teacher initially demonstrates the correct cues for each of the circuit exercises. The teacher identifies the options available for students to decide how and where they enter the activity. Variations in exercises such as knees on floor for the push-up or different numbers of repetitions are examples of choices students may make. Task sheets provide a diagram of the activity as well as performance cues. Students are placed in pairs and dispersed throughout the teaching area. Allow the learners time to assess their level though trial and error and begin the activity. Each time, the learner reassesses and sets new challenges based on the levels available and the achievement of performance criteria.

The teacher's role is to circulate throughout the learning space and provide feedback only on the decision of the students. You might ask, "How are you doing at the level you have selected?" The students' responses will help you inquire about the decisions made and how successful the students feel they are. With this style it is important not to start out by overtly challenging the decision made but to assist the learner.

Muscular Endurance Exercise Circuit

DESCRIPTION

Using Corbin and Lindsey's muscular endurance circuit, students perform the stride jump, trunk lift, 90-degree push-up or knee push-up, and curl-up with twist. Make sure students warm up before starting the circuit. These are the instructions:

Modified push-ups for muscle endurance workout.

- **Stride jump:** Stand with your left leg forward and right leg back. Hold your right arm at shoulder height straight in front of your body and your left arm straight behind you. Jump by moving your right foot forward and left foot back. As your feet change places, your arms switch position. Keep your feet about 18 to 24 inches (45 to 60 centimeters) apart. Continue jumping and alternating feet and arms for 30 seconds to 1 minute.

- **Trunk lift:** Lie facedown with your hands clasped behind your neck. Pull your shoulder blades together, raise your elbows off the floor, and then lift your head and chest off the floor. Arch the upper back until your breastbone (sternum) clears the floor. You may need to hook your feet under a bar or have someone hold your feet. Do not lift more than 12 inches (30 centimeters) off the floor. Hold for 3 seconds and repeat.

- **90-degree push-up:** Lie facedown with your hands under your shoulders, fingers spread, and your legs straight. Your legs should be slightly apart and your toes tucked under. Push up until your arms are straight. Keep your legs and back straight. Your body should form a straight line. Lower your body by bending your elbows until they are each parallel to the floor, then push up until arms are extended. Repeat for 30 seconds to 1 minute.

- **Knee push-up:** This is the same as the 90-degree push-up except that instead of having your legs straight and being on your toes, you contact the ground with your knees. Repeat for 30 seconds to 1 minute.

- **Curl-up with twist:** Lie on your back with your knees bent to about a right angle (90 degrees), your feet flat on the floor. Extend your arms down along your sides. Flatten your lower back to the floor. Tuck your chin and lift your head. Then raise your shoulder blades, twisting to the left and reaching with both arms outside your left leg. Curl up until both shoulder blades are off the floor. Curl down to the starting position and repeat the exercise, this time twisting to the right. Continue alternating from left to right for 30 seconds to 1 minute.

EQUIPMENT

Floor mats.

Adapted, by permission, from C.B. Corbin and R. Lindsey, 2007, *Fitness for life*, 5th ed. (Champaign, IL: Human Kinetics), 213.

Table 12.2 Developmental Stage 2 Instructional Strategies for Fitness

Instructional style	Teaching considerations	Links to TPSR
Reciprocal	• Students work in pairs and have specific roles (doer, observer). • Students have task sheets and a list of feedback phrases. • Pairs work at their own pace. • Teacher ensures that students are maintaining their roles and intervenes only if there is a safety issue.	• Students can demonstrate respect (Level I) for peers (e.g., not interfering with their participation). • Students can demonstrate participation with effort (Level II) by staying engaged with the muscular endurance circuit. • Students can begin to demonstrate self-direction (Level III) by progressively challenging themselves throughout the activities (e.g., increase time they are at a particular station). • Students develop patience and tolerance as they work with peers (Level IV).
Inclusion	• Students make individual choices to accommodate their ability. • Students are reassessing abilities and making allowances as lesson progresses. • Students' assessment allows them to rechallenge themselves or set goals. • Teacher decides skills to be practiced and provides possible levels in the task.	• Students can demonstrate respect (Level I) for partner and self. • Students practice honesty in selecting appropriate level of entry (Level I). • Students demonstrate effort and participation (Level II) as they reassess and rechallenge themselves. • Students set goals and demonstrate self-evaluation as they reassess throughout the lesson (Level III). • Students learn to deal with agreement or discrepancy between their aspirations and actual performance (Levels II and III).

Group Meeting

The group meeting during the second developmental stage should continue to provide students with an opportunity to have a voice in the learning process but involve them more in leading the discussion. Because you have modeled leading the discussion in developmental stage 1, you can help the students assume more responsibility by asking questions like these:

- "What sorts of questions did I ask you about the lesson?"
- "What questions do you have of your peers from the lesson?"

Another strategy is to have students write their questions or comments on a slip of paper and then exchange with partners and engage in small-group discussions. You can then bring them back to the large group and ask for culminating thoughts from the day's lesson. Don't be disappointed if it takes a bit more time to get students to this developmental stage. Be consistent, be caring, and be a good model for your students and they will begin to assume more responsibility.

Reflection

Key to this stage is that students begin to lead more of the discussion. Students can be cued to questions that address the particular level they are working on for this stage (Level III) and begin to scaffold to goals for the next levels (IV and V). These are examples of reflection questions:

- "How did you feel you and your partner worked independently of teacher direction?"
- "What might you improve on?"
- "As we move toward more independence, what goals can you set to show more leadership in class?"

Having students begin activity at a level they choose is key for the inclusion style.

Again, students can begin to generate these types of questions once you have modeled them. We encourage readers to note the many examples in *Teaching Personal and Social Responsibility Through Physical Activity, Third Edition,* of different ways to engage students in reflection time. Methods such as exit slips, journaling, and tapping in (students tap on a poster that lists the levels to indicate where they are) can be quite effective and keep this part of the lesson fresh.

Developmental Stage 3

Transitioning students to developmental stage 3 within the confines of physical education settings can be difficult. At this stage students should routinely demonstrate behaviors consistent with Levels I to III and actively seek out opportunities to lead. Students are increasingly provided with opportunities to lead their peers in skill development, awareness talks, and group meeting settings. These opportunities for caring and leadership take center stage during developmental stage 3. Accordingly, relationship time activities should transition from individuals positively interacting with partners and small groups to collaborative learning experiences led by student leaders with the support of the teacher.

Relationship Time

As students begin to work within developmental stage 3, you can provide for them to lead the activities during this segment of the lesson. Predetermined volunteers or leaders can be ready with an activity

(Model in Action 12.4). In addition, the activity within this stage ought to include increasing amounts of problem solving as well as communication and working together.

Awareness Talk

During the third developmental stage, the teacher releases the responsibility for the awareness talks to student leaders. The student leaders identify the theme, guide the questioning, and draw the connection to the lesson focus. Commonly used themes during developmental stage 3 include self-direction, leadership, and transfer. As you have been consistent in modeling this aspect of the lesson throughout the developmental stages and have allowed for more and more student leadership, it is highly likely that students will use the familiar "What?", "So what?", "Now what?" format. You then truly become a guide on the side. Your nonverbal behavior can really be important here. Remain involved by demonstrating active listening, nodding your head, and making eye contact with whoever is speaking. This models to the students behaviors they too can maintain in the process.

Lesson Focus

Developmental stage 3 activities should provide students with the opportunity for leadership experiences and include strategies for encouraging transfer to other aspects of the curriculum. Model in Action 12.5 offers students opportunities to exhibit behaviors consistent with responsibility Levels I through IV.

MODEL IN ACTION 12.4

Bonk

DESCRIPTION

This is a super activity for having groups work together and problem solve. Groups of 10 will work, but we suggest that as the maximum size. Cards with letters A through F are placed as indicated in the accompanying figure. Students are to figure out the patterns the teacher (or another student) has created. Students can step in any direction but must always begin with letter A, B, or C. All patterns must end with letter D, E, or F. Letters cannot be skipped. For example, the pattern A-C-F is not permissible as it skips the letter B. If the student steps on a letter that is not a part of the solution, the facilitator says "Bonk"! It's then time for the next student.

As a team the students work together to keep track of what patterns have been tried as they process to the full solution. Patterns get progressively more difficult. Sample patterns are B-C-F-E; A-D-E-C-F; A-E-B-D-E-F.

F	E	D
C	B	A

EQUIPMENT

Cards or floor spots with letters.

VARIATION

When a student is bonked, have her follow the pattern up to that point in reverse order.

Teaching strategies for developmental stage 3 include providing students with opportunities to emphasize previous levels but, more importantly, focus on Levels IV (caring and leadership) and V (outside the gymnasium). Table 12.3 presents considerations for teaching the Fitness Exercise Circuit activity using the self-check style, but as with the activities presented earlier, teaching this circuit can easily incorporate the practice/task, reciprocal, or inclusion styles.

Student-Centered Teaching

It is often a challenge to move students to developmental stage 3 within the confines of traditional physical education and youth sport settings. Physical education especially presents a challenge because you work with populations that have diverse motivations toward course content. If you are fortunate and skilled enough to guide your group to this level, much of your time will be spent using student-centered teaching styles. In the next section we present one example of student-centered teaching that can be modified to fit other styles on the spectrum based on the content, your students' learning style, and your preferred teaching style.

Self-Check Style

To use self-check style for this activity, create task sheets that briefly describe the circuit and provide learning cues (similar to task sheets for the practice/

task and reciprocal styles). Demonstrate the activity and focus students on their task sheets. Once students are in pairs and have read their sheets, they can begin. Students are responsible for moving through the circuit at their own pace. They are also responsible for their own feedback based on the criteria for the exercises as noted on the task sheets. The teacher's role is to ask questions related to the student's process of self-checking or self-assessing.

Group Meeting

As with the awareness talk, this portion of the lesson is mostly student led. You can assist by cueing the students regarding the levels they are working on, as well as reminding them of what sorts of questions have been asked in previous classes. Questions that focus on how the lesson was conducted, how the activity met the students' needs or provided challenge, and how the style of teaching engaged them are all examples of program-related discussion questions. You can encourage small-group discussion and then bring everyone back to the larger group. Most importantly, allow students to direct this process while you remain as a support.

Reflection

Allowing students to lead the discussion using the various methods outlined in this chapter or in small groups provides them with the choice and leader-

MODEL IN ACTION 12.5

Fitness Exercise Circuit

DESCRIPTION

This circuit activity includes exercises from Corbin and Lindsey's flexibility and muscular endurance circuits (Models in Action 12.2 and 12.3) but adds one or more of the following: rope jumping, brisk walking, and jogging. Students perform muscular and cardio exercises for 30 seconds to 1 minute and flexibility exercises for 15 seconds. Make sure students warm up before starting the circuit.

EQUIPMENT

Floor mats, jump ropes.

Table 12.3 Developmental Stage 3 Instructional Strategies for Fitness

Instructional style	Teaching considerations	Links to TPSR
Self-check	• Teacher values students' ability to self-evaluate their performance. • Teacher values students' ability to work independently of teacher and peers. • Students have demonstrated competency in the skill.	• Students can demonstrate leadership outside the gym (Level V) by gaining self-awareness about their proficiency. • Students demonstrate leadership (Level IV) by maintaining honesty about their performance.

ship opportunities inherent to this developmental stage. Students might begin to read each other's journals and provide feedback, assist each other in goal setting, or create strategies to transfer the levels to experiences outside of the program. Again, the teacher remains connected to the process as an active listener and support.

Keeping SITE

As discussed in chapter 1, the key to TPSR is keeping SITE of four thematic objectives (student relationships, integration, transfer, and empowerment) throughout your lessons and program. Using the content from this chapter, reflect on the following questions:

Student Relationships

1. What aspects of the variation in teaching styles assisted in enhancing student–teacher relationships? How?
2. What aspects of the variation in teaching styles assisted in enhancing student–student relationships? How?

Integration

1. What are elements within this chapter that facilitate development of personal responsibility in students? How?
2. What are elements within this chapter that facilitate development of social responsibility in students? How?

Transfer

1. What were elements within the chapter that might assist in transfer of TPSR outside of the class but within the school or program? How?
2. What were elements within the chapter that might assist in transfer of TPSR outside of the school or program? How?

Empowerment

1. What elements of your lessons support an empowering pedagogy for students?
2. What pedagogical choices can you make to promote autonomy and a sense of control in your students?

TPSR in Action

In the Trenches

Courtesy of Angela Beale and NY State Education Department 21st CCLC Hempstead Public Schools and Students

Now that you have seen how TPSR can be used in a variety of sports and physical activities, let's look at some real-world examples of the use of TPSR. We have solicited program descriptions from a few of our colleagues, who outline interesting variations in the use of the model.

David Walsh, who studied under Don Hellison, leads off with a description of the Kinesiology Career Club, his San Francisco in-school program that threads the TPSR model through physical education and the development of career aspirations in ninth-grade students.

Angela Beale at Adelphi University on Long Island, New York, provides the next example of TPSR. Angela has used TPSR to create Project Guard: Make A Splash E.N.D.N.Y. (End Needless Drowning New York), an after-school swimming program for inner-city youth at the high school level. In addition to facilitating student development in elements of the model, her program is a link for youth to learn how to swim and acquire lifesaving skills.

Our third example comes from Brian Clocksin with his description of Moving and Shaking with Hofstra. Brian uses the TPSR model in this before-school program to teach elementary-age students math concepts in a physically active environment. The program also serves as a connection to Brian's preservice teachers in work with youth in a physical activity setting.

Meredith Whitley, who is also at Adelphi University on Long Island, New York, rounds out our set of examples. As a doctoral student at Michigan State University, Meredith infused the TPSR model into the Refugee Sport Club, an after-school program for refugee youth between the ages of 9 and 18. Through use of the model, Meredith assists the youth in their transition to U.S. culture.

For each of the four examples, the contributor first provides a general description of the program, then outlines more specifically how the program uses the specific elements of the TPSR model, and concludes by explaining how the program has maintained SITE of TPSR.

The Kinesiology Career Club

David Walsh

Program Description

The Kinesiology Career Club (KCC) is an extension of TPSR with the primary goal of helping inner-city youth envision and discover meaningful, positive

> All summations have a beginning, all effect has a story; all kindness begins with the sown seed. Thought buds toward radiance. The gospel of light is the crossroads of indolence, or action. Be ignited, or be gone.
>
> —Mary Oliver

"possible futures." The more specific goals of KCC for the youth are as follows:

- To maximize motivation to improve in, stay in, and find relevance in school
- To enhance connection between the TPSR goals of respect, effort, goal setting, and leadership skills and the importance they play in youths' futures
- To chart the necessary steps to first become a professional in kinesiology, which provides practical experience in a specific career
- To chart the necessary steps for their own careers of choice and developing strategies for matriculating and graduating from college

The program takes place in San Francisco at Mission High School, a low-performing inner-city school. It began in spring 2011 and will be ongoing every spring and fall semester. The program runs for 80 minutes every Tuesday and Thursday over the entire semester during second-period physical education. Current KCC students include five girls and nine boys who are all ninth graders. The high school has a diverse population with the following ethnicity breakdown: 14 percent African American, 23 percent Asian, 46 percent Latino, 9 percent Caucasian, and 8 percent other. The KCC students closely reflect this diversity.

As a university–community collaboration, KCC is also part of a course offered at San Francisco State University (SFSU) to graduating kinesiology seniors. Called "SFSU Mentors," six to eight seniors are selected to conduct their capstone kinesiology course in the community by helping me run this program. I am the lead instructor of KCC, and the SFSU Mentors help lead various physical activities—a combination of martial arts, weight training, dance, and fitness activities—and mentor the students on positive "possible futures" in either a 1-to-1 or 2-to-1 ratio for the final 15 minutes of every session.

Use of TPSR Model

The KCC goals progress through four phases. Each phase allows for the systematic application of TPSR within the program, as well as providing opportunities for students to engage the model as they move through the program.

Phase One Goals

In phase one we use TPSR daily format and strategies to introduce the program, including the various physical activities. This phase focuses on Level I, respect, and Level II, effort. We aim to begin building relationships with the students, have them voice their opinions about the program content and structure, and introduce the field of kinesiology. We also introduce the combined TPSR reflection time and mentoring time, a significant component of the positive "possible futures" emphasis that takes place throughout the program. We talk about our own choice to study kinesiology, connect the physical activities in KCC to the basis and foundation of the field of kinesiology, bridge Levels I and II to the idea of being successful in kinesiology, encourage the students to talk about their own career interests, and begin to get to know and develop relationships with them.

Phase Two Goals

Once phase one goals are mostly achieved, phase two begins to empower the students to take on the advanced TPSR responsibilities (Level III, goal setting; Level IV, leadership). Students are asked to set goals for martial arts, weight training, dance, or fitness skills. They are also encouraged to take on small leadership experiences by way of teaching the activities they worked on during goal-setting time. We encourage the students to consider a career in at least one of the many subdisciplines of kinesiology, connect the physical activities and goal setting and leadership in the program to being successful in the field of kinesiology, and begin to chart the steps to earning a college degree in kinesiology. Phase two also aims at having students reflect on what they are currently doing in school and out of school that could either help or hinder their futures.

Phase Three Goals

Once phase two goals are mostly achieved, phase three continues to empower the students to work on TPSR Levels I through IV. Goal-setting time and leadership roles are extended so that students take on more responsibility. We introduce the potential transference of the steps to a career in kinesiology to the development of responsibility traits necessary for the students' future careers of choice. The idea is to link phase two experiences of understanding how to be successful in kinesiology to understanding what success would mean in the students' own careers of choice. Students actively reflect on what they would like to pursue as a career and effectively discover ways to link what they learned about kinesiology to their own future career interests. We also introduce the importance of having both potential hopes and potential fears—as suggested by the theory of possible selves (Oyserman, Terry, & Bybee 2002)—and doing the hard work as well as having the positive attitude and preparation needed for success.

Phase Four Goals

After students have mostly achieved phase three goals, phase four continues to empower them to work on responsibility Levels I through IV. We introduce Level V, outside the gym, and address how what the students do in school, at home, and in the streets affects their futures. Phase four discussions focus solely on the students' careers of choice. We further reinforce the connection between the TPSR levels and what might prove necessary for the practical realization of their possible futures, including both potential hopes and fears. We provide additional insight into the degree of hard work, positive attitude, and preparation needed for the realization of their possible futures.

Additional Program Elements

Since KCC is run through in-school physical education, we have to integrate traditional physical education elements such as uniform requirements and fitness testing into the program. Unlike after-school programs that students may choose to attend, attending KCC is mandatory. Mission High School has been very supportive of the program and has given us complete autonomy with respect to fulfilling the goals of KCC. It is a collaboration we plan to continue for several years.

Even though KCC has some goals that differ from those of a regular TPSR program, we are able to keep a TPSR focus by systematically implementing the components of a regular TPSR daily format. Each session has relationship time, an awareness talk, physical activities designed as a way for the students to experience the responsibility levels, a group meeting, and a reflection time. Some of the KCC goals require alteration of the TPSR components. For example, a KCC awareness talk includes how the levels relate to the students' futures, and discussions focus on the field of kinesiology. Reflection time takes place with the guidance of SFSU Mentors, which students document in a journal. Students are asked to reflect not only on the levels but also on how they are performing in school and are exploring a "possible future," first in kinesiology and then in their own careers of choice. An effective strategy has been providing information on the various subdisciplines of kinesiology to give the students the opportunity to find relevance in at least one of them. Some students easily identify with kinesiology as a "possible future" while others connect only with being physically active as an important issue in their lives. As the program progresses, discussions about their own career interests seem to get more detailed and authentic.

Keeping SITE

Though KCC has different goals and purposes, it is still an extension of TPSR. It is crucial for us to keep SITE of the four TPSR themes. KCC includes TPSR's prioritization of the instructor–student relationship through the concern for each student's emotional, social, and physical well-being. KCC is also empowerment based, giving students various leadership roles, providing goal-setting time, giving them a voice in the program's direction, and enabling them to evaluate both themselves and the program. The difference is in how the TPSR levels are integrated into the physical activities as a way to explore a career in kinesiology. Once this is established, then transference of the levels to enhance the students' understanding and exploration of their own careers of interest can occur. KCC is still in its early phases of development and will change as the program evolves, but TPSR will continue to be the foundation and core of the program.

Project Guard: Make A Splash E.N.D.N.Y. (End Needless Drowning New York)

Angela Beale

Program Description

Project Guard: Make A Splash E.N.D.N.Y. (End Needless Drowning New York) was born out of a desire to establish a social and personal growth framework in physical education programs serving at-risk youth in underserved communities. Our school has federal Title 1 status; thus we serve a high percentage of students from low-income homes. Statistics for our school population are 38 percent eligible for free

> Can we be like drops of water
> falling on the stone,
> Splashing, breaking,
> disbursing in air
> Weaker than the stone
> by far but be aware
> That as time goes by the
> rock will wear away
> And the water comes again.
> —Holly Near

lunch, 17 percent limited English proficiency, 86 percent annual attendance rate, 64 percent graduation rate, 9 percent teacher turnover rate, 55 percent black or African American, and 44 percent Hispanic or Latino. While physical education should strive to develop in students an awareness of physical activities that can be used throughout their lives, it should also inform students of their responsibility to promote a just and equitable community by engaging procedures that promote safety. With the large number of aquatic environments (natural water resources, public and residential pools) in the Long Island area, a viable solution for our underserved school districts would be to provide a way to decrease the number of injury deaths attributed to drowning while also facilitating strategies for the school district to sustain such a program. Thus, the mission of the program is to

- expand the physical education options of an underresourced, predominantly minority school district beyond the traditional physical education curriculum,
- improve students' physical fitness and promote lifelong enjoyable physical activity,
- increase minority participation in aquatics through participation in American Red Cross certified lifeguard training and Make-A-Splash (learn-to-swim) programs, and
- provide students with lifeguard training and water safety skills.

Additionally, the students engage in a variety of activities designed to facilitate their critical thinking and problem-solving skills through participation in professional development assignments specifically created for them. Our initial focus was to establish the program within the physical education curriculum at the high school, but because of minimal buy-in

Participants in Project Guard: Make A Splash E.N.D.N.Y. (End Needless Drowning New York) learn lifeguard and water safety skills.

Courtesy of Angela Beale and NY State Education Department 21st CCLC Hempstead Public Schools and Students

of the faculty at the school, the institutionalization of this program became problematic. After our initial year and with the support of the school district, administration, and physical education department, we successfully altered our initial plan and have proceeded over the past two years with outside funding; thus we are now an after-school program.

Use of TPSR Model

The integration of TPSR with occupational skills development, swimming, and lifeguard training allows instructors to help students apply concepts about responsible choices in swimming and guarding to other parts of their lives. Project Guard: Make A Splash E.N.D.N.Y. has been able to create not only a fun but also a relevant school-based learning experience. That is, I am able to utilize real-world occupational opportunities to facilitate student learning in the classroom. Additionally, students are developing and gaining a skill that can save their lives. Furthermore, I have students who epitomize responsibility, involvement, caring, discipline, and character; they are able to create and establish valuable friendships and working relationships that they can sustain for a lifetime.

You might ask, How do you measure your impact on the community or population served? During the program's three-year tenure we have surveyed approximately 300 participants, and some of our participants have become American Red Cross certified lifeguards ($N = 7$); they and other students have earned American Red Cross instructional swimming certificates ($N = 200$). All students earn American Red Cross CPR and First Aid certificates.

Keeping SITE

What makes the Project Guard: Make A Splash E.N.D.N.Y. program unique is the use of the TPSR instructional approach with its four thematic objectives:

- Respecting the rights of self and of others
- Participation and effort; teamwork
- Self-direction and goal setting
- Leadership and helping

With an overwhelming sense of "Yes, we can," we hope to help our participants gain the qualities needed to make responsible choices in aquatic environments, in lifeguarding, and in other parts of their lives. However, as everyone knows, it is easy to "talk the talk"; "walking the walk" is what makes TPSR unique and challenging for instructors and participants alike. In the Project Guard: Make A

Splash E.N.D.N.Y. program, I found that as in any teaching experience, one should enter with a plan; however, a plan not backed with a belief will be a plan unrealized. By keeping SITE of these themes I entered with the attitude that I would succeed, not because I had something to prove, but because I have a true desire to make an impact. I acknowledge that every program is unique and that not everything I suggest may be relevant for everyone, but I offer the following suggestions:

- Planners and instructors must have resiliency regarding the process and understand that TPSR is dramatic and true to its name.

- Planners and instructors must believe in the TPSR instructional approach and its relevance to participants.

- Planners and instructors must understand that consistency with the use of TPSR is key. You have to do it every day, and this is what makes it challenging.

- Planners and instructors must understand that leaders lead by example. Students will hold you accountable for your actions, and that's when you know it's working.

Project Guard: Make A Splash E.N.D.N.Y. is a work in progress, but we believe that through positive student–teacher interactions, true integration of the themes throughout the program's philosophy and goals, and experiences within the program that students can transfer to their everyday lives, they will leave our program empowered with a pride in themselves that is theirs and no one else's.

Moving and Shaking With Hofstra

Brian Clocksin

Program Description

I begin with the quote from Cummings for two reasons. First, it speaks to my first encounter with Don Hellison and the TPSR model. I was coaching youth and college swimming at the time and decided to attend an AAHPERD national teaching conference. As part of a roundtable discussion session, Don presented his model for working with youth. The model resonated with me, and I began to think of how it aligned with my teaching and coaching philosophies. I went to his table to learn more and to begin planning how I would use this model. The message I left

> We do not believe in ourselves until someone reveals that deep inside us something is valuable, worth listening to, worthy of our trust, sacred to our touch. Once we believe in ourselves we can risk curiosity, wonder, spontaneous delight or any experience that reveals the human spirit.
>
> —E.E. Cummings

with was simple: "Do something, do not overplan, do not think about making it perfect, act and adapt."

Secondly, the Cummings quote hits on my motivation for working with youth. Too often youth are not provided with the opportunity to risk curiosity or wonder or are not shown that they are worth listening to and worthy of trust on the part of adults.

I started the Moving and Shaking with Hofstra (MASH) program five years ago at Walnut Street Elementary School. Walnut Street School (Uniondale School District, Uniondale, NY) is classified as a high-needs school (96.2 percent ethnic minority, 40 percent eligible for free or reduced lunch, and 21 percent students with limited English) by the state of New York. Additionally, 34 percent of students are overweight (BMI equal to or greater than age-adjusted 95th percentile) with an additional 48 percent at risk of becoming overweight; these figures are well above the national averages (18 percent and 34 percent, respectively). Walnut Street Elementary serves 550 children in grades K through five.

MASH started as an after-school program that integrated math concepts with physical activity for fourth- and fifth-grade students. The next two years targeted fifth-grade students, and the past two years have targeted fourth graders, with a few fifth-grade peer leaders. The program runs for 75 minutes, once or twice per week, for 10 weeks each semester. This past semester we shifted to a before-school program to avoid conflict with other school-based programming (e.g., tutoring, band, student government).

Use of TPSR Model

From the beginning of the program, the TPSR model has served as the foundation for interpersonal interactions, program structure, and overall climate. The daily structure follows the TPSR lesson format (relationship time, awareness talk, lesson focus, group meeting, and reflection time); the awareness talks, group meetings, and reflection times are linked to the TPSR themes. Students are made aware of the levels of personal and social responsibility and provided opportunities to define these levels in their own terms.

During the first year of the program, lessons were crafted with developmental stage 1 in mind. Our primary goal was to get students to maintain control of their actions and words and to respect the rights of others to participate (Level I) while participating with effort (Level II) in the activities we presented. Using a more teacher-centered (developmental stage 1) format during this first year allowed us to get a sense of the school climate and of the students.

The next three years of the program progressed through developmental stage 2 activities. Students once again defined characteristics of individuals at each of the responsibility levels and completed self-assessments and reflections each day of the program. Students were provided opportunities to work independently (Level III, self-direction) during skill practice as a more student-centered teaching style was employed (task style, reciprocal style). Awareness talks and group meetings targeted transferring skills and behaviors developed during the program back to the classroom. Connections were made with the school's Community of Caring campaign and the Pillars of Caring (trust, respect, responsibility, compassion) used throughout the school. During the third year of this cycle we shifted from fifth-grade students to fourth graders. This transition provided opportunities for students to return to the program as peer leaders during their fifth-grade year.

This past year, the fifth year of programming at the elementary school, we have made an effort to provide opportunities for students to take on leadership roles (Level IV and developmental stage 3). We have used the fifth-grade peer leaders to lead awareness talks and model appropriate behaviors during activities. This has been an exciting transition for the program, as the fourth-grade students quickly sought out opportunities to lead as well. Awareness talks are now completely led by students, although I still provide the daily theme and starter questions to facilitate these discussions. Reflective homework assignments are used to make a connection between program outcomes and life outside of school (transfer).

The responsibility levels of elementary students are often ephemeral. Students who demonstrate Level IV (caring and helping) behaviors one moment can struggle with Level I (respect) behaviors the next. That being said, these students have a tremendous capacity for growth and compassion and also an innate desire to "risk curiosity, wonder, spontaneous delight or any experience that reveals the human spirit." When provided the opportunity, elementary students can flourish as leaders.

For example, one of our procedures is for students to self-check in by signing their names on the attendance sheet. One day Natalie showed up with a notepad and pencil and took over the attendance process. She wrote down each participant's name, introduced herself if she didn't know someone's name, and presented the completed attendance to me once the relationship time had ended. This is only one of many spontaneous displays of leadership and caring we have seen during the program.

A secondary purpose for running the program was for it to serve as a teaching lab for preservice teachers in our PETE (physical education teacher education) program. By demonstrating a student-centered approach to teaching, I hoped that my preservice physical education students would be more willing to try a variety of teaching styles when working with kids. Students use the TPSR lesson format throughout my methods courses, and I use the format to organize my lectures as well. Students are invited to observe and participate in the MASH program throughout the semester. The PETE students have demonstrated an understanding of the model and a willingness to try the lesson format during peer teaching opportunities in class.

Keeping SITE

For practitioners looking to use the TPSR model within their program, I would echo the message I took from Don: Get started. First, identify one aspect of the model (e.g., levels, lesson format) and integrate it into the program. Just as this may be a shift in how you approach teaching, it is often a new experience for the students, and it will take some time for students to understand their role in the model. Too often students are not provided opportunities to demonstrate self-direction (Level III), show leadership skills (Level IV), or reflect on their learning. To ask them to perform these skills on the first day is unrealistic and will lead to frustrated students and teachers. Using the developmental levels approach will make integration of the model into your program easier. Aside from integrating aspects of the model into the program, teachers must demonstrate and establish a learning environment that promotes respect and encourages reflection. Keeping SITE of TPSR themes (student–teacher relationships, integration, transfer, and empowerment) can facilitate the development of such an environment.

As with practitioners, PETE faculty interested in integrating the model into the preparation of preservice teachers need to be mindful of the philosophical shift this often requires in how classes are organized and what is required of students and teachers. As with working with youth in physical activity settings, there is a learning curve for the PETE students. However, by using the model as a means by which to teach your methods class (or activity class), you can help students transition from a theoretical understanding of the model to a more practical understanding of what the model looks like in action. I model the lesson format (relationship time, awareness talk, lesson focus, group meeting, and reflection) each day during lecture and attempt to move students from developmental stage 1 to stage 3. This is often a challenge to accomplish during one course across the semester. In an ideal setting, all classes in the PETE program would integrate the TPSR model for teaching the content. This would allow for sequential learning experiences that could give students opportunities to demonstrate self-direction and leadership and could promote transfer of this teaching philosophy into student teaching experiences and beyond.

The Refugee Sport Club

Meredith Whitley

Program Description

The Refugee Sport Club (RSC) is an after-school program that I began with young refugees in Lansing, Michigan, in the spring of 2009. Following the pilot RSC that spring, I expanded to two programs—a club for middle school students and a club for high school students to be offered each fall and spring. Over the past two and a half years, I have been fortunate in receiving the help of a number of undergraduate and graduate students who have served as cofacilitators of the RSC programming; and this past fall, a talented colleague, Elizabeth "Missy" Wright, has joined our leadership team.

The clubs meet at the facility of a local nonprofit organization in Lansing that serves refugees from the surrounding community. Each RSC meets for one hour each week after school in the gym. Over the past three years, we have had participants from a variety of countries (e.g., Burundi, Tanzania, Eritrea, Burma) who speak many different languages (e.g., Kirundi, Swahili, Congolese, Ethiopian). Some have been residing in the United States for over three years while others have just arrived and are in the midst of transitioning into a new culture and society. The age

> Give children recognition, they will have lofty aims.
>
> —M.K. Soni

range of our participants tends to be between 9 and 13 for the middle school RSC and between 13 and 19 for the high school RSC; a high percentage are males.

Through RSC's sport-based programming, we hope that the participants are developing in three critical domains: physical, psychological, and socioemotional. To make sure we are accomplishing this mission, we focus on a number of specific goals in our weekly sessions. First, we focus on having fun each and every session; experiencing enjoyment can be quite powerful for refugees who may be struggling as they transition into a new life. With this in mind, we are determined to create an environment in which the participants can enjoy themselves and just be kids.

We would also like the young refugees to experience and learn different sports, as we feel it is important for them to learn how to play "American" sports (e.g., basketball, volleyball, football). With this knowledge and experience, they will be able to participate in physical education classes, athletic teams, and pickup games after school.

Another goal is for the participants to feel as if they are valued members of a team. Research has shown that refugees often feel isolated when they relocate to a new country, and we believe that creating a strong sense of team is incredibly important.

An additional focus is on building strong relationships between the adult leaders and the participants. Researchers have found that opportunities to build trusting relationships with adults can be transformational for young refugees.

Lastly, the final set of goals for the RSC is based solely on the developmental levels of the TPSR model. Throughout each program, we focus on helping the participants become more respectful people, better teammates, and stronger leaders and on transferring these three skills to environments outside the gym.

Use of TPSR Model

To reach the goals just outlined, we follow the basic guidelines of the TPSR model, beginning with a focus on the individuality of each participant and recognizing and building on strengths instead of deficiencies. We create opportunities in each session for the participants to teach us something new, with the understanding that each has knowledge and experience that we do not. By learning from the

Meredith Whitley with participants in the Refugee Sports Club. Note the thumbometer posters on the wall.

Photo by G.L. Kohuth/Michigan State University

participants, we demonstrate that we can all learn from each other, leading to an environment that is empowering for all participants. We also work hard to create decision-making opportunities so that the participants can practice making decisions and then reflect on their decision-making process, hopefully leading to a better understanding of how to make good choices.

Along with following these basic guidelines, RSC programming focuses on four of the five developmental levels within the TPSR model: Level I, respect; Level II, teamwork; Level IV, leadership; and Level V, transfer. The decision to exclude the third level, self-direction, was purposeful, as we are limited both by time (8 to 10 weeks for each RSC) and by the challenge of teaching these concepts to English language learners. Another change we made to the developmental levels was to focus on teamwork instead of participation in Level II. This decision was based on a recommendation from Don Hellison and colleagues, who found that participants in extended-day programs like ours tend to have high levels of participation but can benefit from an emphasis on teamwork and collaboration.

As for the implementation of the programming within each session, we follow the format recommended by Hellison but with some modifications: Our sequence is relationship time, awareness talk, physical activity, group meeting, reflection time, and a

second relationship time. Although this basic format provides the structure for each session, we have made some critical changes to tailor our programming to the refugee population with whom we are working.

First, instead of relying solely on discussions during the awareness talk and group meeting, we often incorporate flash cards so that the participants can read the terms we are discussing. During the awareness talk we use flash cards for "respect," "teamwork," and "leadership"; flash cards used during the group meeting list the activities we participated in that day or aspects of those activities (e.g., "basketball," "team huddles," "high fives"). We have learned from past participants that the flash cards helped them understand the concepts we are discussing, allowed them to participate in the discussions with more confidence, and even helped with their English language learning. Another strategy we use during the awareness talk to overcome the language barrier is for the participants to break up into smaller groups and develop skits that demonstrate the concepts they are learning, such as how to be respectful on the soccer field or how to be a good teammate in volleyball. During this creative process, the participants are able to work together and explain concepts to each other in different languages, which allows them to teach each other.

During the physical activity portion of the program, we do not follow the rules of each sport all that closely, often modifying the rules when we feel this is appropriate. The idea is to create the most welcoming environment we can so that participants do not feel frustrated, uncomfortable, or embarrassed as they learn new sports. Many young refugees who have been in the country for two or three years have become very good at basketball while there are others who have never played the sport before. Our aim is to create the most welcoming environment for all of our participants.

Another seemingly minor change that we have made is the inclusion of team huddles at the end of the awareness talk and at the very end of each session. Instead of having everyone say "1-2-3 Refugee Sport Club!" we ask for the 1-2-3 count in different languages. We have found that the young refugees get very excited when asked to count in their own language.

While the RSC has not been formally assessed, we have reason to believe that the program is having a positive impact on our participants and that we are fulfilling our mission to enhance physical, psychological, and socioemotional development. Over time we have seen visible changes in the participants' behaviors as well as changes in what they say when they are in the gym. For example, one young man did not have much capacity for controlling his emotions when he began attending; he would get frustrated and upset when he did not play well or when the ball was stolen from him, and the ensuing emotional breakdown often included physical violence. Over time, we worked with him to help him become more aware of his emotions and of how he could become a more respectful teammate. His behavior and attitude changed and he became more aware of and in control of his emotions. In addition, participants have reported that the program has affected them in a variety of ways, with some focusing on how they enjoy being part of a team and others on how much they like learning a new sport. Still others have talked about how they better understand the concepts of respect, teamwork, or leadership and have a better idea of how these concepts apply outside of the gym.

Keeping SITE

Given that the RSC is focused on keeping SITE, we have worked hard to make sure that we have strong student–teacher relationships. This includes the cultivation of a caring climate in which all the adults show how much they care about the individual student. This means that the adults must bring a high level of energy into the gym and spread their attention across the board, trying to make sure that they build relationships with each participant in ways that reflect that person's individuality.

As for the emphasis on integration within SITE, we focus on integrating what we are teaching into the physical activity portion of the program. This includes, for example, stopping a soccer game to highlight someone's respectful behavior or asking questions about leadership during a time-out.

We also emphasize the transfer piece of TPSR, with discussions at the end of each session that explore how the participants could apply concepts and skills outside of the gym (e.g., in the classroom, with their friends, at home). We use "transfer sheets" and ask the participants to write down one way they will evidence respect or teamwork or transfer their in-program experience to environments outside of the gym over the next week.

Lastly, empowerment is part of the backbone of this program. We strongly believe in the importance of empowering the students to take responsibility for their lives, beginning with taking responsibility in the gym. While this starts out with simple decisions (e.g., what sport to play, what rules should guide the game), over the course of a program this empowerment transitions into opportunities for the young refugees to take leadership positions as captains.

Ultimately, we hope that youth who participate in the RSC program will develop knowledge and skills that will help them not only within but also outside the program as they transition to new lives in the United States.

Summary

The program descriptions in this chapter demonstrate the varied uses of TPSR. As shown by these examples, from a swim program in New York to a career club in California, TPSR can serve as a powerful tool toward positive youth engagement.

Common to all of these programs was the recognition that SITE needed to be maintained in their development and implementation. In each case it was considered important to connect youth to the program leaders as well as to each other. The programs do this in a variety of ways, from making use of the developmental stages as youth participate in the elements of the lesson (e.g., youth begin to lead the awareness talks) to using different styles of teaching that allow the youth to self-pace and support each other. Each program integrates TPSR within all of its elements. Incorporation of the elements varies depending on the needs of the program. For example, while Meredith elected to omit Level III in her program, Brian uses all levels of the model in Moving and Shaking with Hofstra. Transfer is probably the trickiest element of the model, as it is difficult to facilitate; it is also difficult to know when you have accomplished transfer. However, most of the program leaders note some level of transfer over the course of their program. Lastly, all these programs seek to empower youth via use of participant choice through alteration of teaching styles, give young people an opportunity to return to the program as peer leaders, and focus on creating environments in which the youth feel cared for.

What?

Our goal for this chapter was to underscore the key elements of use of the TPSR model beyond the pages of this text. The accounts of these programs provide a glimpse into the variety of uses of the model. It is important that however you incorporate the TPSR model into your program, you make it your own. It is not necessary to use all elements of the model; you can modify TPSR depending on your program needs, as well as on how TPSR connects with your personal philosophy. It is also vitally important to recognize that the content being taught serves only as the initial hook to get the kids' interest. Whether we are teaching basketball, martial arts, or pickleball, successful use of the model is predicated on our awareness as program leaders and teachers that it is necessary to give up some control as we allow and help kids to take more responsibility.

We hope that reading this text has resulted in your reflecting on your own practices as you work with youth. We hope that as you work with and through this reflection, you challenge or rechallenge yourself to create a learning environment in which kids learn more than the X's and O's of the game—that they learn about themselves in relation to each other and their community.

So What?

1. Compare and contrast how SITE is achieved in each of the programs discussed.
2. Using the chapter as a model, outline a youth program that capitalizes on one of your interests or passions.
3. For the program outlined in question 2, would you use all the TPSR levels? Why or why not?

Now What? Suggested Readings

Leading from within: Poetry that sustains the courage to lead. (2007). Jossey-Bass.

Watson, D.L. (2006). Reflections on refugee youth: Potential problems and solutions in the physical activity setting. *Teaching Elementary Physical Education, 17,* 30-33.

What Matters
in Youth Leadership

We started this book on TPSR by asking the same question Don Hellison did a number of years ago: "What is worth doing?" We are hoping that the discussions undertaken throughout this text have given you a good handle on the answer to that question. We're hoping you better recognize that through purposeful decision making on your part, about not only what content you teach but also how you teach it—and about how you create connections between yourself and your students and between students—you can keep SITE of the TPSR model and through sport and physical activity help youth develop qualities that will assist them beyond the gymnasium.

As we conclude this book, the question to return to is "Why does it matter?" In this chapter we examine some of the emerging literature on "mattering" and discuss how this construct relates to assisting youth in the development of qualities connected to the TPSR model. In so doing, we want to end by linking TPSR to leadership development in youth and subsequent success.

Mattering

The need to feel a sense of connectedness and belonging is a fundamental need of all humans. When we feel we are important to others, we feel appreciated; we thus perceive that we matter to others. Rosenberg and McCullough were among the first researchers to define "mattering" or "the degree to which individuals perceive themselves to be important to others" (Rosenberg & McCullough as cited in Dixon, Scheidegger, & McWhirter 2009, p. 304). Clearly, the concept of mattering relates to Maslow's hierarchy of needs. Once the primary needs of safety and physiology are satisfied, the need for belonging emerges. "Mattering is related to belonging in that a sense of belonging is necessary to foster feelings of mattering; likewise, greater feelings of mattering may increase a sense of belonging" (France & Finney 2009, p. 104). However, simply belonging to a group is not sufficient to engender feelings of mattering. Rather, it is the *nature* of that belonging that brings about one's sense that one matters.

Elliott, Kao, and Grant (2004) posit that two superordinate categories comprise mattering. The first involves being the focus of another person's attention or awareness. For example, a teacher might indicate her awareness of a student by commenting that she noticed the student was absent from class the day before. Being noticed is more than simply having regular contact with someone but also includes the idea that one's presence is important. Obviously, we can discuss awareness that is not positive; students

who act out during class to get attention are indeed ensuring that they matter but are doing it in a negative way.

The second category of mattering implies a relationship between the person and the others to whom the person matters. This aspect of mattering is bidirectional; as the saying goes, it takes two. The relationship category of mattering has two additional subcomponents: *importance* and *reliance*. To take the previous example a step further, the teacher might say that she noticed the student's absence and then go on to comment that the absence mattered to her because she enjoys the student's positive energy in class. This suggests that the student not only is noticed (awareness) but also has importance.

Ego extension is also used to qualify awareness. Under this paradigm, awareness is demonstrated when those around us are excited by our successes and achievements or disappointed by our failures or losses (Dixon, Scheidegger, & McWhirter 2009). The teacher in our example could show sadness or concern when the student explains that he was absent because of a death in his family, thus the teacher communicates an emotional connection or demonstrates ego extension. Another example is the shared sense of achievement by both teacher and student when the student reaches his goals.

Lastly, we matter to others if they look to us to fulfill a need or level of satisfaction. This subcomponent of mattering, *reliance,* again underscores the bidirectional nature of the relationship; there is a constant give and take. We can summarize the components of mattering as "awareness of others that is engendered by some intrinsically captivating characteristic; importance arises out of a sincere concern for the person's welfare; and reliance flows from a sense that others appreciate the resources that one has to offer" (Elliott, Kao, & Grant 2004, p. 342).

Although the concept is relatively new, research on mattering has shown some very impressive correlations, particularly in adolescents. Mattering has been shown to be negatively correlated with depression and anxiety in adolescents; that is, the more adolescents perceive that they matter to others, the less likely they are to feel depressed or anxious (Dixon, Scheidegger, & McWhirter 2009; Taylor & Turner 2001). It has also been found that adolescents who feel that they matter to their family are less likely to use marijuana (Elliott et al. 2009) and have longer life expectancies (Elliott et al. 2008). Lastly, and perhaps most directly relevant to our context, mattering appears to relate to school functioning. Students' sense of mattering has been positively correlated with reduction in misconduct in schools. In addition, a sense of mattering associated with teachers has been shown to have a positive effect on academic achievement (Bloch 2009) and is positively associated with self-esteem and social support (Elliott, Kao, & Grant 2004).

When as teachers, coaches, recreation specialists, or other professionals we elect to use TPSR as our pedagogy, we are choosing to create an environment in which youth will more likely feel that they matter. These youth are more likely to feel connected to each other and to the teacher and more likely to apply what they have learned in our classes or programs to other environments or to transfer skills. Throughout this text and particularly in part II, we drove home the message of keeping SITE with TPSR. When we think about the core themes of TPSR in combination with concepts around mattering, this really makes sense. It is those seemingly small things a teacher does—things like smiling and making eye contact, patting a student on the back, asking how a student is doing (student–teacher relationship), as well as the power of such modeling to encourage the students to exhibit similar behaviors with their classmates—that underscore students' perceptions that they not only matter to others but are also important.

When we as educators, coaches, or youth workers provide our youth with choices—about activities or drills, the pace of practices, whom they partner with,

and so on—we also empower them. But we are not only empowering them in terms of self-regulation and stick-to-itiveness; we are also creating space in which they can begin to empower others and feel empowered by their peers or are facilitating ego extension. The integration of the TPSR core values throughout our practice and work with youth clearly lies at the foundation of the concept of mattering. It is the sum total of behaviors encouraged through TPSR that allows for youth to be better able and thus more likely to exhibit personal and social responsibility outside of our programs.

Leadership Examined

We have all heard people say that someone is "a born leader" or "a natural leader." Traditionally, leadership has been conceptualized from two perspectives: It can be seen as a trait or behavior or from an information-processing viewpoint. The notion that sport is connected to the development of leadership abilities is also common. If sport builds character as is often said, then indeed, that character is or would be indicative of characteristics consistent with qualities of a leader. Throughout this book, we have used the TPSR model as a foundation for positive youth development in a physical activity setting. In line with

Are leaders born or made? Probably a little of both.

the goals of TPSR, our ultimate hope is that qualities developed in our programs will be demonstrated in other environments by the youth who attend.

Leadership in many ways is like quality. Both are difficult to describe or measure, but you know it when you see it. Northouse (2007) suggests four aspects of leadership: "(a) leadership is a process, (b) leadership involves influence, (c) leadership occurs in a group context, and (d) leadership involves goal attainment" (p. 3). Leadership as a process emphasizes that leadership is not simply a one-way street, as is often assumed. Leadership from this perspective can be viewed like a teeter-totter with a leader on one side and followers on the other. Both are affected by the other. Influence must exist for there to be leadership; influence refers to *how* the leader affects the followers. Group context relates to the environment in which leadership takes place; leaders can exert influence in a class or a school or community. Lastly, "Leaders direct their energies toward individuals who are trying to achieve something together" (Northouse 2007, p. 3). So leaders engage in a process with a group (small or large) of people who have a common purpose or goal and are working toward achievement of that common purpose.

Leadership as viewed from a trait perspective focuses more squarely on qualities or behaviors that have been identified as key to what makes a person a leader. Theories that developed around this perspective came to be known as "great man" theories because they focused on identification of innate qualities. Characteristics such as intelligence, self-confidence, determination, integrity, and sociability have been identified as common qualities of leaders. While this is not an exhaustive list, these are the often cited qualities, and few of us would deny that these qualities are necessary for an effective leader. However, the caveat with this perspective is that traits are innate; thus this view restricts leadership to those born with certain qualities. Clearly, the components suggested by an information-processing perspective are more inclusive of the interaction between individual and context. This underscores that leadership is more developmental—that is, that people are born and leaders are developed. This perspective also connects well to the components of the TPSR model and our view of youth development. Obviously it falls outside the purpose of this text to fully discuss trait versus information-processing components of leadership; interested readers can refer to Northouse (2007) and Avolio (2011) for thoughtful overviews of that literature.

Leadership Development in Youth

Using the TPSR model as a foundation and based on their combined 40-plus years of experience working directly with youth, Martinek and Hellison (2009) conceptualized youth leadership development as a four-stage model.

- **Stage 1:** Youth learn to respect themselves and others; they are better at self-direction; they participate and demonstrate stick-to-itiveness; and they begin to explore leadership roles.

- **Stage 2:** Youth actively begin to see themselves as leaders. In this stage youth start to assume responsibilities for teaching parts of the lesson; thus they become responsible for their peers' development.

- **Stage 3:** Youth are responsible for the planning and execution of the lesson, evaluation, and management of younger participants. This stage fully incorporates youth in a teaching role for younger-aged participants, termed "cross-age leadership" by Martinek and Hellison.

- **Stage 4:** The final stage, self-actualized leadership, has the youth begin to reflect and act on their personal interests and possible futures (Martinek & Hellison 2009). Youth who are afforded the opportunity to peer teach are likely to reflect on their successes and failures and thus begin to develop awareness of their leadership abilities. It is through these combined experiences across time that youth begin to also develop a sense of their possible futures.

Each of Martinek and Hellison's (2009) stages is a function of the hoped-for eventual outcome of youth participation in a program that keeps SITE of TPSR values. The leap from participant to leader may seem large; but if we conceptualize our programs as youth development programs and recognize the impact of the core values of SITE, in combination with caring adults who underscore that youth matter, it is not so big a leap after all. Youth who have an opportunity to test themselves in a setting that is caring begin to develop confidence, self-esteem, and self-direction. These are qualities of leaders—people who seek out continued challenge, in relation to not only their own development but also the development of their communities. They begin to see reciprocation of community as a necessity to their continued strength as individuals as well as individuals within a community.

Community of Success

In his book *Outliers* (2008), Malcolm Gladwell provides an alternative view of what success is and how we become successful. He discusses the "rags to riches" story of success as one that conceptualizes success in individual terms. It is the individual's determination, hard work, and intelligence that leads the person out of the ghetto and into the corporate boardroom. This idea is more or less consistent with the trait theory of leadership. Gladwell offers the alternative view that while traits like intelligence and determination are ingredients necessary for success, they must be present, and present at the right time. Gladwell suggests that when we look deeper, the seeming individual agency of success is based on a community of success that is already present. This, in combination with certain positive twists of fate, can produce the sort of success stories we see with a Bill Gates or a Michael Jordan.

We believe that TPSR programs provide that sort of twist. Programs based on the TPSR model create communities of caring teachers, coaches, and youth who have a shared value in the common goal of becoming personally and socially responsible people.

Summary

This chapter concludes the book by reconsidering the question "Why does it matter?"—examining what it means to be a leader and how we can help kids become leaders. While instructive, the traditional conceptualization of leadership as trait specific, versus a more developmental perspective of information processing, is not particularly useful in the context of leadership development in youth. Rather, what counts is the sum total of programs that keep SITE of TPSR values, allowing for caring adults to connect with programs that provide opportunities for youth to assume increasing levels of responsibility and demonstrate care to their community, whatever "community" (team, program, and so on) means to them. What matters is that youth feel they matter. Then it is possible to facilitate development of traits that yield leaders.

Engaged kids and teachers are the right ingredients for a community of success.

What?

While the reader is directed to Martinek and Hellison's book (2009) for a more in-depth discussion of youth leadership, our goal for this chapter was to finalize notions around the value of TPSR beyond the goals of our individual programs. Certainly, as educators and coaches, we all hope to instill in youth the qualities of a leader. But, as we have seen, this can occur only if we have provided youth with experiences through which they can explore who they are and are becoming in a safe and caring environment—an environment in which they matter.

So What?

1. Reflect back to a time when you felt that you mattered. What are the things you can do in your program to ensure that the youth you work with feel that they matter?

2. Reflect on leaders you have encountered in your life. What were the qualities that made them leaders? Do you believe leaders are born or made? Why?

3. What can you do in your current program to ensure that youth are given opportunities to explore their leadership abilities?

Now What? Suggested Readings

Gladwell, M. (2000). *The tipping point.* New York: Little, Brown.

Goldsmith, M. (2007). *What got you here won't get you there.* New York: Hyperion.

Holt, N.L. (ed.). (2008). *Positive youth development through sport.* New York: Routledge.

References and Resources

Ames, C. (1992). Classrooms, goals, structures, and student motivation. *Journal of Educational Psychology, 84*, 261-271.

Ames, C., & Archer, J. (1988). Achievement goals in the classroom: Students' learning strategies and motivational processes. *Journal of Educational Psychology, 80*, 260-267.

Arnold, P.J. (1999). The virtues of moral education, and the practice of sport. *Quest, 51*, 39-54.

Avolio, B.J. (2011). *Full range leadership development.* Thousand Oaks, CA: Sage.

Battistich, V., & Hom, A. (1997). The relationship between students' sense of their school as a community and their involvement in problem behaviors. *American Journal of Public Health, 87*, 1997-2001.

Battistich, V., Schaps, E., Watson, M., Solomon, D., & Lewis, C. (2000). Effects of the child development project on students' drug use and other problem behaviors. *Journal of Primary Prevention, 21*, 75-99.

Battistich, V., Schaps, E., & Wilson, N. (2004). Effects of an elementary school intervention on students' "connectedness" to school and social adjustment during middle school. *Journal of Primary Prevention, 24*, 243-262.

Battistich, V., Solomon, D., Kim, D., Watson, M., & Schaps, E. (1995). Schools as communities, poverty levels of student populations, and students' attitudes, motives, and performance: A multilevel analysis. *American Education Research Journal, 32*(3), 627-658.

Battistich, V., Solomon, D., Watson, M., & Schaps, E. (1997). Caring school communities. *Educational Psychologist, 32*(3), 137-151.

Battistich, V., Solomon, D., Watson, M., Solomon, J., & Schaps, E. (1989). Effects of an elementary school program to enhance prosocial behavior on children's cognitive-social problem-solving skills and strategies. *Journal of Applied Developmental Psychology, 10*(2), 147-169.

Battistich, V., Watson, M., Solomon, D., Lewis, C., & Schaps, E. (1999). Beyond the three R's: A broader agenda for school reform. *Elementary School Journal, 99*, 415-431.

Bloch, S.S. (2009). Mattering in school: Students' perceptions of mattering to teachers and functioning in school. Paper presented at the annual meeting of the American Sociological Association, Hilton San Francisco, San Francisco, CA, August 8. www.allacademic.com/meta/p307776_index.html.

Bradshaw, C.P., Rodgers, C.R., Ghandour, L.A., & Garbarino, J. (2009). Social-cognitive mediators of the association between community violence exposure and aggressive behavior. *School Psychology Quarterly, 24*(3), 199-210.

Brown, J. (2004). *Tennis: Steps to success* (3rd ed.). Champaign, IL: Human Kinetics.

Buchanan, A.M. (2001). Contextual challenges to teaching responsibility in a sports camp. *Journal of Teaching in Physical Education, 20*, 155-171.

Clanton, R.E., & Dwight, M.P. (1997). *Team handball: Steps to success.* Champaign, IL: Human Kinetics.

Clements, R. (2009). Four considerations for urban physical education teachers. *Journal of Physical Education, Recreation and Dance, 80*, 29-31.

Clocksin, B., Watson, D.L., Walsh, D., Dunn, R., Doolittle, S., Beale, A., McCarthy, J., & Whitley, M. (2011). Half-day workshop: Teaching personal and social responsibility. Presented at the National Convention for the American Alliance of Health, Physical Education, Recreation and Dance, San Diego, March 29.

Cohen, J. (2001). Social emotional education. In J. Cohen (ed.), *Caring classrooms/Intelligent schools* (pp. 3-29). New York: Teachers College Press.

Cook, P.J., & Laub, J.H. (1998). The unprecedented epidemic in youth violence. In M. Tonry and M.H. Moore (eds.), *Youth violence. Crime and justice: A review of research* (vol. 24, pp. 27-64). Chicago: University of Chicago Press.

Corbin, C.B., & Lindsey, R. (2007). *Fitness for life* (5th ed.). Champaign, IL: Human Kinetics.

Dasho, S., Lewis, C., & Watson, M. (2001). Fostering emotional intelligence in the classroom schools: Strategies from the Child Development Project. In J. Cohen (ed.), *Social emotional education* (chapter 6, pp. 87-107). New York: Teachers College Press.

DeBusk, M., & Hellison, D. (1989). Implementing a physical education self responsibility model for delinquency-prone youth. *Journal of Teaching in Physical Education, 8*, 104-112.

Dixon, A.L., Scheidegger, C., & McWhirter, J.J. (2009). The adolescent mattering experience: Gender variations in perceived mattering, anxiety and depression. *Journal of Counseling & Development, 87*, 302-310.

Elliott, G.C., Cunningham, S.M., Becker, L., Reuland, T., & Gelles, R.J. (2008). Mattering and subjective life expectancy among adolescents. Paper presented at the annual meeting of the American Sociological Association, Sheraton Boston and the Boston Marriott Copley Place, Boston, MA, July 31. www.allacademic.com/meta/p240799_index.html.

Elliott, G.C., Cunningham, S.M., Colangelo, M., & Gelles, R.J. (2005). Mattering to the family and violence within the family by adolescents. Paper presented at the annual meeting of the American Sociological Association, Marriott Hotel, Loews Philadelphia Hotel, Philadelphia, PA, August 12. www.allacademic.com/meta/p20483_index.html.

Elliott, G.C., Cunningham, S.M., Cowhig, F., Horton, D., & Gelles, R.J. (2009). Perceived mattering to family and marijuana use among adolescents. Paper presented at the annual meeting of the American Sociological Association, Hilton San Francisco, San Francisco, CA, August 7. www.allacademic.com/meta/p308578_index.html.

Elliott, G.C., Kao, S., & Grant, A. (2004). Mattering: Empirical validation of a social psychological concept. *Self and Identity, 3*, 339-354.

France, M.K., & Finney, S.J. (2009). What matters in the measurement of mattering? Construct validity. *Measurement and Evaluation in Counseling and Development, 42*, 104-120.

Fry, M.D., & Newton, M. (2003). Application of achievement goal theory in an urban youth tennis setting. *Journal of Applied Sport Psychology, 15*, 50-66.

Futrell, M.H., Gomez, J., & Bedden, D. (2003). Teaching the children of a new America: The challenge of diversity. *Phi Delta Kappan, 85*, 381-385.

Garbarino, J. (1997). Educating children in a socially toxic environment. *Educational Leadership, 54*(7), 12-16.

Gass, M.A. (1995). *Book of metaphors,* vol. 2. Dubuque, IA: Kendall/Hunt.

Gladwell, M. (2008). *Outliers: The story of success.* New York: Little, Brown.

Goleman, D. (1995). *Emotional intelligence.* New York: Bantam Books.

Hammond-Diedrich, K.C., & Walsh, D. (2006). Empowering youth through a responsibility-based cross-age teacher program: An investigation into impact and possibilities. *Physical Educator, 63*, 134-142.

Hellison, D. (1973). *Humanistic physical education.* Englewood Cliffs, NJ: Prentice Hall.

Hellison, D. (1985). *Goals and strategies for teaching physical education.* Champaign, IL: Human Kinetics.

Hellison, D. (1995). *Teaching responsibility through physical activity.* Champaign, IL: Human Kinetics.

Hellison, D. (2003). *Teaching responsibility through physical activity* (2nd ed.). Champaign, IL: Human Kinetics.

Hellison, D. (2011). *Teaching personal and social responsibility through physical activity* (3rd ed.). Champaign, IL: Human Kinetics.

Hellison, D., & Cutforth, N.J. (1997). Extended day programs for urban children and youth: From theory to practice. In H.J. Walberg, O. Reyes, & R.P. Weissberg (eds.), *Children and youth: Interdisciplinary perspectives,* Vol. 1 (pp. 223-249). Thousand Oaks, CA: Sage.

Hellison, D., & Walsh, D. (2002). Responsibility-based youth programs evaluation: Investigating the investigations. *Quest, 54*, 292-307.

Hellison, D., & Wright, P. (2003). Retention in an urban extended day program: A process-based assessment. *Journal of Teaching in Physical Education, 22*, 369-381.

Johnson, L. (2002). "My eyes have been opened": White teachers and racial awareness. *Journal of Teacher Education, 53*(2), 153-167.

Keltner, D. (2009). *Born to be good. The science of a meaningful life.* New York: Norton.

Kenny, B., & Gregory, C. (2006). *Volleyball: Steps to success.* Champaign, IL: Human Kinetics.

Kolb, D.A. (1984). *Experiential learning.* Englewood Cliffs, NJ: Prentice Hall.

Li, W., Wright, P.M., Rukavina, P.B., & Pickering, M. (2008). Measuring students' perceptions of personal and social responsibility and the relationship to intrinsic motivation in urban physical education. *Journal of Teaching in Physical Education, 27*, 167-178.

Luxbacher, J. (2005). *Soccer: Steps to success* (3rd ed.). Champaign, IL: Human Kinetics.

Magyar, M., Guivernau, M., Gano-Overway, L., Newton, M., Kim, M.S., Watson, D.L., & Fry, M. (2007). The influence of leader efficacy and emotional intelligence on personal caring in physical activity. *Journal of Teaching in Physical Education, 26*, 310-319.

Martinek, T., & Hellison, D. (2009). *Youth leadership in sport and physical education.* New York: Palgrave Macmillan.

Martinek, T., Schilling, T., & Johnson, D. (2001). Transferring personal and social responsibility of underserved youth to the classroom. *Urban Review, 33*, 29-45.

Meece, J.L., & Kurtz-Costes, B. (eds.). (2001). Schooling of ethnic minority children and youth [Special Issue]. *Educational Psychologists, 36*.

Midura, D.W., & Glover, D.R. (2005). *Essentials of team building: Principles and practices.* Champaign, IL: Human Kinetics.

Mosston, M., & Ashworth, S. (2002). *Teaching physical education* (5th ed.). New York: Benjamin Cummings.

National Association for Sport and Physical Education. (2004). *Moving into the future: National standards for physical education* (2nd ed.). Reston, VA: NASPE.

National Association for Sport and Physical Education. (2008). *National initial physical education teacher education standards.* Reston, VA: NASPE.

National Center for Health Statistics. (2012). *Health, United States, 2011: With special feature on socioeconomic status and health.* Hyattsville, MD. Retrieved from http://cdc.gov/nchs/hus.htm. Last accessed July 29, 2012.

Newton, M., Duda, J.L., & Yin, Z. (2000). Examination of the psychometric properties of the Perceived Motivational Climate in Sport Questionnaire-2 in a sample of female athletes. *Journal of Sport Sciences, 18*, 275-290.

Newton, M., Fry, M., Watson, D.L., Gano-Overway, L., Kim, M.S., Magyar, M., & Guivernau, M. (2007). Psychometric properties of the caring climate scale in a physical activity setting, *Revista de Psiologia del Deporte, 16*, 67-84.

Newton, M., Watson, D.L., Gano-Overway, L., Fry, M., Kim, M.S., & Magyar, M. (2007). The role of a caring-based intervention in a physical activity setting. *Urban Review, 39,* 281-299.

Newton, M., Watson, D.L., Kim, M.S., & Beacham, A.O. (2006). Achievement goal theory and the taking of Personal and Social Responsibility Model in a sample of underserved youth. *Youth & Society, 37,* 348-371.

Noddings, N. (1984). *Caring: A feminine approach to ethics and moral education.* Berkeley: University of California Press.

Noddings, N. (1988). An ethic of caring and its implications for instructional arrangements. *American Journal of Education, 96,* 215-230.

Noddings, N. (1992). *The challenge to care in schools: An alternative approach to education.* New York: Teachers College Press.

Noddings, N. (1995). Teaching themes of care. *Phi Delta Kappan, 76,* 675-679.

Noddings, N. (2010). Moral education in an age of globalization. *Educational Philosophy and Theory, 42,* 390-396.

Northouse, P.G. (2007). *Leadership theory and practice.* London: Sage.

Ommundsen, Y., Roberts, G.C., Lemyre, P.N., & Treasure, D. (2003). Perceived motivational climate in male youth soccer: Relations to social-moral functioning, sportspersonship and team norm perceptions. *Psychology of Sport and Exercise, 14*(4), 397-413.

Oyserman, D., Terry, K., & Bybee, D. (2002). A possible selves intervention to enhance school involvement. *Journal of Adolescence, 25,* 313-326.

Palmer, P.J. (2007). *The courage to teach: Exploring the inner landscape of a teacher's life.* San Francisco: Jossey-Bass.

Parker, J. (1995). Secondary teachers' views of effective teaching in physical education. *Journal of Teaching in Physical Education, 14,* 127-139.

Parker, M., Kallusky, J., & Hellison, D. (1999). High impact, low risk: Ten strategies to teach responsibility. *Journal of Physical Education, Recreation and Dance, 70*(2), 26-28.

Priest, S. (1999). *The semantics of adventure programming.* In J.C. Miles & S. Priest (eds.), *Adventure programming* (pp. 111-114). State College, PA: Venture.

Sachs, S.K. (2004). Evaluation of teacher attributes as predictors of success in urban schools. *Journal of Teacher Education, 55,* 177-187.

Schempp, P., & Mattsson, P. (2005). *Golf: Steps to success.* Champaign, IL: Human Kinetics.

Schilling, T.A. (2001). An investigation of commitment among participants in an extended day physical activity program. *Research Quarterly for Exercise and Sport, 72,* 355-366.

Solomon, D., Watson, M., Battistich, V., Schaps, E., & Delucchi, K. (1996). Creating classrooms that students experience as communities. *American Journal of Community Psychology, 24,* 719-748.

Solomon, M.A. (1996). Impact of motivational climate on students' behavior and perceptions in a physical education setting. *Journal of Educational Psychology, 88,* 731-738.

Standage, M., Duda, J.L., & Ntoumanis, N. (2003). A model of contextual motivation in physical education: Using constructs from self-determination and achievement goal theories to predict physical activity interventions. *Journal of Educational Psychology, 95,* 97-110.

Taylor, J., & Turner, R.J. (2001). A longitudinal study of the role and significance of mattering to others for depressive symptoms. *Journal of Health and Social Behavior, 42,* 310-325.

Treasure, D.C. (1993). A social-cognitive approach to understanding children's achievement behavior, cognitions, and affect in competitive sport. Unpublished doctoral dissertation, University of Illinois, Urbana-Champaign.

Tuckman, B. (1965). Developmental sequencing in small groups. *Psychological Bulletin, 63,* 384-399.

Tummers, N.E. (2009). *Teaching yoga for life: Preparing children and teens for healthy, balanced living.* Champaign, IL: Human Kinetics.

U.S. Department of Education, National Center for Education Statistics. (2003). *Digest of Education Statistics 2002* (NCES 2003-060), chapter 2.

Vivola, A.M., Matjasko, J.L., & Massetti, G.M. (2011). Mobilizing communities and building capacity for youth violence prevention: The National Academic Centers of Excellence for Youth Violence Prevention. *American Journal of Community Psychology, 48,* 141-145.

Wallhead, T.L., & Ntoumanis, N. (2004). Effects of a sport education intervention on students' motivational responses in physical education. *Journal of Teaching in Physical Education, 23,* 4-18.

Walsh, D. (2007). Supporting youth development outcomes: An evaluation of a responsibility model-based program. *Physical Educator, 64,* 48-56.

Walsh, D. (2008a). Helping youth in underserved communities envision possible futures: An extension of the teaching personal and social responsibility model. *Research Quarterly for Exercise and Sport, 79*(2), 209-221.

Walsh, D. (2008b). Strangers in a strange land: Using an activity course to teach an alternative curriculum model. *Journal of Physical Education, Recreation and Dance, 79*(2), 40-44.

Walsh, D., Ozaeta, J., & Wright, P.M. (2010). Transference of responsibility model goals to the school environment: Exploring the impact of a coaching club program. *Physical Education and Sport Pedagogy, 15,* 15-28.

Watson, D.L., Newton, M., & Kim, M.S. (2003). Recognition of values-based constructs in a summer physical activity program. *Urban Review, 35*(3), 217-232.

West Stevens, J. (2002). *Smart and sassy: The strengths of inner-city black girls.* New York: Oxford University Press.

Wissel, H. (2012). *Basketball: Steps to success* (3rd ed.). Champaign, IL: Human Kinetics.

Wright, P.M., & Burton, S. (2008). Implementation and outcomes of a responsibility-based physical activity program integrated into an intact high school physical education class. *Journal of Teaching in Physical Education, 27,* 138-154.

Wright, P.M., & Li, W. (2009). Exploring the relevance of a youth development orientation in urban physical education. *Physical Education and Sport Pedagogy, 14,* 241-251.

Wright, P.M., White, K., & Gaebler-Spira, D. (2004). Exploring the relevance of the personal and social responsibility model in adapted physical activity: A collective case study. *Journal of Teaching in Physical Education, 23,* 71-87.

Adventure Education Resources

These are but a small sampling of the types of resources available describing games and initiatives that can be used throughout your program.

Anderson, M., Cain, J., Cavert, C., & Heck, T. (2005). *Teambuilding puzzles.* Brockport, NY: FunDoing Publications.

Bower, N.M. (1998). *Adventure play.* Needham Heights, MA: Simon & Schuster.

Cain, J., & Jolliff, B. (1998). *Teamwork and teamplay.* Dubuque, IA: Kendall Hunt.

Cavert, C. (1999). *Affordable portable: A working book of initiative activities and problem solving elements.* Oklahoma City: Wood 'N' Barns Publishing.

Frank, L.S. (2004). *Journey toward the caring classroom.* Oklahoma City: Wood 'N' Barns Publishing.

Kreidler, W.J., & Furlong, L. (1995). *Adventures in peacemaking.* Hamilton, MA: Project Adventures Inc.

Panicucci, J. (2002). *Adventure curriculum for physical education: Middle school.* Hamilton, MA: Project Adventures Inc.

Panicucci, J. (2008). *Achieving fitness: An adventure activity guide.* Hamilton, MA: Project Adventures Inc.

Rohnke, K. (1984). *Silver bullets: A guide to initiative problems, adventure games, and trust activities.* Dubuque, IA: Kendall Hunt.

Rohnke, K. (1989). *Cowstails and cobras II: A guide to games, initiatives, ropes courses and adventure curriculum.* Dubuque, IA: Kendall Hunt.

Rohnke, K. (1993). *The bottomless bag revival!* (2nd ed.). Dubuque, IA: Kendall Hunt.

Rohnke, K. (2004). *Fun 'n games.* Dubuque, IA: Kendall Hunt.

Rohnke, K. (2010). *Silver bullets: A guide to initiative problems, adventure games, and trust activities* (2nd ed.). Dubuque, IA: Kendall Hunt.

Index

Note: The letters *f* and *t* after page numbers indicate figures and tables, respectively.

About the Authors

Doris L. Watson, PhD, is an associate professor in the department of educational psychology and higher education at the University of Nevada at Las Vegas. In addition to her teaching responsibilities, Watson serves as assistant chair and graduate coordinator.

Watson has over 20 years of experience in sport pedagogy and physical education teacher education. Her areas of expertise include student learning and development, working with and in diverse organizations, community-based research, and issues in preparing culturally responsive leaders in higher education. She has published work on creating a caring environment in a physical activity setting and facilitation of personal and social responsibility through physical activity.

Watson has two decades of experience in facilitating TPSR-based after-school and summer programs for underserved youth ages 8 to 15 years. She has worked with the NCAA Youth Day in creating a curriculum based on the TPSR model. She has also taught and conducted TPSR workshops in Nepal, Ireland, and Trinidad. Also a certified high- and low-ropes facilitator, Watson works with people ages 8 to 40-plus, sport teams, and professionals.

Brian D. Clocksin, PhD, is chairman of the department of movement and sports science and associate professor of movement and sports science at the University of La Verne in La Verne, California. Clocksin previously taught at Hofstra University in Hempstead, New York, as an associate professor in the department of physical education and sport science, where he taught courses in physical education methods, adapted physical education, adventure education, and motor behavior. In addition to his teaching duties, Clocksin served as the graduate coordinator for the department of physical education and sport sciences. He also ran Moving and Shaking with Hofstra (MASH), an after-school physical activity program for fourth- through fifth-grade students that used the TPSR model.

Clocksin has published 10 articles in peer-reviewed journals and 6 abstracts and invited articles. He is a regular presenter at national, regional, and state conferences on adventure education and decreasing childhood obesity through physical activity interventions. Clocksin is an active member of the American Alliance for Health, Physical Education, Recreation and Dance (AAHPERD). He served as the chair for the Council for Adventure & Outdoor Education/Recreation (CAOER) and as a board member with the American Association for Physical Activity and Recreation (AAPAR). Clocksin also served as a program reviewer and auditor for the National Council for Accreditation of Teacher Education (NCATE) and the National Association for Sport and Physical Education (NASPE) certification programs. He is currently a reviewer for the *Journal of Teaching in Physical Education, The Physical Educator, Journal of School Health,* and *International Journal of Aquatic Research and Education.*

Clocksin has facilitated TPSR-based after-school, summer, and in-school programs since 2002 with elementary students. He has led workshops on the use of TPSR in physical activity and sport settings and prepares physical education teacher education candidates to use the model. While at Hofstra University, Clocksin directed the adventure education program, facilitating groups ranging from second-graders to corporate leadership teams.

You'll find other outstanding
physical education resources at
www.HumanKinetics.com

In the U.S. call 1.800.747.4457

Australia 08 8372 0999

Canada. 1.800.465.7301

Europe . . . . . +44 (0) 113 255 5665

New Zealand 0800 222 062

HUMAN KINETICS
The Information Leader in Physical Activity & Health
P.O. Box 5076 • Champaign, IL 61825-5076